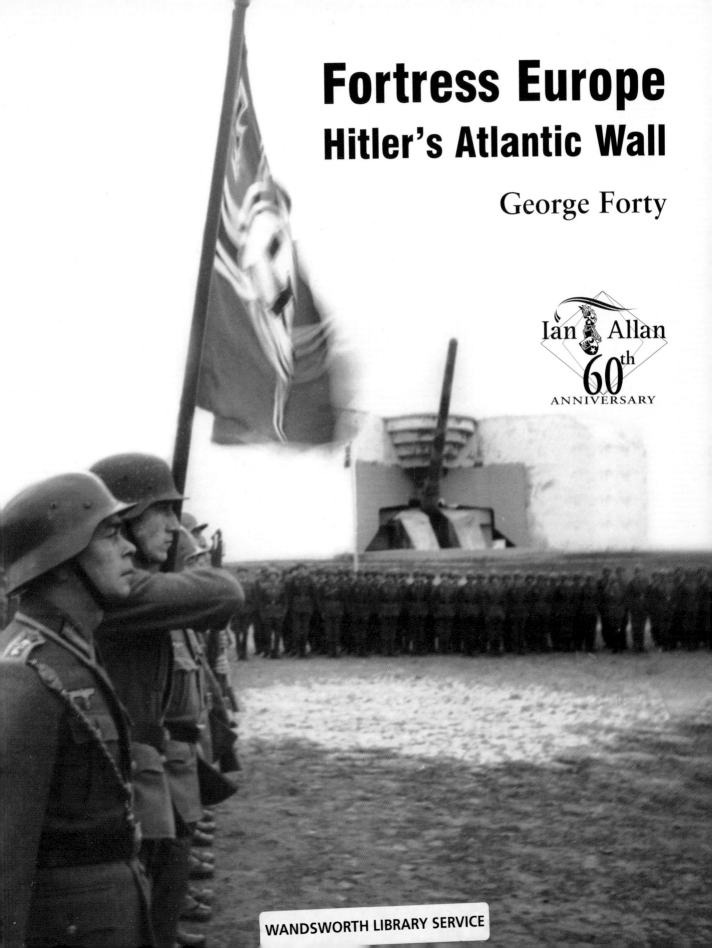

Fortress Europe
Hitler's Atlantic Wall

George Forty

First published 2002

ISBN 0 7110 2769 2

Published by Ian Allan Publishing

an imprint of
Ian Allan Publishing Ltd, Hersham, Surrey KT12 4RG.

Printed by Ian Allan Printing Ltd, Hersham, Surrey KT12 4RG.

Code: 0211/A2

Front cover: Image by Casebourne Rose Design Associates

Rear cover: (Clockwise from top left)
An artillery observer uses high powered binoculars to look for targets from an artillery observation tower in Guernsey. *Ludwig Spaeth via Guernsey Museums & Galleries*

Utah Beach. GIs shelter in a captured German trench on the edge of the beach as they make their way forward over the top of the next obstacle. *US Army via Real War Photos A-122*

Members of the fire control staff plotting targets in their control room on Guernsey. *Ludwig Spaeth via Guernsey Museums & Galleries*

Wounded Canadians wait on the beach next to an empty blockhouse to be transferred to a casualty clearing station. *Canadian Official No 337757-N (PL)*

Feldmarschall Erwin Rommel inspecting the Atlantic Wall defences. *IWM — HU 3060*

Title page:
The unveiling of Batterie Todt. Near the village of Haringzelles, about a kilometre south of Audinghen, was the battery of four artillery turrets, each containing a massive 38cm gun. It was originally called Batterie Siegfried, then renamed in honour of the head of the Organisation Todt. Least damaged of the Channel batteries, it now houses a museum. *Bundesarchiv*

Above: This coastal gun looks far too small for its massive camouflaged emplacement. *Bundesarchiv*

Below: Hitler's Atlantic Wall. A typical scene of a small French seaside town prior to the Allied invasion. Note the beach obstacles extending into the sea, concrete anti-tank wall, barbed-wire entanglements, and so on. And of course there are plenty of well-camouflaged gun positions. *Bundesarchiv*

Inset: A 17cm SK L/40 gun near Sangatte. Note the camouflage painting on the casemate. *Bundesarchiv*

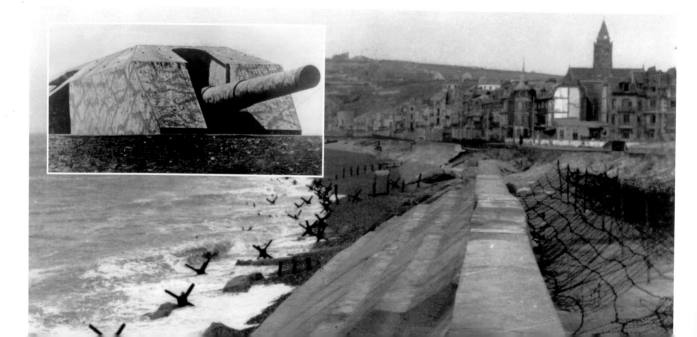

Contents

Above: This German gun position has been camouflaged to look like a seaside villa, complete with painted windows and curtains. *Bundesarchiv*

Introduction & Acknowledgements

Throughout the history of warfare, either one side or the other has built defensive fortifications, varying from simple scrapes in the ground to massively complex earthworks such as Maiden Castle in Dorset; from ditches and mud walls, to complex stone structures like Hadrian's Wall in northern England and the most amazing and enormous wall of all time — the Great Wall of China; together with a vast array of castles, watchtowers, and so on, to highly complex modern structures with mines, razor wire — even ground-installed atomic demolition munitions — in an attempt to defend themselves and their territories from the incursions of their enemies. One of these fortifications, built during World War 2, was given the title 'The Atlantic Wall' and it has been a source of abiding interest to many military historians ever since. It is to be the subject of this book.

When I began my research for the project I was immediately struck by the large number of books that had already been written about it — Mr Svein Wiiger Olsen of Drammen, Norway, listed no fewer than 676 books and articles in the 2001 edition of his *Atlantic Wall Bibliography*. Granted most of them were in a mixture of European languages other than English, but that just goes to show how universal the interest still is in this remarkable piece of architecture. It is also true to say that the majority of these books and articles confine themselves to one particular location on the 5,000-plus kilometre length of the Atlantic Wall, or deal with just one aspect of it — for example, how the fortifications were built or what weapons they contained. Obviously, if one is going to go into the 'nitty-gritty' of one of these aspects then this is sensible. However, in doing so one is liable to get immersed in facts and figures and perhaps lose sight of the human side of the equation. In this book I have followed the style of previous books in Ian Allan Publishing's 'At War' series and tried to show the human side of the Atlantic Wall, starting with the builders, then the defenders and finally the attackers and destroyers (in battle) of parts of the Wall. To close the saga of the Wall, as I did in my similar recent volumes for Ian Allan Publishing, *Channel Islands at War* and *Battle of Crete*, I have given some information about the amazing structures which still remain to be visited, and also details of the large tourist industry which has grown up to cater for those who wish to visit such historical sites.

The Atlantic Wall failed to keep out the Allied invasion; perhaps it was never intended to do so, but rather to act as a tripwire so as to give warning, then to delay the invader and gain sufficient time to allow for counter-attack forces to be moved into position to deal with any threat. If this was the case — and it does seem to be a reasonable theory — then it failed for a variety of reasons, some of which had little to do with its construction and manning, but rather with the way it fitted into the overall German defence plans and, most especially, how it was adversely affected by the almost continual inter-service rivalry which plagued the German armed forces. All these points are examined in this study.

Acknowledgements

As this book is a 'pictorial evocation', that is to say full of photographs and personal stories, I have many people to thank for their generous assistance. First and foremost I must mention

Herr Kurt Hanson of Wiesbaden, who has been a continual tower of strength with advice, translations and other assistance. I owe him my grateful thanks for his continued support over the past two years. Also Dr Jean-Pierre Benamou OBE, MSM, Conservateur of the Musée de la Bataille de Normandie at Bayeux, whose help, advice and photographs have been invaluable; Luc Braeuer at Le Grand Blockhaus, St Nazaire; D. C. Davies at the Musée du Mur de L'Atlantique, Batterie Todt; Mrs Ivy Forty; Maj (Retd) & Mrs Tonie Holt; William Borchardt of the Panzer Turm Research Group; Soren Byskov of the Fisheries and Maritime Museum, Esbjerg, Denmark; Aleks Deseyne of Domein Raversijde, West Flanders; Svein Wiiger Olsen; Dr John Verbeek of Den Haag; P. van Noort Collectiebeheer Fort a/d Hoek van Holland; Michael Ginns MBE of CIOS Jersey, who has once again given me his generous support as have all my other friends and contacts in the Channel Islands, Lt-Col (Retd) Leif Ipsen; and Mrs Margaret Pinsent (editor of the Journal of the Fortress Study Group). My thanks also go to the Departments of Photographs at the Imperial War Museum, the National Archives of Canada and the Bundesarchiv, to the Department of Sound at the IWM, the MOD Whitehall Library, and PRO Kew. Also I must thank those ex-soldiers and wartime workers who have allowed me to quote from their reminiscences, including: Tony Carter, Gilbert van Grieken, Juan Taule, Harry Haendler, Roland Fischer, Gerard Koch and Hans Sippli. The staff of the US 1st Division Museum at Cantigny, Illinois, in particular Mr Andrew E. Woods, Research Assistant, have been most helpful both in supplying photographs and by allowing me to quote from Harley A. Reynolds' riveting account of his D-Day landing on 'Bloody Omaha'. Finally, I wish to thank my son Jonathan and my wife Anne, who have as always been of tremendous help and support, and suffered in silence during seemingly endless tours of 'fascinating' derelict bunkers!

George Forty
Bryantspuddle, Dorset
August 2002

Above: Somewhere on the Belgian coast was this camouflaged gun position containing a Feldkanone 418(f). Note the all-round traverse, which had to be set by hand, three of the gun crew pushing the heavy 10,000+kg gun around — not an easy task. *Bundesarchiv*

Above and opposite left: 'To the Normandy Front' reads the sign on the outskirts of Paris, whilst the one in Arromanches seems to have more appeal to these off-duty members of the garrison — I wonder why. *J. P. Benamou Collection and IWM — HU 20742*

Chapter 1
The Reasons Why

Above: Map showing the extent of the Atlantic Wall, which reached along the coast from Norway to the Spanish border.

Last Major Defensive Line

If one discounts the somewhat ethereal 'Iron Curtain' of the Cold War, although parts of it such as the Berlin Wall portion were solid enough, then the Atlantic Wall can be considered as being the last great defensive line to be built in Europe. However, unlike its predecessors, such as the Maginot and Siegfried Lines (the latter also known as the West Wall), its enormous length — over 5,000km (3,125 plus miles) stretching from Norway to the Spanish/French border — the vast range of different types of fortifications used; the massive work force employed; the incredible amount of concrete, steel and other materials used; and finally, the length of time it took to build (1940–45), all make it unique among European defensive lines.

The fact that much of it still remains is a testament to the work of its builders, despite the fact that a large number of those employed in the actual building work were from the occupied countries including both paid workmen and unfortunate slave labourers, all forced to work for the Nazis.

Although the intention may have been to create a continuous wall that would stand up to an enemy invasion anywhere along the northern coastline of Europe (and later, partly along the Mediterranean coastline as well), I doubt if even Adolf Hitler or his most optimistic Nazi planner ever imagined that this was entirely possible — or if they did so, then they must have been

seriously deluded. However, all this work was done for a purpose, so it is relevant to look first at why it was built. What must also be kept in mind is that from time to time the demands of the other battle fronts, especially the insatiable Russian Front, required more and more of Germany's limited resources, so on numerous occasions, the requirements of the less critical western European area had to take a back seat. This was inevitable, because Germany did not possess unlimited resources even though the Nazis made use of foreign labour to a considerable degree and took over all the raw materials, weapons and other resources that were available in the countries it conquered.

Operation 'Sealion'

There was in truth no single underlying event that led to the initial building of major defences along the western European coast. However, a number of distinct phases can be seen within the period of their construction and these all had their own 'Reasons Why'. We should perhaps go back to the days of 1940 when Hitler's Third Reich was master of Europe — that is apart from one annoying small group of islands off the north-west coast of the continent. Despite the fact that the British Expeditionary Force (BEF) had been forced to make a disastrous withdrawal from France in May/June 1940, the stubborn islanders showed no signs of surrendering as their major ally France had done, crumbling in a few short weeks under the shock of the German Blitzkrieg. However, steps were already in hand to deal with them — the planning for Operation 'Seelöwe' ('Sealion'), the amphibious assault on England (enshrined in Hitler's Directive 16 — 'On preparations for a landing operation against England', issued on 16 July 1940) was well advanced and this included the installation of four heavy naval batteries in the Calais–Boulogne area. The original purpose of these batteries was, therefore, not to defend the coast, but rather to back up the intended invasion. This is confirmed in a treatise on the Organisation Todt (OT), written postwar by Franz Xaver Dorsch, Deputy Chief of the OT (see Bibliography) in which he says:

'The first rather large, combined work of the OT after the construction of the West Wall was the installation of the heavy batteries at Cap Gris-Nez. According to an official announcement of the Naval Warfare Command, this work was part of Operation 'Sealion'. It was supposed to have provided the necessary fire support to the units that were committed for a landing operation in England. It should not go unmentioned at this point that Hitler declared, when inspecting the batteries on 23 December 1940, that he never gave a serious thought to Operation 'Sealion'. The value of the batteries, even without taking 'Sealion' into consideration, was no doubt afforded by the fact that a blocking of the Channel, up to a certain degree, for enemy ships was thereby given support.

'The naval commandant (Admiral Fischer) personally took it upon himself to designate the locations of the batteries. The construction work itself was under the OT-Einsatzstab on the Channel coast in Audinghen, which I personally directed.'

Interestingly the initial OT workers were housed in a former British Army camp near Étaples, some 15km south-west of Boulogne, 'a corrugated iron barracks in which most of the workers who had been quickly assembled could be given shelter at once'.

In fact in Directive 16, Hitler gave his approval for this action when he said:

'The largest possible number of extra-heavy guns will be brought into position as soon as possible in order to cover the crossing [to support 'Sealion'] and to shield the flanks against enemy action at sea. For this purpose railway guns will also be used (reinforced by all available captured weapons) and will be sited on railway turntables. Those batteries intended only to deal with targets on the English mainland (K5 and K12) will not be included. Apart from this the existing extra-heavy platform-gun batteries are to be enclosed in concrete opposite the Strait of Dover within the limits of their range. The technical work will be the responsibility of the Organisation Todt.'

Even when 'Sealion' was postponed indefinitely after the failure of the Luftwaffe in the Battle of Britain and Hitler's decision to invade Russia, no formal order was immediately given for the systematic building of defences anywhere along the coast, but rather major construction effort was given over to the building of submarine pens in places like Brest, Lorient and St Nazaire.

Blocking the Strait of Dover

As part of the 'Sealion' operation, both the Oberkommando der Wehrmacht (OKW — German Armed Forces High Command) and Hitler fully appreciated the need to blockade the Strait of Dover and considered the task perfectly possible, because only 21 miles of sea separated the two coastlines. In his book

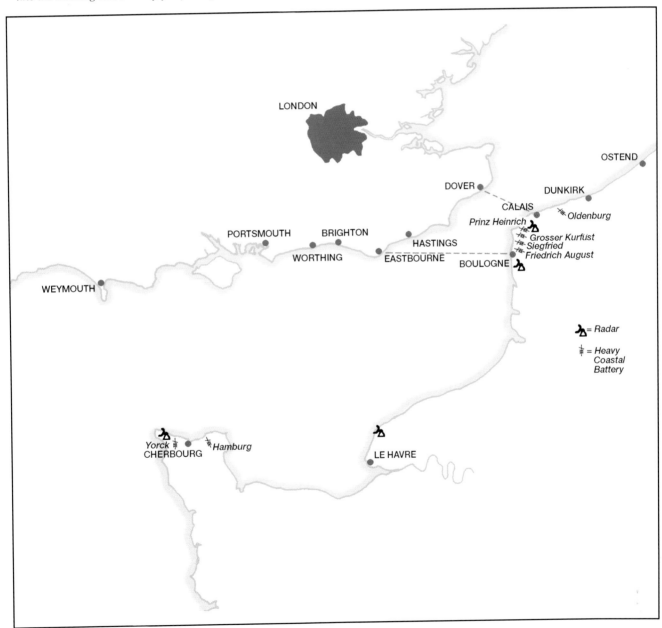

Above: Map showing the locations of the original heavy coastal batteries.

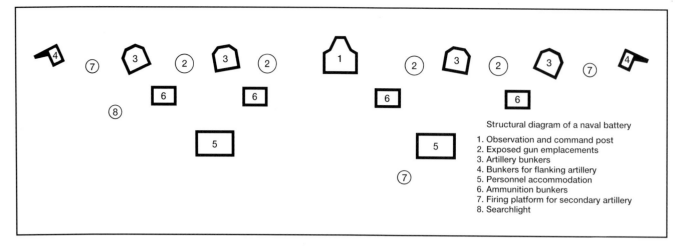

Structural diagram of a naval battery

1. Observation and command post
2. Exposed gun emplacements
3. Artillery bunkers
4. Bunkers for flanking artillery
5. Personnel accommodation
6. Ammunition bunkers
7. Firing platform for secondary artillery
8. Searchlight

Above: Typical layout of an artillery battery.

Invasion of England 1940, Peter Schenk explains that the issue of the use of coastal batteries was brought up at a meeting on 15 July 1940, with Hitler at the Berghof, when it was agreed that every available piece of Army and Navy heavy artillery would be set up in suitable selected positions along the Channel coast to support 'Sealion'. The Navy reckoned that it would take at least three months for this work to be completed and the Organisation Todt was given the task of carrying it out. They began on 22 July 1940. To quote Peter Schenk:

'The battery Grosser Kurfürst at Pillau was dismantled and re-erected at the Pas de Calais, where three guns were ready to fire by 31 July. At the beginning of August, the four 28cm traversing turrets of this battery were fully operational, as were all the Army's railway guns. The latter comprised six 28cm K5 guns in two batteries and a 21cm K12 gun with a range of 115km. These two types were only for land bombardment while the other railway guns could be used . . . against maritime targets. These were the eight 28cm Kurze Bruno in two batteries; two 28cm Schwere Bruno; three 28cm Lange Bruno, the latter of which were set up at Cherbourg. Six 24cm K3 guns (motorised), six Czech 24cm guns (motorised) and 10 21cm K39 guns (motorised) were also erected at the Pas de Calais. These too were only of limited use against naval targets. The Army guns were placed under Navy command to ensure uniform fire.'

By mid-August three more heavy naval batteries had become operational: Friedrich August (3 x 30.5cm guns), Prinz Heinrich (2 x 28cm guns) and Oldenburg (2 x 24cm guns). Two other batteries — Hamburg and Yorck (both 24cm guns) were also installed on the Cherbourg peninsula. Finally, the following month Siegfried (2 x 38cm guns) was ready. This last battery would later be renamed Todt, in honour of the work done by Fritz Todt's organisation. In addition to these heavy batteries, the Army and the Navy together deployed some 444 medium and light guns in batteries along the Dutch–Belgian–French coastlines, their main task being to protect coastal shipping routes and ports/harbours. As well as the guns, some fire control radars[1] were installed, to work with the heavy batteries at Blanc Nez, Cap d'Alprech, Cap de la Hague and Cap d'Antifer (near Le Havre).

One could therefore count this work as the first phase of construction of the Atlantic Wall, in that a certain amount of construction work on gun positions was commissioned. This was perfectly in line with normal German field works construction policy which will be explained in a future chapter. Taking Belgium as an example, the ports of Blankenberge, Zeebrugge, Ostend and Nieuport, despite the fact that they were at that time all less important than the large French coastal ports, soon also became protected by naval artillery batteries (Marine Artillerie Abteilungen — MAA), and Army batteries. As the sketch above shows, the usual organisation and layout of such a battery consisted of an observation and command post, four to six gun emplacements, ammunition bunkers and troop accommodation, anti-aircraft guns, searchlights and, in some cases, radar.

All this activity had not gone unnoticed by the British, as Winston Churchill commented in *Their Finest Hour* (Volume 2 of his *History of the Second World War*):

'We watched with attention the growth of the German heavy batteries along the Channel coast during August and September. By far the strongest concentration of this artillery was around Calais and Cape Gris-Nez, with the apparent purpose of not only forbidding the Straits to our warships but also of commanding the shortest route across them.'

He then details the batteries as Schenk does, then continues:

'Besides this no fewer than 35 heavy and medium batteries of the German Army, as well as seven batteries of captured guns, were sited along the French coast for defensive purposes by the end of August.'

Churchill goes on to write about the British defences, saying that he took a personal interest in the whole of the business of the defence of Dover. On the other side of the Channel Adolf Hitler was also paying visits to the coastal areas. His personal train was attacked by the RAF near Boulogne on 23 December 1940 and had to be diverted into a convenient, safe railway tunnel close by, with flak guns protecting it at either end!

Marching against England

Although 'Sealion' was postponed in the autumn of 1940, an earlier operation — 'Green Arrow' ('*Grüne Pfeil*') had already taken place, namely the relatively peaceful occupation of the British Channel Islands by German forces, 30 June–3 July 1940.

The Channel Islands, especially Alderney, would have an important place in the eventual Atlantic Wall, so it is relevant to look briefly at this operation, which the Germans no doubt thought of at the time as a logical first step to the successful invasion of the United Kingdom. After some dithering and mind changing in Whitehall, it had been decided to leave the Channel Islands undefended. However, no one told the Germans until after they had carried out an armed reconnaissance (on 28 June) during which they bombed and machine-gunned St Peter Port in Guernsey and St Helier in Jersey, killing 44 civilians and wounding many more. Fortunately this was the only bloodshed during the initial occupation of the islands, by a small force from 216th Infantry Division, which was then occupying the Cherbourg peninsula area, together with Naval Assault Group *Gotenhafen* (Kriegsmarine Abteilung 'Gotenhafen')[2] and some Luftwaffe light anti-aircraft guns. Commanded by Major Albrecht Lanz, CO of 2nd Battalion, 396th Regiment (216th Infantry Division), who became the first island Commandant of Guernsey, the force landed peacefully by air at Guernsey airport on 30 June, then went on to visit and formally take over Jersey, Alderney and Sark together with the other tiny uninhabited islets of Herm, Brechou, Jethou and Lithou. So at least some of the German forces could legitimately say, in the words of their song, that they had been '*fahren gegen England*' ('marching against England') successfully.

The Channel Islands became a special place as far as Hitler was concerned and, as we will see later, he rated them so important as to station the largest infantry division in the entire German Army there. The fortunate garrison would in fact have an almost bullet-free occupation and become known as the 'Canada Division' by the rest of the German Army, who were rightly convinced that they would all end up in POW camps there or in the UK.

The Channel Islands would be the only part of the British Isles to be occupied by the Germans and the islanders would have to put up with five long years of occupation until they were liberated on 9 May 1945, with the German surrender and the arrival of British troops. Some of the fortifications built on the Channel Islands were unique within the Atlantic Wall and will be covered in some detail later.

'Softly Softly'

Whilst all this activity was taking place, France and the other occupied western European countries had rather faded into the background. As Professor Alan Wilt says in the opening chapter to his book on the Atlantic Wall:

'The Wehrmacht wanted a minimum of trouble during the initial period of adjustment. For this reason, although the Germans had placed the Netherlands and Belgium under occupation governments, numerous Dutch and Belgian officials continued to function in an administrative capacity. The Germans also treated France with deference, for the French, though beaten, still retained a considerable naval fleet as well as several unconquered colonies. And her civil servants, as in the Low Countries, could administer the country with only nominal German control, thus freeing the Wehrmacht to dispose of Britain.'

He goes on to explain how the Germans occupied only that part of metropolitan France which lay closest to England and the Atlantic coast, letting the Vichy government control the south-eastern part of France and even allowing it to retain an armed force of some 100,000 men so as to help with the maintenance of law and order. In 1940, therefore, the need for defences along the Atlantic coast was probably the last thing on the minds of the German planners.

Allied Strategy — A Second Front?

The most contentious issue between the USSR and the rest of the Allies was undoubtedly Joseph Stalin's continually repeated demands from 1941 onwards, that they should open a 'Second Front' in the West on the mainland of Europe, in order to divert pressure from his hard-pressed Red Army, which was by then fighting the advancing German forces deep inside the USSR. Initially there was no reaction, however, as the assault which had begun on 22 June 1941 continued to succeed, and the German penetrations extended nearer and nearer to the outskirts of Moscow itself, there was growing pressure from the population of Britain, and then in the USA, to invade Europe. Fortunately the Soviets were able to hold on and withdraw deeper and deeper into their vast country, whilst Churchill remained unwilling (and initially of course unable) to commit large-scale forces to a major assault, without first conducting considerable forward preparation and planning. Following on from visits by the Soviet Foreign Minister, Molotov, to London in early 1942, to press again for the opening of the Second Front, Churchill once more travelled to meet President Roosevelt in June 1942. Churchill reiterated the British view that a landing in Europe was impossible in 1942, but proposed in its stead a plan to invade North-West Africa (Operation 'Torch'). Initially the US Joint Chiefs of Staff opposed the proposal, but the obvious weakness of Britain and the Allied war machine (US industry was still getting into gear and the massive expansion of US armed forces had only just begun) forced them to reconsider and accept 'Torch' the following month. The next major conference was held near Casablanca in January 1943 and, despite the absence of Stalin who was too busy dealing with the defence of Stalingrad to make the journey, the main topic discussed was the opening of the Second Front in Europe. Churchill and the British Chiefs of Staff — supported to a degree by Roosevelt — opted for an invasion in southern Europe to build upon their obvious success which was by then apparent in North Africa. However, the American service chiefs, led by General Marshall, wanted to go for a cross-Channel invasion to occupy northern France in 1943. Once again the British considered this to be premature, especially as there was also much for the Allies to worry about in the Pacific war with the Japanese. After some 10 days of arguing, it was eventually decided to opt for the invasion of Sicily (Operation 'Husky'), to be followed later by the invasion of Italy (Operations 'Baytown' and 'Avalanche'), whilst a cross-Channel invasion was once again put on hold, although it was agreed that a planning staff (COSSAC — Chief of Staff to the Supreme Allied Commander) would be established and that the build-up of US troops in UK would be accelerated.

It was not until the third Anglo-American conference, held in Washington in mid-May 1943, (code-named 'Trident'), that the target date for the cross-Channel invasion was finally agreed as 1 May 1944. This date was confirmed at the first Quebec conference (code-named Quadrant) held in August 1943, despite the fact that Churchill still favoured an offensive through Italy and into the Balkans, rather than in North-West Europe. Stalin did not attend that conference either, but the Soviets still pressed just as hard for the Second Front. Operation 'Overlord' was the code-name given to the Allied invasion of occupied North-West Europe, whilst the assault phase, namely the landing by a 150,000 strong invasion force, was code-

Right:
The occupation forces on parade. Here a detachment of Luftwaffe field troops from one of the Luftwaffe field divisions (authorised by Hitler in 1942 to absorb excess Air Force personnel) marches through Villedieu-les-Poêles, Brittany. *J. P. Benamou Collection*

Below:
President Roosevelt and Winston Churchill discussed the Soviet demands for a Second Front during their meeting at Casablanca in French Morocco in January 1943. This photo was taken at the Villa Dar-es-Saada, Casablanca. *IWM — NA472*

named 'Neptune'. In February 1944, SHAEF (Supreme Headquarters Allied Expeditionary Force), the HQ of the Supreme Allied Commander, General Dwight D. Eisenhower, was activated and 'Overlord's' air, land and sea commanders produced the initial joint plan for 'Neptune'. Changes, such as the expansion of the assault force from three divisions to eight (including three airborne) and the subsequent need for more landing craft that were by then in short supply, together with climatic and geographical considerations, led to the date for the invasion being narrowed down to the period 4–6 June 1944. D-Day was initially fixed for 5 June, but then had to be delayed for 24 hours due to bad weather.

Der Feind Hört Mit!

The Germans had a saying during the war, 'Der Feind Hört Mit!' ('The Enemy Listens'), their equivalent to Britain's 'Careless Talk Cost Lives' campaign, so they were no strangers to the world of spies and spying. They had in the Abwehr a sophisticated military intelligence and counter-intelligence organisation which had been formed just after the Great War. Despite the fact that the Versailles Treaty had forbidden Germany from establishing an intelligence organisation, a counter-espionage group had been set up as early as 1920 within the Defence Ministry. It was known as Abwehr (Defence) and in 1933 its duties were expanded to include espionage.

Below: 'Achtung! Der Feind hört mit!' The warning that the enemy is always listening appears on this bunker wall, close to the telephones, just to remind users to watch their security. *J. P. Benamou Collection*

It was later vastly increased in size and scope after the appointment of Admiral Canaris in 1935, so that by the beginning of World War 2, it was an extremely large and sophisticated intelligence network. Therefore it would be illogical to think that the Allied high level discussions, planning and preparations for the Second Front went unnoticed by the Abwehr secret agents, although there were relatively few German spies actually operating in Britain, and then only briefly until all were captured.[3]

Undoubtedly, knowledge of what the Allies were planning as regards the launching of the Second Front had its effect upon the need to build new defences to protect North-West Europe. Thus it became rapidly clear to Hitler and the OKW that it would in future be necessary to defend the western coastline of their 'Empire', so that they could continue to give the bulk of their attention to the campaign in the East. This led to the publication of an OKW directive on 14 December 1941, which detailed the building of the *Neue Westwall*, (New Westwall). It was issued with Hitler's full approval, but signed by Field Marshal Keitel (Chief of Staff of OKW) and its opening paragraph set out the concept thus:

> *'The coastal regions of the Arctic Ocean, North Sea and Atlantic Ocean which we control are ultimately to be built into a "New Westwall" in order that we can be sure of repelling any landing attempt, however strong, using the smallest possible number of permanently stationed troops.'*

The directive went on to explain that the aim was to construct a series of coastal batteries to ensure long-range coastal defence. In addition, it explained that it had been decided to build bunkers of the *verstarkt feldmassige* (V.f) type, that is to say, reinforced field fortifications, that were different from the ordinary, usually temporary field fortifications (made of earth, wood and masonry) The V.f type would be built of masonry or reinforced concrete with ceilings and walls between 0.30m and 1.5m thick. In view of the fact that at that time there was little enemy air activity, open, circular gun emplacements were chosen. With the construction of the 'New Westwall', all the existing coastal artillery batteries were to be improved and extra protection from *Stützpunkte* ('strongpoints') would be given to coastal areas considered to be under threat.

Priorities were given for the construction in certain specific areas. Norway was given top priority, firstly, because it was difficult to use mobile reserves there, then because of the terrain and weather, and finally, because there was an urgent need to increase the number of harbour defences available so as to protect coastal shipping. Belgium and France's western coasts were then given second priority, with the open coasts of the Netherlands and Jutland third. Most of the construction of these coastal defences would be under Army control, but the Navy was made responsible for Norway and for all measures which involved sea warfare. Air defence was naturally put under the Luftwaffe,,whilst the actual construction work in all areas was to be handled by the Organisation Todt.

Directive 40

As the war dragged on, the OKW was forced to send more and more reinforcements to other areas such as the Mediterranean and of course to the Eastern Front which continually demanded additional troops, so the defences in the West were inevitably weakened. This danger was appreciated by Hitler and the OKW and gave rise to them drawing up a plan for the defence of the

Above: 'Pinpricks and propaganda coups.' British commandos storming an enemy position at Maaloy are silhouetted in the white smoke of a phosphorous grenade exploding to their flank. IWM — N520

western coasts. The Küstenverteidigung (Coastal Defence) Directive 40 of 23 March 1942 enshrined this plan and as it is the main reason for the building of the Atlantic Wall, I have given it almost an entire chapter to itself which follows on next. However, before going into the detail of the main policy, it is worth while looking at another of the 'Reasons Why' the Wall was built.

Pinpricks and Propaganda Coups

On 2 July 1940, just two days after the Channel Islands had been occupied by German forces, Winston Churchill sent a note to Major-General Hastings Ismay, who was then his personal chief of staff and a member of the Chiefs of Staff Committee, in which he commented on the way in which the Germans had carried out their operation and recommended that plans should be immediately formulated to land secretly by night on the islands to kill or capture some of the invaders. There should be, he said, a ready source of information about the islands available from ex-inhabitants who had been evacuated or who were currently serving with British forces.

A few days later his memo would be acted upon and resulted in the first operation to be undertaken by the newly forming unit — the Commandos. Sadly it was a complete disaster from start to finish; some of the launches which were to be used to ferry the commandos from the destroyers which took them to the Channel Islands were found to be unfit and had to be left behind, whilst others were damaged en route by the buffeting they received from the destroyers' wakes; then the naval officers

in charge of the remaining launches almost missed Guernsey completely due to problems with their navigational instruments; next the chosen enemy targets on Guernsey were found devoid of any enemy, and finally, after the raid had been aborted, due to tide problems, and the commandos had to swim out to the destroyer, it was discovered that three of their number could not swim, so had to be left behind to be captured by the Germans! All this would result in a scathing missive from the PM to HQ Combined Forces, which included the words: 'Let there be no more silly fiascos like those perpetrated in Guernsey.'

Fortunately this incident was followed by a completely successful raid on the Lofoten islands in northern Norway on 4 March 1941, during which factories producing glycerine were destroyed. More importantly, the current settings for an Enigma code machine were found aboard a German armed trawler. This was followed on 26 December 1941 by another raid on the Lofoten islands designed to divert German attention during a further commando raid — the bloody encounter at Vaagso on 27 December 1941. This small-scale operation against the German-occupied islands at the entrance to Nordjord in central Norway, was designed to prevent German troops from being moved from Norway and sent to the Eastern Front. German military installations were wrecked and the supporting Royal Navy ships neutralised several of the nearby shore batteries.

Despite being only a 'pinprick' it was a great morale boost to the British public and was described in the British press as 'The Perfect Raid'.

Other small-scale commando raids would follow, including a fair number on the Channel Islands and the French coast, with varying degrees of success. However, all these amphibious operations would be overshadowed by the attacks on St Nazaire on the night of 27–29 March 1942 and the even larger Dieppe raid on 19 August 1942. Clearly the raids prior to St Nazaire and Dieppe had their effect upon the German psyche — they enraged Hitler to such an extent that they caused him to issue the infamous order that all captured commandos should be executed. Therefore, they must have had their part to play in the formulation of Hitler's subsequent Directive 40. The St Nazaire and Dieppe raids, however, took place after that directive had been written, so therefore can be fairly described as being the first two significant assaults upon the German Atlantic Wall, and as such deserve to be dealt with separately and in more detail than is possible in this opening chapter.

To summarise therefore, there were a number of 'Reasons Why' the Atlantic Wall was built, although the main one was obviously to protect *Festung Europa* from any major Allied invasion. The building took place over a long period, the main impetus being the all important Directive 40 which we will now examine in some detail.

Notes
1. These were DeTeGerät fire control radars designed to locate sea targets.
2. A Naval Assault Group is probably best described as being the Kriegsmarine equivalent of the Royal Marines.
3. See *After the Battle* Issue No 11: 'German Spies in Britain' for details.

Above:
Burning oil factories at Vaagso, where 98 prisoners were taken and considerable damage caused, 27 December 1941.
IWM — N459

Above left:
Commodore Lord Louis Mountbatten, Adviser Combined Operations (appointed by Churchill on 4 October 1941 to succeed the then Director, Admiral of the Fleet, Sir Roger Keyes), talks to commandos after the Vaagso raid.
IWM — N505

Left:
Commandos returning from a successful raid on the Lofoten Islands on 4 March 1941.
IWM — A3321

Right:
A 17cm SK L/40 of Battery M II, near Sangatte, Pas de Calais, seen here in 1942, still in an open firing position where it was located in the summer of 1940. Note the sandbag wall erected to give the gun crew some protection, the camouflage netting and the fabric muzzle cover. Also, the range-finder in the background. *Bundesarchiv*

Below left, below right and bottom:
Hans Sippli, who served in the Marineartillerie (Naval Artillery) took these photos whilst he was stationed on the Mole at Zeebrugge during the summer of 1940. The AA machine gun is a Dutch Mitrailleur M20, a version of the British Lewis gun. See Chapter 8 for an account of Hans Sippli's service. *Hans Sippli*

Chapter 2

Directive Number 40

The following Directive was issued by the Führer's Headquarters on 23 March 1942, under the title: 'Competence of Commanders in Coastal Areas'.

OKW/WEST/Operation No 001031
DIRECTIVE NUMBER 40

I. General Considerations

1. In the coming months, the coastline of Europe will be vulnerable to the danger of an enemy landing in strength. The time and place of such landing operations may not be dictated by operational considerations only. For example, setbacks in other areas, obligations to Allies and political considerations, may persuade him to take action which might appear unlikely from a purely military point of view.

2. Even enemy landing operations which have limited objectives could have serious repercussions on our own plans if they result in the enemy gaining a foothold on the coast. Our coastal sea traffic could be interrupted and they may pin down significant numbers of our Army and Air Force in dealing with them, which may require them to be withdrawn from other important areas. Capturing one of our airfields or establishing a bridgehead would be particularly dangerous.

3. There are many important military and industrial locations all along the coastline or close by, some of which are equipped with especially valuable plant, which may tempt the enemy into making surprise local attacks.

4. Particular attention must be made to preparations in England for amphibious landings on open coastline, because they have at their disposal numerous armoured landing craft, able to carry armoured fighting vehicles and heavy weapons. The possibility of parachute and airborne attacks on a large scale must also be considered.

II. General Operational Instructions for Coastal Defence

1. Coastal defence is a task for everyone and calls for especially close and complete co-operation between all units of the three services.

2. In addition to naval and air reconnaissance, the intelligence service must endeavour to obtain early information on the state of enemy readiness and their preparations for any amphibious landing operation. All suitable air and sea units will then concentrate on attacking enemy embarkation locations and their convoys, so as to defeat and destroy them as far from our coast as possible. However, it may be that by clever camouflage and/or by taking advantage of bad weather conditions, the enemy may achieve a surprise attack. All troops who may be exposed to such surprise attacks must be at a *state of permanent readiness*. One of the most important duties of commanding officers of such units must be to overcome a lack of vigilance among their troops which, as experience has shown, is bound to increase as time passes.

3. As recent battle experience has shown, the responsibility for planning and the implementation of all defensive matters formulated in the defence of the coast — including coastal waters within range of medium coastal artillery — *must* lie unequivocally and unreservedly in the hands of a single commander. This commander must be able to make use of all available forces and weapons of all branches of the armed forces, of organisations and units outside the armed forces, and of our civilian headquarters in the area, for the sole purpose of destroying enemy transports and landing forces. He will use them so that the attack collapses if possible, *before* it reaches the coast, or at the latest, on the coast itself. Enemy forces that do manage to land must be destroyed or thrown back into the sea by an immediate counter-attack. Everyone carrying weapons, no matter what branch of service or non-service organisation they belong to, must do this. Additionally, the working of the naval shore establishments must be guaranteed, in so far as they are not themselves involved in the fighting on land. This applies equally to Air Force ground staff and anti-aircraft defence of airfields. No headquarters is to initiate a withdrawal in such circumstances. All German troops stationed on or near the coast must be armed and trained for battle. The enemy must also be prevented from securing a foothold on any islands that present a threat to the mainland or to coastal shipping.

4. The distribution of forces and the building of defensive works must be carried out so that our strongest defence positions are located in those sectors most likely to be selected by the enemy for landings (fortified areas). Other coastal sectors that may be threatened by small-scale surprise attacks will be defended by a series of strongpoints, supported, where possible, by the coastal batteries. Important military and industrial plant will be included within these strongpoints. The same principles will apply to off-shore islands, whilst less-threatened areas will be kept under observation.

5. The coast will be divided into sectors as decided by the three services in mutual agreement, or, should the situation demand it, by the responsible commander (see Para III-1 below) whose decision will be final.

6. The fortified areas and strongpoints must be able, by virtue of proper distribution of forces, completion of all-round defence and by their supply situation, to hold out for some time even against a superior enemy force. Fortified areas and strongpoints *will be defended to the last man*. They must never be forced to surrender from lack of ammunition, rations, or water.

7. The responsible commanders (see Para III-2 below) will issue orders for keeping the coast under constant observation and will ensure that reconnaissance reports from all three services are quickly evaluated, co-ordinated and sent to the headquarters and civilian authorities concerned. As soon as there is any evidence that an enemy operation is imminent, then the commander is authorised to issue the necessary instructions for co-ordinated and complementary reconnaissance on sea and land.

8. There can be no question of peacetime privileges for any

Hitler plans. The Führer and Field Marshal von Brauchitsch study a map together with Keitel (left), Jodl (behind) and an unidentified officer (possibly von Brauchitsch's adjutant). *IWM — HU75487*

headquarters or formation of the armed services in coastal areas, or for any non-military organisations and units. The accommodation, security precautions, equipment, immediate readiness for action, and the use they make of the ground in their area will entirely depend upon the need to meet any enemy attack as quickly and in as great strength as possible. Where the military situation demands it, the civilian population will be immediately evacuated.

III. Competence of Commanders

1. The following are responsible for the preparation and execution of plans for coastal defence in the areas under German command:
   (a) In the eastern area of operations (excluding Finland): the army commanders appointed by the Army High Command.
   (b) In the coastal area of the High Command Lappland: C-in-C High Command, Lappland.
   (c) In Norway: Commander Armed Forces, Norway.
   (d) In Denmark: Commander of German troops in Denmark.
   (e) In the occupied western territories (including the Netherlands): C-in-C West.
   (For coastal defence the responsible commanders in (d) and (e) will be directly subordinate to the High Command of the Armed Forces.)
   (f) In the Balkans (including the occupied islands): Commander Armed Forces South-east.
   (g) In the Baltic Territories and the Ukraine: Commander Armed Forces Baltic Territories and Ukraine.
   (h) In the home theatre of war: the commanding admirals.

2. The commanders named in paragraph III-1 above will have for these tasks, full powers of command over staffs commanding all armed forces, the German civil authorities, and the non-military units and organisations in the area. In exercising this authority they will send out the necessary tactical, administrative and supply instructions, and ensure that they are obeyed. In all matters relating to land fighting training of units will follow their dictates and all necessary information will be put at their disposal.

3. Among the orders to be given and measures to be taken the following *must* be given top priority:
   (a) The inclusion inside fortified areas of strongpoints of all important military and industrial establishments that are concerned with defence, especially those of the Navy (e.g. submarine bases) and Air Force.
   (b) The co-ordination of coastal reconnaissance.
   (c) The defence of fortified areas and strongpoints by infantry.
   (d) The defence by infantry of all isolated positions outside the fortified areas and strongpoints — e.g. coastal lookout posts and air-attack warning posts.
   (e) Artillery defence against land targets. NB: The Navy has priority in the installation of new batteries, or in the conversion of existing batteries.

(f) The defensive preparedness, development and supply facilities of installations, including isolated positions away from these installations. (This includes being equipped with all the necessary weapons needed for defence such as mines, hand grenades, flame-throwers, barbed-wire, etc.)

(g) The signals communications network.

(h) Methods of ensuring that troops are always on the alert and that infantry and gunnery training is being carried out in accordance with the special defence requirements.

4. Similar authority is conferred upon local commanders, up to sector commanders, in so far as they are responsible for the defence of a part of the coast. The commanders designated in paragraph III-1, will in general, appoint commanders of army divisions employed in coastal defence as local commanders with full powers. In Crete, the Fortress Commandant Crete, will appoint them. As far as other duties allow, local commandants or Air Force/Navy commanders will be made responsible for the general defence of individual sectors or sub-sectors, especially air and naval strongpoints.

5. All naval and air units employed in strategic warfare are subordinate to the Navy or Air Force. In the event of enemy attacks on the coast they are required to comply with the orders of the commanders responsible for defence, in so far as tactical considerations permit. They must therefore, be included in the distribution of all the information they require for the duties, and close liaison will be maintained with their headquarters.

IV. **Special Duties of the Branches of the Armed Forces in the Field of Coastal Defence**

1. Navy
   (a) Organisation and protection of coastal traffic.
   (b) Training and employment of all coastal artillery against targets at sea.
   (c) Employment of naval forces.

2. Air Force
   (a) Air defence of coastal areas. The use against enemy landings of suitable and available anti-aircraft guns, under the orders of the commander responsible for local defence, will not be affected.
   (b) The completion of ground organisations and their protection against air attack and surprise attack by land; the latter in cases where airfields are not included in coastal defences and are therefore insufficiently protected.
   (c) Operational employment of aircraft. Attention to be paid to duplication of command implied by these special duties.

V.
Orders and instructions which run contrary to this directive are hereby cancelled with effect from 1 April 1942. New operational orders which will be issued by commanders on the basis of my directive, are to be submitted to me through the OKW.

Signed: *Adolf Hitler*

Bones of Contention

To a degree, Directive 40 reiterated much of what had been said in Keitel's earlier directive of the previous December. However, it clearly was the true starting point from which the Atlantic Wall proper was conceived. Reading it through one has to congratulate its writers in the OKW staff for dotting all the 'i's and crossing all the 't's in their desire to produce a set of rules that could not be misinterpreted. However, human nature and inter-service rivalry soon led to differences of opinion emerging, some of which were so fundamental as to almost invalidate the whole *raison d'être* of the Wall itself and to make the Allies' task of breaking through it all the simpler. Whilst these differences are best commented upon at the end of this study when they have become more apparent, it is perhaps relevant here at least to air some of the main bones of contention such as:

- Who was really in command?
- Who controls what?
- Where was the main battle to be fought?
- Who controls the mobile reserves and where should they be located?

Who Was Really in Command?

Below Hitler and the OKW, instead of one Supreme Commander as was to be the case on the Allied side, the Oberbefehlshaber West (OBW), Feldmarschall Gerd von Rundstedt, was purely a land commander, having no direct control over any sea or air forces, the senior admiral (Theodor Krancke who commanded Marinegruppe West) still received his orders direct from Oberkommandomarine (OKM — Navy High Command), while the senior Luftwaffe general (Feldmarschall Hugo Sperrle who commanded Luftflotte 3) received his orders direct from the Oberkommando der Luftwaffe (OKL). As Rommel's chief of staff Hans Speidel wryly commented in his book *We Defended Normandy*:

'Operations at sea and in the air could thus be co-ordinated neither by the C-in-C in the West nor by the Army Group commander. The military commanders were only partially informed of the intentions of the other two services and usually too late.'

In any case von Rundstedt, who had gone into voluntary retirement at the end of 1941 after falling out with Hitler, only to be recalled in July 1942 to become C-in-C West, was really only in command 'on paper'; every major decision was actually made by Hitler or 'rubber stamped' on his behalf. It is said that von Rundstedt once caustically remarked that the only troop formation he was actually allowed to move was the guard at the gate of his own headquarters.

Who Controls What?

Just a few days after the issue of Directive 40 the Navy issued an order which contained the following words:

'Even if the fight for the coast extends to the coastal areas within the reach of the Army medium range artillery, control over the bombardment of targets at sea remains in the hands of naval shore commanders who have command over coastal artillery (including Army coastal artillery) in the sector for this purpose. The naval shore commanders are under the operational command of the respective Army divisional commanders only in the battle for the coast.'[1]

This muddled thinking produced a duality of command that might have worked all right in a straightforward situation such as the one that pertained on the Channel Islands, where there was a clear demarcation between sea and land targets, the

Above: 'I do love to be beside the seaside!' Hitler's overweight sidekick Hermann Göring, looks out across the sea from an OP. *HU24288*

Above: Even on the Atlantic Wall there were sometimes dummy weapons. This pretend naval gun would possibly fool high level Allied air reconnaissance. It was located at Fort Le Marchant on Guernsey. *Guernsey Museums and Galleries*

Navy being responsible for engaging the enemy whilst they were on the water, whilst the Army took over once they had landed. Anti-aircraft (AA) guns were obviously excluded and could engage enemy aircraft with impunity. Thus the Navy C-in-C Channel Islands (SEEKO-KI) exercised command over all Navy and Army coastal artillery, controlling their fire as and when necessary. However, this system of command for the defence of the Channel Islands against a determined enemy attack was never fully put to the test, although it does seem to have worked well enough within the tight limits of the small attacks on these tiny islands.

On the French coast, however, it was a different matter. Here the Army wished to group its coastal batteries inland around some 5km from the coast in order to reduce the risk from naval bombardment, whereas the naval commanders wanted their batteries to be situated as close to the coast as possible in order to be able to fire with line of sight directly upon assaulting enemy vessels. The resulting differences of opinion undoubtedly affected results. For example, if one looks in detail at the results achieved by the formidable coastal artillery battery at Longues-sur-Mer (4 x 152mm naval guns), when faced by the Allied armada on D-Day, we can see that it failed to sink or even to damage a single vessel of the enemy amphibious strike force.

Where Was the Main Battle to be Fought?

Whilst Directive 40 clearly stated that all the defensive actions of the commander must be to defeat the enemy attack before it could reach the coast or, at the latest, on the coast itself, this undoubtedly went against the opinions of many of the advocates of mobile warfare. As we shall see, Feldmarschall Rommel, who would later play such a major part in improving the Wall's defences, was quite clear that the shoreline was the right place to defeat the enemy — witness his dictum: 'Die HKL ist der Strand'.[2] His main reason for coming to this conclusion was his personal experience in North Africa of having to move by day under constant enemy air superiority. The casualties both to men and materiel, especially during the Tunisian campaign, had left him with the firm conviction that reserve forces, in particular armour, had to be as far forward as possible, otherwise they would be decimated trying to get their panzers into battle. However, his 'fight them on the beaches' policy was not shared by von Rundstedt and other senior officers, who favoured mobile defence.

Control of Mobile Reserves

This became one of the most contentious issues of the defence strategy. Panzer Group West, commanded by General der Panzertruppen Freiherr Geyr von Schweppenburg, who was completely opposed to Rommel's view that reserves had to be forward, brushed aside Rommel's criticisms of his centralised 'out of harm's way' policy by saying that even if Allied air power affected daylight movement, then the panzers would still be able to move quickly by night. Not only did he fundamentally disagree with Rommel but he also thoroughly disliked the Desert Fox's chief of staff, the brilliant General Hans Speidel, commenting on one occasion that Speidel had never commanded anything larger than an infantry company. In a postwar study he reiterated his criticism of Rommel and his theories on panzer movement thus:

'The following Rommel theories were fundamentally unjustified and have been proved to be false:
(a) "Panzer divisions cannot be moved when the enemy

has air supremacy." Under skilled leadership 12th SS Panzer Division and 2nd Panzer Division reached their operational area without serious losses. Panzer Lehr Division had its considerable losses only because of Rundstedt's express command to move forward by day, an order foreign to air and armoured warfare.*
(b) "A main landing on the Channel Coast is still to be expected." This is a model example of clinging tenaciously to a preconceived opinion.
(c) "Without mobile panzer divisions, landings of fairly great local significance cannot be eliminated." "Pure" panzer divisions cannot fight with their mass and shock effect at all within range of great enemy battle fleets, least of all in flooded and mined terrain. Anyone who fought in Sicily and Salerno (invasion of Italy) will confirm that. Besides, for the sake of logic it must be stated that it is comparatively easier to bring up panzer divisions from a location far to the rear than to move laterally mobile panzer reserves near the front. If the latter is possible, the first must be too."[3]

Such fundamental points of disagreement were bound to have an effect on the success or failure of the German defence plan, especially when the overall land commander, von Rundstedt, had no direct control over sea and air forces. Clearly the seeds of confusion were there from the outset.

Hitler's Table Talk

It is also interesting to note that only a few months after Directive 40 had been issued — on 13 May 1942 to be exact, during the evening meal at his headquarters — Hitler was describing a recent inspection trip he had made to look at the defences in western France:

'I was accosted by one of the workmen', Hitler recalled, '"Mein Führer" he said, "I hope we're never going away from here. After all this tremendous work, that would be a pity." There is a wealth of wisdom in the man's remark, for it shows that a man hates to abandon such safe positions as those on the Channel coast, captured during the campaign in France and consolidated by the Organisation Todt, and retire into the narrow confines of the North Sea.'[4]

Further Directives and Orders from the Führer

Whilst Directive 40 was clearly the most important of Hitler's pronouncements as far as the Atlantic Wall was concerned, it was not the only one that affected the Wall. There are a number of others which were issued subsequently and which had a definite bearing on all or part of the Wall and so need to be looked at here:

- Fortification Order of 20 October 1941, which dealt specifically with the fortification of the Channel Islands.
- Directive 51 of 3 November 1943, which dealt with the situation that was emerging in the West that would lead to what Hitler described as being 'War on two Fronts'.
- Führer Order No 11 of 8 March 1944, which laid down procedures for Commandants of Fortified Areas and Battle Commandants.
- Directive 62 of 29 August 1944, which dealt specifically with the completion of defences in the German Bight.

Above: This massive 28cm Eisenbahngeschütz (railway gun), called 'New Bruno', was located at Zeebrugge in Belgium in August 1942. The gun alone weighed 218 tons. *Bundesarchiv*

Above: Ammunition numbers of the 'New Bruno' gun crew manhandle cartridges on a small railway truck. *Bundesarchiv*

Above: The vast turning dome of the Todt Battery's electric range-finder. Together with subsidiary fire-control posts it could cover an arc of 342°. *Bundesarchiv*

Above: Major Albrecht Lanz, first commandant of the island of Guernsey, steps out of his commandeered car, whilst an island policeman holds open the door. *IWM — HU3616*

Fortification Order for the Channel Islands

The Directive issued by the Führer's office on 20 October 1941 read as follows:

1. Operations on a large scale against the territories we occupy in the West are, as before, unlikely. Under pressure of the situation in the East, however, or for reasons of politics or propaganda, small scale operations at any moment may be anticipated, particularly an attempt to regain possession of the Channel Islands, which are important to us for the protection of sea communications.
2. Counter-measures in the islands must ensure that any English attack fails before a landing is achieved, whether it is attempted by sea, by air or both together. The possibility of advantage being taken of bad visibility to effect a surprise landing must be borne in mind. Emergency measures for strengthening the defences have already been ordered, and all branches of the forces stationed in the islands, except the Air Force, are placed under the orders of the Commandant of the islands.
3. With regard to the permanent fortification of the islands, to convert them into an impregnable fortress (which must be pressed forward with the utmost speed) I give the following orders:
    (a) The High Command of the Army is responsible for the fortifications as a whole and will, in the overall programme, incorporate construction for the Air Force and the Navy. The strength of the fortifications and the order in which they are erected will be based on the principles and the practical knowledge gained from building the Western Wall.
    (b) For the Army: it is important to provide a close network of emplacements, well concealed, and given flanking fields of fire. The emplacements must be sufficient for guns of a size capable of piercing armour plate 100mm thick, to defend against tanks which may attempt to land. There must be ample accommodation for stores and ammunition, for mobile diversion parties and for armoured cars.
    (c) For the Navy: one heavy battery[5] on the islands and two on the French coast to safeguard the sea approaches.
    (d) For the Air Force: strongpoints must be created with searchlights and sufficient space to accommodate such AA units as are needed to protect all-important constructions.
    (e) Foreign labour, especially Russians and Spaniards but also Frenchmen, may be used for the building works.
4. Another order will follow for the deportation to the continent of all Englishmen who are not natives of the islands, i.e. not born there.
5. Progress reports to be sent to me on the first day of each month, to the C-in-C of the Army and directed to the Supreme Command of the Armed Forces (OKW) — Staff of the Führer, Division L.

Signed: *Adolf Hitler*[6]

Directive 51 (3 November 1943)

This Directive from the Führer really came about because of the way the war was going on the Eastern Front. Instead of a swift victory as they had achieved in North-West Europe, the German Blitzkrieg forces were being swallowed up in the vast steppes of Russia, whilst in the Middle East events had also turned against the Germans and their inept Italian partners. Now there was also the inevitability of having to fight on yet another front as the Americans and British built up for the long awaited 'Second Front'. Directive 51 therefore opened with some sombre words:

'The hard and costly struggle against Bolshevism during the last two and a half years, which has involved the bulk of our military strength in the East, has demanded extreme exertions. The greatness of the danger and the general situation demanded it. But the situation has since changed. The danger in the East remains, but a greater danger now appears in the West: an Anglo-Saxon landing! In the East, the vast extent of the territory makes it possible for us to lose ground even on a large scale, without a fatal blow being dealt to the nervous system of Germany.

'It is very different in the West! Should the enemy succeed in breaching our defences on a wide front here, the immediate consequences would be unpredictable. Everything indicates that the enemy will launch an offensive against the Western Front of Europe, at the latest in the spring, perhaps even earlier.'

Hitler then went on to state that he could no longer take responsibility for weakening the Western defences in favour of the other theatres, and that therefore he had decided to reinforce them, in particular the areas from where the 'long-range bombardment of England will begin' — in other words, the secret V-weapon sites — because he considered that it was there that the decisive battle against the enemy landing forces would be fought. Diversionary attacks were noted as being possible on other fronts and he cited Denmark as being a possible location for a large-scale attack, despite the difficulties of launching such an undertaking, because if it were successful then the political and operational repercussions would be considerable.

Such an assault would initially require the whole of the enemy offensive strength being thrown against the German forces holding the coastline. Therefore,

'Only by intensive construction, which means straining our available manpower and materials at home and in the occupied territories to the limit, can we strengthen our coastal defences in the short time which probably remains.'

The directive then went on to delineate the ground weapons that would shortly be sent to Denmark and the other areas in the West, such as heavy anti-tank guns, static armoured fighting vehicles (to be sunk into existing emplacements), coastal artillery, field artillery, mines and other supplies. They would be concentrated at strongpoints in the most threatened areas on the coast, which meant that everyone had to accept that the defences in less threatened areas would not be improved. If and when the enemy attacked, then immediate heavy counter-attacks were to be launched, so as to prevent them exploiting their landings and throw them back into the sea. Such emotive phrases as 'high fighting quality', 'attacking power' and 'mobility' were used to describe these counter-attack forces, whilst 'careful and detailed emergency plans' had to be drawn up. The Air Force and Navy must also play their part, 'with all the forces at their disposal, regardless of losses'.

The Directive then went into considerable detail as to what action the Führer expected the Army, Navy, Air Force and SS to take, requiring them to submit their plans to him immediately for the follow-up action to be taken within the next three months. The Chief of the Army General Staff, the Inspector

General of Armoured Forces and the C-in-C West were specifically named for action under the Army section. The plan for the distribution of weapons, tanks, self-propelled (SP) guns, motor vehicles and ammunition on the Western Front and in Denmark was to be based on the following dictates:

- All panzer and panzergrenadier divisions were to be assured of adequate mobility and equipped with 93 Panzer IV tanks or SP guns, plus strong anti-tank weapons, by the end of December 1943.
- 20th Luftwaffe Field Division was to be converted into an effective mobile offensive formation by the allocation of SP artillery also by the end of 1943.
- The Waffen-SS Panzergrenadier Division *HitlerJugend*, 21st Panzer Division, and the infantry and reserve divisions in Jutland were to be speedily brought up to strength.
- A further reinforcement of Mark IV SP guns and heavy anti-tank guns would be made to panzer divisions in reserve in the West and Denmark; this was also to include the SP artillery training unit in Denmark.
- An additional monthly allocation of 100 heavy anti-tank guns (7.5cm Pak 40 L/46 and 8.8cm Pak 43 L/71) of which half were to be SP, was to be made during November and December to the newly raised formations in the West.
- An increased weapons allocation (to include approximately 1,000 machine guns) was to be made to ground forces engaged in coastal defence in the West and Denmark (to be co-ordinated with the withdrawal of equipment from units in sectors not under attack threat).
- A liberal supply of short-range anti-tank weapons (Panzerfaust and Panzerschreck) was to be made to formations in threatened areas.
- The firepower in artillery and anti-tank guns of units stationed in Denmark and along the coasts of occupied territories in the West was to be increased, whilst Army artillery was to be strengthened.
- No units or formations stationed in the West and Denmark, nor any of the newly raised SP armoured artillery or anti-tank units in the West, were to be withdrawn and moved to other fronts without the Führer's approval.

The Chief of the Army General Staff and the Inspector General of Armoured Forces were to report to Hitler through staff channels, when the re-equipment of the units was completed.

Commander-in-Chief West Von Rundstedt was to carry out a series of exercises in the field and similar training measures to ensure that additional formations could be moved up from sectors that were not under attack and made capable of offensive action. Hitler firmly stated that areas where there was unlikely to be an enemy attack 'be ruthlessly stripped of all except the smallest forces essential for guard duties'. Labour units employed on construction were to open and keep open the lines of communication (roads and railways) which had been destroyed by the enemy, making full use of the local population. This order also applied to the Commander of German troops in Denmark, whilst the Chief of Army Equipment and the Commander of the Replacement Army were to raise regimental-sized battle groups in the home defence area from the men in training depots, or at Army schools and so on, which were to be

Below: Batterie Oldenburg at Calais, where Hans Sippli served in November 1942. *Hans Sippli*

at 48 hours' notice of being called up. All further personnel must be immediately ready to replace the heavy casualties that would be expected.

The Air Force The offensive and defensive power of the formations stationed in the West and Denmark was to be increased. This would be done by taking forces from flying units and AA units engaged in home defence, also from schools and training establishments, for employment in the West and Denmark. Ground establishments in southern Norway, Denmark, north-west Germany and the West were to be organised and supplied so that they were as decentralised as possible, to ensure that units were not exposed to enemy bombing at the start of major operations. This was especially important as far as fighter aircraft were concerned, which needed an increased number of emergency airfields. 'Particular attention will be paid to good camouflage.'

The Navy The Navy was to draw up plans to bring into action all naval forces that were capable of attacking the enemy landing fleet.

'Coastal defences under construction will be completed with all possible speed and the establishment of additional coastal batteries and the laying of further obstacles on the flanks will be considered.'

As with the Air Force the employment of everyone from schools, training establishments and other land establishments on security duties was emphasised. Special attention was to be paid to defence against enemy landings in Norway or Denmark, in particular to plans for using large numbers of submarines in northern sea areas, even if this caused a temporary diminution of these forces in the Atlantic.

The SS The Reichsführer-SS was to test the preparedness of units of the Waffen-SS[7] and the police and make preparations to raise battle-trained formations from those on training, in reserve or recuperating in the home defence area.

Hitler closed Directive 51 with orders to the various senior officers he had named in the directive to report by 15 November, that is in just 12 days, on what steps they had taken and those they proposed to take. As we shall see, although much was accomplished in the next few months, fundamental differences of opinion between the three services and between various senior officers, would fortunately — from the Allies' point of view — lead to final failure of these defence plans.

Führer Order 11

This was a general order issued for guidance to Commandants of Fortified Areas and Battle Commandants, for which there was now a need in various theatres of war, for example in Italy and on the Eastern Front, as well as at various places along the coastline of Western Europe. On 19 January 1944 he designated a number of coastal areas from the Netherlands to the Gironde estuary in south-west France as 'fortresses' and issued special instructions for their defence. Whilst the detail of the areas will be dealt with later, it is worth while naming them here:

The Netherlands Den Helder, Ijmuiden, the Hook of Holland and Vlissingen (Flushing), located at the entrance to the River Scheldt.

France Dunkirk (Dunkerque), Calais, Boulogne, Le Havre, Cherbourg, and St Malo along the Channel coast; the harbours of Brest, Lorient, St Nazaire, La Rochelle (with U-boat pens at nearby La Pallice), and Royan at the mouth of the Gironde along the Atlantic coastline.

Then, on 3 March, the **Channel Islands** were also given fortress status.

The gist of Hitler's Order 11 was as follows:

1. A distinction was to be made between Festeplätze (Fortified Areas or Fortresses) which would be under a Fortified Area Commandant and Ortsstützpunkte (Local Strongpoints) each commanded by a 'Battle Commandant'. The fortified areas were likened to castles of past eras, their aim being to ensure that the enemy did not occupy an area of vital operational importance. They would allow themselves to be surrounded and by doing so tie down the maximum possible number of enemy, who would thus be liable to successful counter-attacks. Local strongpoints on the other hand were within the battle area and would be defended tenaciously in the event of enemy penetration. They would act as a reserve of defence and should the enemy break through, as a corner/hinge for the front, becoming places from which counter-attacks could be launched.

2. Each 'Fortified Area Commandant' was to be specially selected, a tough experienced soldier, preferably of the rank of general, and could not delegate his responsibilities. He would be appointed by, and personally responsible to, the Army Group C-in-C. They would: 'pledge their honour as soldiers to carry out their duties to the last'. The C-in-C Army Group was the only person permitted to relieve a Fortified Area Commandant of his duties or to order him to surrender; however, this could not be done without Hitler's personal approval. Everyone within a Fortified Area was under the orders of the Commandant, be they soldiers or civilians and irrespective of their rank. The Fortified Area Commander had the military rights and disciplinary powers of a Commanding General, with both mobile courts martial and civilian courts to assist him. His staff would be appointed by Army Group, whilst his chief of staff would be appointed by OKH, but in accordance with suggestions from the Army Group.

3. The garrison of a fortified area comprised two elements: the security garrison and the general garrison. The former was to be inside the fortified area at all times. Its strength would depend on the size of the area and the tasks to be fulfilled (for example preparation and completion of defences, holding the area against raids or local enemy attacks). The general garrison was to be made available to the Commandant in sufficient time to permit it taking up proper defensive positions early enough to deal with a major enemy attack. The strength would, like the security garrison, be laid down by the C-in-C Army Group depending upon the size and task(s) of the fortified area.

4. Each 'Battle Commandant' came under the orders of the local forces commander and would be appointed by him and was to receive his operation orders from him. His rank would depend upon the importance of the position and the garrison strength. His duties called for: 'specially energetic officers whose qualities have been proved in crisis'.

5. The strength of the garrison of a 'Local Strongpoint' was to be fixed by the importance of the positions and the available troops. Orders were to be given from the HQ to which the Battle Commandant was subordinate.

Above: Officers of the Army and Marine Artillery at Batterie Oldenburg, Calais, *circa* autumn 1942. *Hans Sippli*

Directive 62

This was the order for the strengthening of the German Bight defences and covered the following main points:

1. The area covered was to be the German coast from the Danish frontier to the Dutch frontier, as well as those North and East Frisian Islands which had not yet been fully fortified, whilst those that had been fortified were to be brought up to a full state of defence.
2. The planning and preparation of all necessary measures for the speedy construction of a second position, that would run from the Danish frontier at a depth of about 10km from the coast.
3. The person responsible for construction was named as Gauleiter Kaufmann of Hamburg. However, this was later changed to make the Gauleiters of Schleswig-Holstein, East Hannover and Weser-Ems responsible for the defences which were located in their areas, whilst Kaufmann would supply them with what resources he had available and also act as their spokesman to X Corps.
4. C-in-C Naval Command North was to assume the direction of purely military tasks, with the Deputy General of X Army Corps responsible for carrying out the following tasks:
   (a) Planning the defensive system and estimating the materials needed for the construction of permanent field fortifications; also for estimating the strength of the garrison needed for a full defence.
   (b) Settling the tactical siting of the defence line in detail.
   (c) Establishing building priorities for the completion of the various sectors.
   (d) Deciding on the form which the construction would take in the light of past experience (technical and tactical) and what material was available.
5. In addition, Deputy General X Corps was to form three more planning staffs composed of officers of all arms, plus Engineer staffs including the Naval Fortification Engineer Organisation stationed in the German Bight.
6. As far as priorities for construction were concerned the following had top priority:

   (a) North and East Frisian Islands.
   (b) The coastal sector opposite Sylt (Hindenburgdamm).
   (c) The Eiderstedt peninsula.
   (d) The river defence of the Elbe–Weser estuary.
   (e) The coast Brunsbüttel–Cuxhaven–Wesermünde–Wilhelmshaven inclusive.
   (f) The Ems estuary with Delfzijl.
7. The remainder of the coastline had second priority.
8. The construction was to comprise a continuous anti-tank obstacle, with an articulated defensive system in depth, which was to be continuously strengthened.
9. The Gauleiter was responsible for procuring and employing civilian labour, accommodating and feeding them (including OT).
10. The OT was to be employed on the basis of direct agreement between the Gauleiter and the OT. Local OT staff would be attached to Kaufmann's staff.
11. Gauleiter Kaufmann was to report to Hitler, via the Head of the Reich Chancery, as soon as possible on his plans for organising the work and raising the labour. Naval High Command North Sea was to report on the 1st and 15th of each month (via OKW) on the state and progress of the construction.

Notes
1. C-in-C Navy, Skl. Qu A II 77/42.Kdos, 'Command Organisation on the Coast' dated 27 March 1942, as quoted in Wilt *The Atlantic Wall*.
2. HKL = *Haupt Kampf Linie* — the main line of resistance.
3. *World War II German Military Studies*, Volume 12.
4. As quoted in Trevor-Roper *Hitler's Secret Conversations 1941–1944*.
5. The heavy battery on Guernsey was Batterie Mirus. The two on the mainland were to be on the Joburg peninsula and near Paimpol on the Brittany coast, but they were never installed, 20.3cm railway guns being put there instead — one in each location.
6. Source: *CIOS Review 1973*, published here by kind permission of CIOS (Jersey).
7. The military arm and the largest of the major branches of the SS.

Above: U-boat pens. As well as gun emplacements, the Germans built a series of massive structures to house their submarines at various places along the Atlantic Wall. The photograph shows building in progress at the French port of Bordeaux in 1942. *Bundesarchiv*

Above: Marine artillerymen of Batterie Oldenburg outside their living accommodation in the sand dunes near Calais. *Hans Sippli*

Chapter 3

Building the Wall — The Germans

Division of Responsibilities

Although the Organisation Todt was responsible for much of the building work, it was actually only one of five elements concerned with the overall building programme. These were:

(a) Individual troops. Normal individual members of Army units, especially infantrymen, were responsible for constructing field fortifications such as weapon pits, foxholes and trenches.

(b) Divisional Field Engineers (*Pioniere*), the Army's badged engineers, were responsible for a wide range of duties such as bridging, ferrying, demolitions, the construction of obstacles and, as far as their responsibilities within the building programme were concerned, all aspects of the distribution, recording and sowing of land mines, plus the location and use of flame-throwers.

(c) Army Construction Battalions (Baubataillone) were responsible for reinforced field-type constructions which were designed to withstand and to give protection from bullets, shell-splinters and blast, but not prolonged bombardment. Where concrete was used, it did not exceed 1m in thickness.

(d) Fortress Engineers and Fortress Construction Battalions (Festungsbautruppen) were responsible for supplying and mounting fortress weapons, conveying heavy loads, some tunnelling, compiling construction progress reports and maps, ordering and supervising tasks undertaken by the Organisation Todt (OT). In overall command of the Fortress Engineers was the Festungspionierkommandeur (Fortress Engineer Commander) General der Pionier der Festungen und der Eisenbahnpioniere Alfred Jacob, holder of the Knight's Cross. Jacob held this post from 1 September 1939 for the entire war. His units contained experts in all branches of military engineering.

Below: The Reichsarbeitsdienst (RAD) got involved in building parts of the Atlantic Wall, such as on the Channel Islands. Here a column of RAD men, spades at the slope, marches along the South Esplanade, St Peter Port, Guernsey. They assisted with the fortification programme on Guernsey and Jersey prior to the arrival of the OT and its foreign workers. *CIOS Jersey*

(e) Organisation Todt (OT) was responsible for quarrying, most tunnelling projects, constructing power stations, railways and roads, supplying building equipment and machinery, organising sea transport (in conjunction with the Navy), loading and unloading ships, supervising civilian construction firms, controlling non-military labour and building fortress-type constructions.

Reichsarbeitsdienst

Before going into more detail about the OT and its German and foreign work force, the Reichsarbeitsdienst (RAD — State Labour Service) must also be mentioned as it was sometimes involved in fortification work. In speeches before he came to power, Hitler had promised that he would overcome unemployment (Arbeitslosigkeit), and did so simply by making labour on behalf of the state compulsory. A law was passed on 26 June 1935 which made it obligatory for all non-Jewish German men between the ages of 18 and 25 to work in the RAD/Männer for six months before their two years' military service (conscription had been reintroduced on 21 May 1935). RAD/M also contained some volunteers as well as the mass of conscripts; these volunteers stayed for at least a year. All were under the command of a cadre of Army officers and NCOs who had already completed their military service. The commander of the RAD from its inception until surrender was Konstantin Hierl, a man of considerable foresight as well as political and organisational skills. The first annual contingents numbered 200,000 men. There was also a RAD der weiblichen Jugend (RAD/wJ) for young women.

Many men were assigned to farms to work under a strict discipline with no distinction being made between workers, artisans, peasants or intellectuals. Women who were called up did housework in peasant homes whilst the men worked in the fields. In this way, Hitler reduced Germany's unemployment from six million to one million in just over a year, producing at the same time a pool of cheap labour as all were paid just a nominal wage. He saw it also as a necessary step towards rearmament — 'men who shouldered shovels would one day carry guns'.

One such member of the RAD, who 'shouldered his shovel' was Erwin Albert Grubba, who recorded his reminiscences on a tape for the Department of Sound Records at the Imperial War Museum (Accession No: 010006/8). Grubba recalled:

'I was called up because my Jahrgang [class/year] was due for call-up: 1925 became due after Stalingrad in 1943. And after the usual military screening, which took place the autumn before, actually in 1942, we knew that some time in the spring of '43, we would be called up. We would have to go, our particular age group. There was no way out of it anyway,[1] because there was no such thing as a conscientious objector in the German Army. So we just went and that was it. We all got our call-up papers. And first of all I had to do a few months in Poland in a labour battalion, you know the Arbeitsdienst, which was paramilitary training as well as general sort of digging anti-tank ditches and God knows what, and guard duties . . . After three months in, I got a fortnight's leave, just at the middle — my birthday. And that's when the RAF struck and demolished our house, lock stock and barrel, and everything I had. So there I was, literally nothing in my pocket except the dirty shirt around my neck and a pair of boots which had been singed in the fire.'

When Grubba reported back, he was sent to the Panzergrenadier depot at Spandau Barracks in Berlin, to begin his proper military service.

Heinrich Stockhoff of Gesmold was in the 1921 age group, so was called up in June 1940 for his medical examination along with some 17 others from the surrounding area. Then, from 29 October to 28 December, he did his service in the RAD. He recalls:

'I did my service with the RAD, in Abteilung K1-196 Messingen. After we had received our uniforms we were taught how to salute. We were also taught how to dig ditches. The ground was very sandy. The boys from the big towns who had been working in shops and offices had problems with the trench digging — but not us country boys! The work was hard and we got very little free time. We weren't allowed to go to church, not even on Christmas Day.'

Another called up in 1940 was Rolf Munninger of Fellbach. He joined Abteilung 306-3 in Rohrbach/Holledu in Bavaria. He remembers that they had 'plenty of sport and training, but also plenty of work too!' For example, they straightened and regulated the River Ilm, dug a trench in which Siemens technicians were to lay a cable from Donaueschingen to Freiburg, built a dam where there had been a bridge between Breisach and Colmar, and repaired bomb-damaged flats in villages in Alsace. Then at the end of his RAD service he was called up for the Army. Without doubt RAD service made the transition from civilian to service life much easier as the men became used to hard work, discipline and obeying orders.

In 1938, the RAD/M was organised in Divisional Districts (Arbeitsgaue) I–XXXII, each commanded by a brigadier, with a staff and an HQ guard company and some eight battalions of 1,200–1,800 men, each under a lieutenant-colonel or a major. The normal work unit was company-sized, containing some 200 men with an HQ and four platoons, each with three 17-man sections under a sergeant/corporal, although the ranks in the RAD were actually different from those of the Wehrmacht. The men all carried spades and their transport was normally by bicycle. Pre-World War 2, the RAD supported the armed forces in the invasions of Austria, the Sudetenland and Czechoslovakia. From June 1938 to September 1939, 300 RAD companies also worked in conjunction with civilian contractors under the OT building the Siegfried Line (Westwall) along the western border from Emmerich (frontier with the Netherlands) to Lörrach (ditto with Switzerland). About 100 companies assisted with similar work on the Ostwall fortifications on the Polish border.

In August 1939 the RAD was at its peak strength, with 360,000 men in 1,700 companies, when general mobilisation was declared. Almost straight away well over 60% (1,050 companies) were transferred to the Army to form Bautruppen (see above). Following on from the end of the Polish campaign, Hitler ordered the RAD to be rebuilt, which meant that the RAD went back to its prewar status of providing pre-military training and, at the same time, supporting Army engineers. By 1940 there were 39 Arbeitsgaue, Numbers XXXIII-XXXIX being in Austria and Bohemia.

Thereafter the RAD was active in all theatres, some companies being sent to France to help build the Atlantic Wall and later on in the war they even manned anti-aircraft batteries, laid minefields and manned and defended fortifications, as well as building defensive earthworks along German borders from August to October 1944. This action caused the Allies to protest that the RAD was abusing its non-combatant status under the Geneva Convention.[2]

Fortress Engineers

In every Defence District (Wehrkreise) in Germany there were Fortress Engineer units, Fortress Construction Battalions, and Construction Battalions. Their units contained experts in all branches of military engineering such as tunnelling, camouflage, reinforced concrete work, geology, artillery. (Note that the German word for a military engineer is *Pionier*, whilst a civil engineer is *Ingenieur*.)

In his book on the OT and Fortress Engineers in the Channel Islands, Michael Ginns lists the nature and size breakdown of Fortress Engineer units as follows:

UNIT	OFFICERS & OFFICIALS	NCOs	OTHER RANKS
Fortress Engineer Command	11	11	27
Fortress Engineer Staff	18	18	30
Fortress Engineer Sector Group	7	9	12
Battalion Staff (including Transport Staff) for a Fortress Construction Battalion	8	14	53
Fortress Construction Company	3	18	150
Technical Park Company	3	17	134
Fortress Engineer Park Company	3	23	224
Staff of a Construction Battalion	8	7	12
Construction Company	4	27	231
Construction Company (motorised)	2	16	157
Rock Drilling Company	5	41	359
Engineer Mining Company	4	24	164
Military Geology Unit	2	3	4

The Organisation Todt

Ministerialdirektor (a civil service grade equivalent to the rank of lieutenant-general) Franz Xaver Dorsch was born in Bavaria on 24 December 1899. In 1934 he was appointed District Advisor to the OT in Berlin, then in 1939 was placed in charge of all construction work on the western frontiers of Germany. Two years later he became Deputy Chief of the OT and in 1944 was assigned as Chief of the Organisation Todt Construction Office, a department of the Armaments Industry, in addition to his other duties. On 7 May 1945 he was taken prisoner by US forces at Tegernsee, Bavaria, and whilst in prison volunteered to write about the OT for the Foreign Military Studies Branch of the US Army Historical Division European Command. This resulted in Document MS P-037, from which I have taken certain quotations, including these opening words on the foundation of the OT:

'When Hitler ordered the construction of the West Wall to be accelerated in the spring of 1938, the fortress engineer staffs in charge of this work were, because of the magnitude of the project and their lack of experience in large-scale construction, quite understandably and excusably at first unable to cope with the business side of the job: the control and allocation of contractors and workmen, the distribution and transportation of materials and the other minor tasks connected with these things. Therefore, he appointed Dr Todt, then Inspector General of the German Highway System, to carry out this task. The reasons for the selection of Dr Todt are obvious.

'Besides his mastery of the principles of construction engineering, Dr Todt, as Inspector General of the German Highway System, was the man who had laid the organisational foundation which enabled the German

Below: The troops who would man the defences often either assisted with the building or built their own basic field fortifications. It was also common practice for troops of divisional artillery batteries to construct their own gun positions, as seen here at Mont Cambrai, Jersey, 1942. *CIOS Jersey*

Above: Divisional field engineers had a wide range of duties, including the construction of obstacles, whilst Army construction battalions were responsible for reinforced field-type constructions. These soldiers are hard at work building defences on the coast of Normandy in 1943. *J. P. Benamou Collection*

Above: Once the concrete casemates had been built, then the guns had to be installed, such as here, near Ostend, during the summer of 1943. *Bundesarchiv*

construction, building materials and construction machinery industry, after years of very low output — one might even say after years of economic decline — to rise to exceptional achievements in a short time in connection with the construction of the national autobahn system, with the result that after 1936 about 1,000km of autobahn were completed every year. This achievement was primarily due to the fact that Todt, who himself was a man from private industry, opened the way to free enterprise from bureaucratic restrictions and encouraged it in every way. Furthermore, in spite of his individual treatment of autobahn engineering, for example with respect to adapting the construction to the landscape and other aesthetic considerations, he succeeded to a far-reaching degree by standardising construction works and construction equipment depots, which, judging by conditions in Germany, certainly had to be regarded as a great step forward in the field of construction engineering. An additional important point was that since the national autobahn covered great distances and were frequently far from any residential areas of any size, it was necessary to quarter large numbers of workmen quickly and efficiently in new, temporary camps. Under the direction of Dr Todt work was done in this field which was a model of its kind. Recognition of this work of Dr Todt's was given expression in the so-called "Law Governing the Accommodating of Workmen in Construction Projects". The general standards for the accommodation of autobahn workmen were thereby declared binding in connection with construction projects in general.'

Dorsch goes on to describe Todt's work in connection with the building of the Westwall, where construction works totalling around 8 million cubic metres of concrete and reinforced concrete had to be completed within a relatively short time, so, just as with constructing major highways, two of the main tasks were rapid labour procurement and workers' accommodation. It would hardly have been possible to find a more suitable man than Todt to solve the economic problems concerned with the construction of the West Wall.

Fritz Todt

Fritz Todt was born on 4 September 1891, at Pforzheim, Baden, into an upper class family. He served in the German Air Force during the Great War, was awarded the Iron Cross and was wounded whilst flying as an observer. Postwar, he joined the Munich firm of Sager & Woerner which specialised in building roads and tunnels, rising to become manager. Soon after Hitler came to power Todt was put in charge of the new state-owned Reichsautobahnen corporation and ordered to build a national highway system — laid out by the military and primarily for military use, but of course with enormous beneficial use for civilians. Todt helped to found the Nationalsozialistischer Bund Deutscher Technik and co-ordinated all the engineers and managers of the German construction industry into a single, enormous entity — Organisation Todt. The quiet withdrawn technocrat eventually held three posts: Minister of Armaments and Munitions; Head of the OT (in charge of highways, navigable waterways and power plants); then, from late 1941, he was also given responsibility for restoring the railways and road system in occupied Russia. In his capacity as head of OT he was, until his death in February 1942, in charge of the major construction works on the Atlantic Wall. However, he did not perform any military functions, as Dorsch emphasises in his treatise:

Above: Founder of the Organisation Todt, Fritz Todt, who held the honorary rank of Generalmajor in the Luftwaffe, having been awarded an Iron Cross in World War 1, whilst flying as an observer. Here Reichsminister Todt wears Luftwaffe uniform. *IWM — MH 6101*

'It is necessary to state this expressly if one is to understand the position of the Engineer Generals at Army High Command and with the Army Corps . . . Todt did not receive any military authority . . . the design, development and construction of fortifications of all kinds, their arrangement in the terrain and the determination of construction deadlines according to military priorities were, as before, duties belonging to the Inspector General of Engineers and Fortifications and the Fortress Engineer staffs subordinate to him.'

Dorsch labours this point somewhat, despite the fact that Todt held the honorary rank of general in the Luftwaffe and liked to wear Air Force uniform when he went visiting sites. However, it is clear from what Dorsch says — or doesn't say — that there was no love lost between the senior members of the OT and the senior generals of the Army. However, he does correctly make the point that an additional reason for Todt being appointed was because the rapid expansion from the small Reichswehr to the much larger Volksheer (People's Army) had led to the Army's command apparatus becoming overburdened. Therefore the Army was glad to be relieved of the task of directing the construction industry and its feeder enterprises, 'a task that was more or less foreign to its nature'.

On 8 February 1942 Todt set out to fly from Rastenburg to Berlin after a meeting with Hitler. His normal aircraft was being serviced and had been replaced by a Heinkel 111 twin-engine bomber, a well tried and airworthy aircraft. A few minutes after leaving Rastenburg airport at 08.00hrs, the Heinkel exploded, killing all on board. Sabotage was suspected but nothing was ever discovered. Interestingly, Albert Speer, who succeeded Todt, was also scheduled to be on the same plane, but had cancelled some hours before, complaining that he had been kept up all night by Hitler.

'When I finally left Hitler at three o'clock in the morning,' Speer wrote later in his autobiography, 'I sent word that I would not be flying with Dr Todt. The plane was to start five hours later, I was worn out and wanted only to have a decent sleep . . . Next morning the shrill clang of the telephone startled me out of a deep sleep. Dr Brandt reported excitedly: "Dr Todt's plane has just crashed and he has been killed." From that moment on my whole world was changed. My relationship to Dr Todt had become perceptibly closer in recent years. With his death I felt that I had lost an older, prudent colleague.'[3]

Below: Albert Speer, successor to Fritz Todt as head of the OT, is seen here during an inspection tour of the Atlantic Wall. He took over when Todt died when the Heinkel 111 in which he was travelling after a conference with Hitler, blew up on 8 February 1942. *IWM — HU3045*

Speer, the Successor

Albert Speer was born in Mannheim on 19 March 1905, so he was some years younger than Todt. Son and grandson of successful architects, he was an instant hit with Hitler, who became a firm admirer of the 1.93m/6ft 4in architect and gave him such commissions as designing the Reichstag building and the Nuremberg stadium in which the most spectacular Nazi ceremonies were performed. In his memoirs he commented that if Hitler had had any friends he would certainly have been considered one of his closest. The shy, retiring Speer hated making speeches and had no interest in fame. However, he did covet power and lost no time in taking over the reins when Todt was killed — and he had to move fast because power-hungry competitors like Göring were waiting in the wings to step in. Speer was responsible for continued miracles and lasted out the war.

Speer is considered by some to be the 'good Nazi', especially as he 'owned up' to his share of what the Nazis had done. However, this did not stop him being found guilty of war crimes and crimes against humanity because he had knowingly used slave labour. Waiving his right to appeal, he spent 20 years in prison and was released in 1966. He died in 1981.

The OT in Essence

From Dorsch's report one can summarise the expansion of the OT. thus its origins begin in the autobahn-building organisation gathered together by Fritz Todt in 1933, which was honed, improved and expanded by Todt over the next five years, when, still without a name, it was sent to assist the Army Fortress Engineers in constructing the Westwall along Germany's border with France. In June 1938 Todt began to recruit a whole raft of civilian firms into his organisation and

organised them into brigades — known as Oberbauleitungen (Senior Construction Administrations). Then, on 18 July 1938, Hitler first called the body the Organisation Todt (OT). The men still did not wear uniforms. For a while the OT remained behind the Westwall repairing railways, roads and bridges, and gaining its status as an auxiliary to the armed forces. Then, as the German forces spread throughout Western Europe, the OT followed, its 200,000 men, still mainly German, performing all the previously mentioned tasks. However, as it grew even larger, the German element became the planners and overseers — now wearing khaki uniforms and special badges (see below), whilst the majority of the labourers were either foreign volunteers or forced labourers. This distinction was made more pronounced when Hitler issued an order to say that in future the menial tasks — such as breaking up stones or carrying bags of cement — were no longer to be done by Germans.

By 1943, the OT was over a million strong and growing fast. The change from Todt to Speer made little difference to the smooth running of the OT, although Speer did put it onto a more regular footing, so that it now had its own weapons (for self-protection, especially in areas where partisans were very active) and its own medical services. However, the grievous casualties suffered by the armed forces did cause a major change, in that more and more German members — officials and overseers — were called up for military service. Their places were taken by foreign volunteers and, in some cases, by ex-penal-unit personnel. The foreigners who joined often did so in order to escape being deported to Germany or (if Jewish) being sent to die in a concentration camp. This led to a wide range of different nations being represented in the OT, as well as ethnic Germans. These included Allied prisoners of war; people from the European countries nearest to Germany — such as the Netherlands, Denmark, Belgium and Norway; and those from further away such as from Italy and the Balkans, Russia and the Ukraine. The largest foreign group were ex-Soviet citizens. Thomas and Jurado's book *Wehrmacht Auxiliary Forces* lists the breakdown of the OT in November 1944, when it had reached its maximum as being:

German	44,000	plus a further 313,000 in contracted firms	= 357,000
Foreign	12,800	plus a further 680,700 in contracted firms	= 693,500
Women (German)	4,000		
POW	165,000		
Petty criminals	140,000	(a category which included Jews)	
TOTAL			1,359,500

As far as the Atlantic Wall was concerned, there were OT workers employed in all areas, stretching from Einsatzgruppe *Wiking* with units in Norway and Denmark, right along to France where there were some 112,000 German and 152,000 French workers, including 17,000 from the French North African colonies.

Odd Nansen was a Norwegian political prisoner, who spent most of the war in prison or concentration camps in various parts of Norway and Germany, such as Grini, Veidal and Sachsenhausen. In his autobiography *Fra Dag Til Dag (Day after Day)* he writes about his first meeting with the OT thus:

'Besides the guards and us prisoners, the camp (No 1380) is teeming with queer creatures half-civilian half-military. They are OT-workers. Most of them are apparently from Vienna, but there are also men from other countries, certainly a number of Czechs. We thought at first they were Russian prisoners of war, but they seem to be detailed men on Arbeitsdienst [Labour Corps Service]. So they are not "prisoners" but "volunteers". These men work on all kinds of jobs in and outside the camp, under the OT's snuff-coloured "officials" with the swastika band round their arms. One of these is also in chief command of the work inside the barbed-wire. The detailed men have been up here since the early part of May. For three months then. In that time they have erected our huts and done a certain amount of work in the camp. It doesn't leave one breathless with admiration.'

Observers on the Channel Islands also had a low opinion of the OT men — not so much from their work ability, but rather from the way its leaders treated their workers. Here are the comments of two such observers, who made recordings for the Imperial War Museum's Sound Archive. First, Mr R. W. le Sueur (Tape No 10715/3/2), a clerk who lived in Jersey who recalled:

'Now the people who were in charge of the work were not the military. The organisation responsible for all this work was called the Organisation Todt. There was a Doctor Todt who was responsible for it. I think he went down as a war criminal in the end. And those who were members of the OT were, they really were a kind of sub-species from what one could make out. They were people who had been crafty enough not to get involved in the armed services. They were people running rackets; they were people who were, in many cases, the foremen, and had just come out of prisons and for whom society had — the sick society of Nazi Germany that is — had suddenly found a place. And they were a pretty revolting bunch of people. And they treated those under their care, those under their charge, in a terrible way.'

Mr E. J. de Ste Croix (Tape No 10103/02/02), who had worked on the docks in Jersey, said when asked what OT meant:

'This was the German construction organisation. They were beasts, there was no two ways about that . . . their manner generally, particularly to the men under their control, could only be described as bestial . . . it was frequently seen that the men had been beaten for the slightest thing.'

OT Uniform

OT personnel wore ex-Czech Army uniform. Odd Nansen described it as being 'snuff-coloured', others called its colour olive-green, khaki or even brown. However, it was very like other German military uniforms being sufficiently similar to normal Army style to be misidentified, and thus its wearers mistaken as combatants — especially by anyone who had not the faintest idea what the inscription 'Organisation Todt' meant. This worked very much to the disadvantage of a number of OT men who were employed in the Dieppe area during the time of the Canadian and British raid in August 1942. They were occupying a large hostel in Pourville, where they had started building weapon pits and pillboxes. Their senior staff lived in the nearby Hotel de la Terrasse. During the raid some of these bunkers were encompassed by the fighting and, consequently, the OT workers were mistaken for German soldiers and killed. Fortunately there were no reprisals, as the information that the OT wore military-style uniforms had never been officially passed on to the British via the Red Cross. Later of course they became a fully-integrated paramilitary force, with a range of weapons for self-defence, so were 'fair game' on the battlefield from then on.

Up to the period just before the start of World War 2, the majority of OT personnel wore civilian clothes. The exceptions were the 'top brass' who would have been uniformed members of the three armed services, RAD or one of the other Nazi organisations, including Specialists (Sonderführer) who were interpreters, radio specialists, cameramen, laboratory technicians and such like, with nominal ranks up to that of battalion commander, but with no actual military rank. Once war started, these men had to be uniformed as has already been explained.

The first type of rank insignia was introduced in 1940 and this was a series of armbands (see examples below). Then in 1942,

arm chevrons and shoulder straps (in pairs) were introduced, with coloured piping on the shoulder straps to identify the branch of the service. Gilt stars (pips) were used on the shoulder straps to denote the senior members such as the commanders of construction units, medical services, communications units, equipment providers and so on. The colours of the piping were black for construction and accommodation control, dark blue for medical, white for equipment, provisions and messing, brown for propaganda, yellow for signals, green for administration, and carmine for musicians.

In 1943 yet another series of rank insignia was introduced, which replaced shoulder straps with arm chevrons, collar patches and armbands. Under the new system OT workers, OT under-leaders, OT leaders, OT staff leaders and OT higher leaders all wore appropriate rank insignia. There is not space to show all these, so just a selection is illustrated below. For full details see Brian L. Davis's most comprehensive book which is listed in the Bibliography.

Left: An OT Vorarbeiter (overseer) talks to one of his workers on the Atlantic Wall somewhere in France. Note the colour of his uniform, his Nazi armband and, lower down, his Organisation Todt armband. *Bundesarchiv*

Bottom left: This excellent photograph of two OT members with an Army Obergefreiter (corporal) in a club in Guernsey, shows distinctly the different colour of their uniforms. *Werner Wagenknecht*

Below: Rank badges of the Organisation Todt.

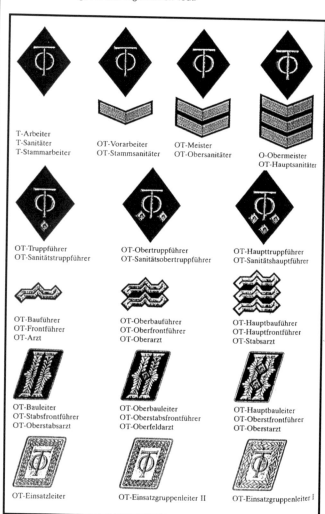

T-Arbeiter T-Sanitäter T-Stammarbeiter	OT-Vorarbeiter OT-Stammsanitäter	OT-Meister OT-Obersanitäter	O-Obermeister OT-Hauptsanitäter
OT-Truppführer OT-Sanitätstruppführer	OT-Obertruppführer OT-Sanitätsobertruppführer	OT-Haupttruppführer OT-Sanitätshauptführer	
OT-Bauführer OT-Frontführer OT-Arzt	OT-Oberbauführer OT-Oberfrontführer OT-Oberarzt	OT-Hauptbauführer OT-Hauptfrontführer OT-Stabsarzt	
OT-Bauleiter OT-Stabsfrontführer OT-Oberstabsarzt	OT-Oberbauleiter OT-Oberstabsfrontführer OT-Oberfeldarzt	OT-Hauptbauleiter OT-Oberstfrontführer OT-Oberstarzt	
OT-Einsatzleiter	OT-Einsatzgruppenleiter II	OT-Einsatzgruppenleiter I	

OT Work in North-West Europe

Dorsch lists the work done by the OT from after the French Armistice onwards as being:

- General repairs to the network of canals, particularly in the region of northern France and Belgium. Within the scope of this work OT also undertook the clearing and repair of various seaports, such as Boulogne, Calais and Dunkirk. Tackled in parallel was the construction of shatterproof oil reservoirs in the various ports in the Bay of Biscay, and construction of bombproof shelters for the more important harbour personnel and quarters for the troops. The OT also took over the construction of airfields in the zone of Regional Air Command for Brussels.
- Emplacing the heavy batteries on Cap Gris-Nez (to support Operation 'Sealion').
- Constructing U-boat shelters.
- Construction of the Atlantic Wall.

Cap Gris-Nez Heavy Batteries

We have already covered these 'Sealion' guns in an earlier chapter. However, from an OT point of view it began with the emplacement of some 20 heavy calibre guns and the construction of subsidiary installations (quarters for personnel, medical facilities, ammunition bunkers and so on) in a semi-permanent manner (2m ferro-concrete work). All this work had to be completed in eight weeks, the guns remaining without cover. The next demand was that, without interfering with their readiness for action, the guns were to be provided with a 3.5m-thick ferro-concrete roof and additional subsidiary installations. The first phase had required the handling of some 30,000 cubic metres of ferro-concrete, but the second phase was much longer, dragged on until the spring of 1941 and involved some 130,000 cubic metres of ferro-concrete, so a total of 160,000 cubic metres was used at Cap Gris-Nez alone.

The U-boat Berths

In the autumn of 1940 OT received orders from Hitler to build bombproof U-boat shelters on the Atlantic coast, beginning at the ports of Brest, Lorient and St Nazaire. In 1943 these were extended to include shelters at Marseilles and Toulon in the Mediterranean. In the main the Engineer and Fortification General drew up the patterns for the types of shelter, then these were forwarded to the OT for it to draft and work out the construction plans in detail. Some 96 bombproof berths were built, including requisite workshops, covered locks and other subsidiary installations. Work on a further 33 was under construction when the invasion began.

Work on the Atlantic Wall

In the autumn of 1941 the OT received orders to start construction work on the Channel Islands, as Hitler feared the enemy might regain possession of the islands which would then be a constant menace to the north coast of France and be able to provide an excellent 'jumping off place' for the enemy once the invasion began. Then in 1942, came the full directive (Order 40), which was as Hitler put it: 'the clear-cut conception of the Atlantic Wall defence system'. He went on to explain that the development of the Wall was based upon the following basic principles:

1. Under all circumstances interference with traffic in the U-boat bases was to be prevented, even if an invasion should initially be successful. Work on unfinished bases must continue and the bases equipped for all round defence.

2. Every port that could serve for large-scale landings must be rendered inaccessible to the enemy, so as to compel him to carry out all landing operations on the unprotected coast and hence under less favourable conditions than within a harbour. Therefore the all-round defence of all ports within the framework of the Atlantic Wall was essential.[4]

3. Defensive power must be concentrated as far forward as possible, that is close to the coastline, so as to tackle the enemy at his weakest moment, namely whilst landing. It also meant being able to reach as far as possible seawards with artillery.

4. Wherever possible guns were to be provided with ferro-concrete roofs as protection against air attacks. The objection to this was that it would considerably restrict fields of fire and make all-round fire impossible, but Hitler discounted this with the remark that in the event of an air attack meeting with only limited success, the guns could be put out of action by just a few large fragments. (As we shall see later, this proved to be incorrect.)

5. The basic principle underlying the technical equipment, the choice of location and the type of installations was the same as in the case of the Westwall, namely that: 'The final struggle for a position is fought by the infantry,' and therefore provision had to be made for adequate and secure shelter space for them, where they could weather out the shelling and bombing preceding any enemy close combat attacks, without their combat efficiency being reduced.

Prior to Minister Speer talking with Hitler, Dorsch had given him an estimate of 450,000 cubic metres of ferro-concrete per month as being the highest figure the OT could handle — after a few months getting things under way. Later Speer, as the Chief

Above: Advertisements for firms hiring labour from the Channel Islands.

of OT, and in order to be on the safe side, reduced this figure to 300,000 cubic metres per month on all projects including the U-boat pens. In fact, the amount of ferro-concrete work done by the OT between July 1940 and July 1944, was a staggering 17,600,000 cubic metres, plus 25 million cubic metres of ground work handled amongst the OT's other duties. However, he is careful to stress that the OT did not carry out the work itself, but rather had all the work entrusted to it carried out by firms of building contractors. Even the manpower employed by the 'Mobile OT' was supplied by firms.

The OT was not directly under the command of the Wehrmacht, but was treated as a subsidiary organisation (Wehrmachtsgefolge), because, lacking the facilities granted in the war zone and the occupied territories, it would have encountered extreme difficulties. As a subsidiary organisation to the Wehrmacht, OT personnel could travel on Wehrmacht tickets and it could have its supplies shipped on Wehrmacht consignment notes. It also had the right to demand Wehrmacht billeting facilities, to use Wehrmacht telephone and cable lines and all other installations of the Wehrmacht. Naturally it was subject to the directives issued by the Wehrmacht command agencies in respect of its actions in the war zone and so forth. Direct subordination of the OT to any one of the branches of the Wehrmacht was not possible because the organisation had to work not only for all three branches of the Wehrmacht but also, for example, on a comparatively large scale for the Ministry of Armaments, a further reason why it needed its own facilities for its connections with the building industry and for procurement of supplies and so on. Hence the OT accepted definite contracts from the Armed Forces and then had to fulfil them on its own responsibility.

As far as the Atlantic Wall was concerned an agreement was reached at the end of 1942 concerning the construction work, between the General of Engineers and Fortifications in OKH, Alfred Jacob, and HQ OT. According to this the sites were to be chosen solely by Fortress Engineer staffs, whilst the building contractors then to do the work were chosen by the OT Construction Group Chief.

'A decisive factor' to quote from Dorsch's account:

'in the Atlantic Wall construction was the approval given on 22 August 1942, by the Chief of Staff OB West, General Kurt Zeitzler, to construction work being continued until 1 May 1943 in such manner as though no landing by the enemy were expected by that date. This approval made the serial mass production of the construction parts possible on a purely building economical basis, without regard to the combat efficiency of the installations at any given moment, whereby an increased capacity was brought about. Thus, in April 1943, the record was reached — 870,000 cubic metres of ferro-concrete work being completed in that month.'

He goes on to explain that the reason for the decrease in output after that date was due to the necessity, starting in May 1943, to repair the Möhne and Eder Valley dams which had been destroyed by the RAF, a considerable part of the construction capacity being transferred from the Wall to Construction Group 'Ruhr' (it took OT four and a half months to repair the dams). Dorsch also says that, in all, some 10,400,000 cubic metres of ferro-concrete work were built into the Atlantic Wall.

In reply to criticisms that the Atlantic Wall was too thin or not deeply enough organised, Dorsch points out that from the constructional point of view it would hardly have been possible under the circumstances pertaining after 1942 to achieve any better capacities for ferro-concrete work except at the expense of other military or war industry structures. Had work begun immediately after the French armistice, then the picture would have been entirely different. Dorsch says that, towards the end of 1943, he had drawn Hitler's attention to the fact that it would be necessary to slow down work on the Wall, because in the case of an emergency it would be impossible to man it. Hitler asked him how many bunkers would be available in the completed Wall and how many men they could accommodate on the average. He had replied that at best there would be 15,000 bunkers with a capacity of six men in each, to which Hitler replied (to Keitel) that this figure would not even suffice to hold the staffs! Actually the OT handed over 9,671 'ready to occupy' bunkers (minimum 2m ferro-concrete), and 5,976 field-type bunkers, so the total was 15,647. In addition, the concrete work had been done on a further 1,386 permanent and 205 field bunkers before the invasion began.

Of course the OT was not left alone at any time to concentrate on the Wall. Dorsch mentions the building of U-boat bases, E-boat bases, various structures for the Air Force, plus such work as the bauxite mines in Brignoles, near Marseilles and tungsten mining at Fougères. He also mentions the launching sites and servicing installations for V-1 and V-2 missiles including dummy sites, construction of the so-called Millipede (*Tausendfüssler*) — a long-range gun with 12 x 160m barrels.[5] In addition to 'other work' the OT also had to put up with enemy interference, the V-weapon sites at St Omer, for example, being repeatedly attacked with heavy bombs and totally destroyed.

Wages

The German and foreign labourers employed building the Wall were, according to Dorsch, 'paid at the current wage tariffs'. He goes on to say that, 'It is worthy of mention, for instance that the Dutch OT specialist worker received a higher wage than a corresponding German OT specialist worker employed alongside of him.' Payment for materials used also took place, 'on the basis of properly regulated contracts and proper lawful purchase'. Despite Dorsch's statements, the reality was somewhat different — as can be seen by the comments of a French OT volunteer in the next chapter.

Notes

1. In fact, after the outbreak of war, volunteers for the Wehrmacht were called up immediately and did not do any RAD service.
2. See Thomas and Jurado *Wehrmacht Auxiliary Forces*.
3. *Inside the Third Reich* by Albert Speer.
4. Clearly the Germans had no inkling whatsoever about the construction of the prefabricated Mulberry Harbours which the Allies would use on the Normandy coast.
5. It is not clear whether this was the same as the 'Site V-3' which can still be seen at Mimoyecques, just south of Calais, where thousands of deported workers and German political prisoners dug tunnels to house the 'London Cannon' — five tunnels sheltering five 130m-long cannons, which were supposed to fire once every six seconds. Due to Allied bombing, this device, which was supposed to shell London from the French coast, was never used, but the site is now visitable (see chapter 12).

Top left:
A group of engineers from the Army and OT study plans of the Atlantic Wall, January 1943.
IWM — HU66987

Top right:
OT funeral party for an OT overseer at St Brelade, Jersey, *circa* 1943. Note the miners' lamps which suggests that the deceased was probably killed in a tunnelling accident. The official on the right wears NSKK uniform, that is the Nationalsozialistisches Kraftfahrerkorps (Nazi Motor Corps). *CIOS Jersey*

Above:
Members of the OT celebrate Hitler's birthday in a hotel in Guernsey, at a workers' staff party. *IWM — HU25962*

Left:
Der Frontarbeiter. The cover of the special OT newspaper, issue dated 24 July 1943. *J. P. Benamou Collection*

work was dull and monotonous so that an environment was soon created where petty bickering was resorted to in an attempt to break the monotony. One day the conscript labour force, who considered they should be better treated than the slave labourers, staged a demonstration outside the OT offices demanding more food. The OT guards responded to this by firing shots over the heads of the protesters, who were shouting for more food or no work. This response rapidly put an end to the demonstration but the point must have been taken as the food provided to the workers was improved.

'The scene at the construction site reminded the young man of pictures he had seen in children's history books of the building of the pyramids. There seemed to be thousands of men crawling about like ants, or perhaps a colony of bees, all over the huge concrete structure that was to form the submarine pens. Materials such as reinforcing steel bars, bags of cement, sieves, wooden shuttering and supplies of water to mix the concrete had to be handed up a huge ramp made of tree trunks.'

The first time van Grieken went up the ramp he was terrified as the whole structure shook and rattled as though it were about to collapse; however, it was still there some six months later when he was leaving for Guernsey, so he concluded that the engineers who had designed it knew what they were doing.
The German decision to move the conscript workers was put into effect without warning. One day in mid-November (1941) an OT NCO read out a list of names, including Van Grieken's and told the men to report at 6am for transport elsewhere. No details were given. Once more packed into a crowded train the workers were left to speculate on their likely destination. They had heard on the German news bulletin of the German attack on Russia and fervently hoped they were not going to be sent there, particularly with the winter coming on.
Their fears were not allayed by the fact that at every station they stopped en route, there were armed guards to ensure no one got off. They arrived at St Malo at about 03.00hrs the next morning, piled onto lorries and were taken to a barracks at St Servan, just to the south of the walled town of St Malo. After spending some uncomfortable days and nights there, once again a guard came in one evening, read out a list of names and told them to parade in the yard at 05.00hrs the next morning, with all their possessions. Again no destination was given.

'At 5.30 in the morning, the Germans were ready to move off. This time they were taking no chances of anybody escaping. The conscript workers were marched off, with armed guards posted at 10yd intervals on both sides of the column, and taken to St Malo harbour where they were loaded into the hold of a small coastal freighter — where they were going they had no idea and, once again, speculation was the main topic of conversation as the men waited to find out what their masters had in store for them.'

After a first stop in Jersey, they finally docked in Guernsey and Gilbert soon found himself standing on the windy quayside in St Peter Port, main town of the island, where he would spend the rest of the war years.

'Soon some lorries arrived and the conscript labourers were loaded aboard. Their destination was L'Ancresse, where they were to be accommodated in requisitioned houses and bungalows. The accommodation provided was spartan in the extreme, providing little in the way of comfort. Each room, according to size, was furnished with up to six wooden double tier bunk beds with wood slats as a base. The only bedding provided was a straw-filled palliasse and two Army blankets. No chairs, table, carpets or other furniture were provided.

'Each morning the labourers were taken by lorry to Pleinmont where, high on the cliffs, they were put to work preparing a site for the construction of a coastal battery... The group Van Grieken was put to work with consisted of about 50 men, some conscript forced labourers and some slave labourers. The slave workers were Moroccans, Algerians and Greeks who had been living in occupied France, had been rounded up by the Germans and, together with petty criminals found in French prisons, drafted into the OT for construction work. Their condition was pitiful. Clothed in little more than rags, underfed and denied any proper sanitary facilities, they were accommodated in what were, to all intents and purposes, miniature prison units and given the minimum of subsistence rations. The conditions under which the slave workers were housed were so bad that a German doctor, after an outbreak of typhus in one of the camps, warned the German authorities of the danger to their own troops if the sanitary conditions of the slave workers' camps were not improved. The work the men were given to do was backbreaking. Only hand tools, pickaxes and shovels were provided for the men to prepare the site, located on a granite outcrop. Each swing of the pickaxe might loosen half a shovel load of granite, if that, so the progress of the work was slow. If the OT guards thought the slave workers, in particular, were not working fast enough they were more than ready to urge them to greater lengths with the aid of a pickaxe handle or a whip.

'Each midday the conscript workers were lined up and given a ration of thin watery soup fit only for drinking; there was nothing in it to spoon up. This "meal" had to be taken while working. There was no lunch break. The slave workers were also given soup which they had to drink out of any receptacle they could find: old food tins, a disused saucepan, anything that would hold liquid. The OT slaves were usually so ravenous they would battle to reach the food lorry, but the old hands held back as they knew the soup at the bottom of the container was thicker. The OT guards went off elsewhere for their food that was undoubtedly more substantial and sustaining than that given to the workers.'

At the end of each day the slave workers would be taken back to their camps, given their usual meagre ration and left to sleep on the floor of whatever building they were billeted in. The conscript workers fared better, although not a lot. Van Grieken and his group were taken back to their billets and lined up in the kitchen which had been set up in a garage of the bungalow where they lived. There they were given a ration of warm food: vegetable, lentil or macaroni soup, sometimes boiled potatoes and vegetables with a tiny piece of meat. At the same time they were given half a pound of bread with some butter and jam and, occasionally, a piece of meat. This was to be their breakfast for the next morning. They would take the warm food back to rooms to eat. After that they were free to do what they liked, but as there was little attraction to be found at L'Ancresse, particularly in wintertime, and because of the strenuous nature of the day's work they had done, most of the workers simply went to bed to prepare themselves for another day of picking and shovelling at the battery site.

A French Volunteer

Another conscript/volunteer was a French electrician who had his own reasons for volunteering for OT employment, having made two abortive attempts to escape from France. He then volunteered at the Bureau de Placement at Orléans on 30 June 1942, for work in the Channel Islands, in the hope that he would be able to steal a boat and cross to the UK. In fact he managed to get away from France on 30 March 1943, after serving on the Channel Islands, and was interviewed by MI19 (RPS) on reaching England. As well as telling his story of what had happened to him, he was also able to give his interviewers a lot of valuable information about the islands and their defences. In brief the story he told was as follows. From Orléans he was sent to Celle St Cloud near Paris, where he was lodged in a workers' camp for two nights before joining a convoy of workers who were going by train to St Malo. He found himself with some 300 Algerians, French and Belgians, the whole train being given over to these workers. The Algerians were, he said, 'Petain's offering to the Germans'. They had been recruited either in North Africa or Marseilles and promised the earth in the matter of pay, food and lodgings, then packed off in cattle trucks to serve the Organisation Todt.

'These miserable creatures were treated by the Germans worse than animals and were the chosen objects of the foulest brutalities. Any pains or discomforts suffered by the French volunteers were insignificant in comparison with the miseries of these Arabs.'

They arrived at St Malo on 4 July 1942, spent 24 hours in a barracks near the port and then left by night in a cargo ship, with about 150 on board. On arrival at St Peter Port (Guernsey), they were met by some uniformed OT officials, taken to the workers' canteen — a building called 'Rose Marie' — and given a meal. Then they were taken to a bare uninhabited house behind a church where they stayed for some 15 days before being found regular quarters in a similarly bare and deserted house in the south of the town.

After two days they were assigned to various sub-contractors' firms; he went to work for Selbach of Koblenz. This company was not a building firm but rather a supplier of all types of building materials. It was in fact the main builders' merchant for the OT on the island and kept vast stocks of cement, timber, iron and other items at various dumps throughout Guernsey. Initially he was employed as a labourer on the upkeep of the permanent way of the narrow gauge railway that the Germans had laid between St Sampson and St Peter Port to be used exclusively to move building materials. As he was moderately well educated he was soon given an office job and spent his time between the firm's two offices in St Peter Port and St Sampson. There were about 70 OT men in the firm who wore uniform; however, only 15 had been with Selbach prewar.

Above: French colonial troops, now prisoners of war but working for the OT, together with other OT workers, marching on their way to start work on the St Saviour tunnels, Guernsey. They are watched by troops of the German garrison, who are standing in front of St Saviour's School. The photo was taken in the summer of 1940, not long after the occupation began. *Gilbert van Grieken*

Above: Juan Taule (arrowed) with a group of Spanish forced labourers 'acquired' by the OT. He worked first on the submarine pens at La Rochelle, before being shipped over to Jersey. *J. Taule*

'They drew their authority as OT officers from the island chief of the OT, a German called Klaus. The interpreter for Selbach was an Alsatian called Sakseder (phonetic spelling) a wicked rogue who pinched and stole from the workers. As interpreter he acted as censor of the workers' letters and parcels from home and invariably took something out of each parcel for himself. He was a fanatical Nazi and was rumoured to be well in with the local Gestapo. Among the OT foremen was an Italian, called Roger Santini, a youth of 23 who preferred to work for the OT rather than to join the Italian Armed Forces. A German foreman called Nicolas Hewer, a former brasserie proprietor from Koblenz aged 50, was a confirmed grumbler. He hated the war and admitted it was already lost, but nonetheless was unsympathetic toward the foreign workers under his charge. In contrast, another German foreman remained a staunch Nazi even after losing his four sons on the Russian front. He later volunteered himself to go to Russia as a soldier.'

During the months he spent on the island (July 1942–March 1943), he witnessed a notable increase in the average age of the Germans in the OT. Before he left many of 40–45 years had been drafted away to the Army, being replaced with 55–60 year olds. There had been some Luxemburgers amongst the uniformed OT who were volunteers for the German labour service. Some of them were sent away for Army service. There were also Spanish volunteers — but they were of course 'Franco Spaniards'. In fact Republican Spaniards made up a high percentage of the foreign labour — he reckoned that their firm had 150 Spanish Republicans, 250 Belgians, 200 French, 300 Algerians and 20 Poles. There was also a small percentage of islanders, but they kept a semblance of independence and were more like sub-contractors to the OT. However, this did not stop them from being deported.

Conditions of work, food and living conditions were very similar to those already outlined by Gilbert van Grieken. They worked every day, seven days a week, from 07.00–19.00hrs,

with just half an hour break in the middle of the day, when they ate the same watery soup as the others. Living conditions were also as for the Dutchmen, with bunk beds, straw mattresses, no lighting of any sort and no proper internal sanitation.

'We had no changes of clothing either, and I wore the same suit of clothes and the same underwear from July 1942 to March 1943. When my shoes wore out I was given wooden clogs.'

He also mentions there being a typhus epidemic which broke out in January 1942. A total of 14 Arabs died before it was brought under control, but it did not spread to the military or the civilian population.

'The main benefit accruing to the workers from the typhus was an order from the Wehrmacht to the OT to treat the men more kindly. This was the rumour at least! The evidence was that from January until March 1943, there were no reported cases of beatings up by OT foremen.'

The informant also gave some details on pay. He could never get a clear idea of his rates of pay as some money was paid over to his wife (and child) in France. This happened irregularly which annoyed him. However, he found that some other nationalities' pay was even more chaotic. Some Belgians told him that their families had not been paid by the OT for over six months. Personally he was always paid in marks, German currency being used all over the Channel Islands, and he seldom saw British coins. When he was transferred to the office job he was given a contract at 200Rm a month. Of this he received only 52Rm himself, whilst the balance supposedly went to his family through a bank in St Malo. He was meant to be paid every fortnight.

Spanish Nationalists

Among the forced labourers were several thousand Spanish Nationalists who had fought in the Spanish Civil War against Franco. One of these was Juan Taule who had escaped over the frontier into France and was 'given' (his own word) to the Germans by the French authorities in late 1940 in exchange for the release of French POWs. He was initially employed working on the submarine base at La Rochelle, but after some six months was taken over to Jersey and billeted in Elizabeth Castle, St Helier. First of all, he worked on sea walls around the castle, then moved to various other locations, staying longest at Camp Udet, Route de Orange, where he worked on bunkers and sea walls at La Carrière Point, St Ouen's Bay, and other places. Working conditions were not good and food was scarce, especially in 1943–44. Fortunately the foreman who was with the gang all the time was, as Taule put it: 'one of the "good" Germans' and treated them reasonably well: 'We were lucky to get him.' Juan Taule actually worked for the German company Kehl & Co, who had set up a branch on the Channel Islands, in line with many other German building firms.

'Compared with most of the OT work force', comments Michael Ginns,

> 'the Spaniards were in a class of their own; coming from all walks of life, there were clerks, tradesmen and even doctors in their ranks. The OT operated a "divide and rule" policy and would offer inducements of pay and better living conditions to the Spaniards if they would co-operate more closely. Whether any did or not is open to question, but certainly in the Channel Islands a number followed their own trades . . . in 1945 they were transferred to England.'

Which is where Mr Taule still lives.

Local Labour

The Channel Islands perhaps provides a microcosm of the situation that faced many ordinary workers in many parts of Occupied Europe, in that, whilst normal civilian jobs were scarce or badly paid, the OT could offer good wages for even the most mundane of tasks (such as lorry driving). In order to try to stop men from seeking to work for the Germans, the States of Jersey Department of Labour, for example, created work schemes, such as forestry and road construction. However, the Germans craftily imposed a ceiling on the amount that such workers could be paid, making it virtually impossible for anyone to maintain a family on the size of the wage packet offered (single man — £1.50 a week, married — £2.50), whilst when the OT arrived it could offer jobs at £5.00 a week. It is hardly surprising that some 530 local men volunteered to work for the OT. And there was another reason too, as Michael Ginns explains:

> 'Known in the vernacular of the day as "working for the Jerries" and from whatever source the local labour came, employment by the OT gave access to a large pool of commodities that were otherwise unobtainable, and at the end of the working day nearly everybody took something home with them, be it tools or bottles of scarce petrol or diesel fuel.'

However, this form of 'respectable stealing' from the Germans had an effect on island life and in a letter from the Liberation Forces to the Under Secretary of State at the War Office in June 1945, it was stated that: 'the whole moral tone of the Island has been weakened — stealing is prevalent.' (PRO Document WO 199/2131)

Mr G. Prigent, a young 18-year-old builder who lived in Jersey at the time of the occupation, was called up with other young islanders to go to work for the OT. In a tape (No 10711/3), which he recorded for the Imperial War Museum in 1989, he said:

> 'Being a builder I was called up to go and work for them. It wasn't a gun emplacement but they were putting these 24,000 gallon fuel tanks — they had removed them from the harbour to St Peter's Valley. They were going to bury them under ground and then cover them with concrete. They were to refuel the aircraft at the airport. It happened to be a cold November day when I got there. Everybody — not everybody — three or four of the chaps were standing round a brazier warming their hands. A couple of Irish chaps were playing cards. This German soldier said to me: "You come, you have to paint the tanks." I knew I could paint them but there were already three painters in the shed, so I said "I'm no painter, there's one, two, three painters in the shed. Why should I paint them while they are sitting around the fire?" So the officer came, with red stripes. I said, "I couldn't care less. I'm no painter. I have been called up. I'm a builder, plasterer, concrete worker, not painting." So we had a few words. I gave him back the paintbrush and the bucket of red oxide paint. I decided to walk home. At nine o'clock that evening I was arrested as an undesirable troublemaker.
>
> 'I was taken down the harbour. When I got on this boat in the harbour I met three or four other Jersey lads and this Walter Gallscin that I went to school with. We went to Guernsey. We stayed overnight in Guernsey. The next night, on another boat, we went up to Alderney. A year or so before I was sent to Alderney they had called up young chaps to go over to Alderney to work. But they had a German ration. They got double pay working in Alderney than if they were working here. So I thought I was classed as one of those. When we arrived at the docks these chaps went one way, guard was waiting down the bottom of the harbour, he said to me, "You come with me." So I went alone up to an OT farm. So I thought, "There's nobody in here I know." They were all Russians, Poles, French.'

After working on the farm for some weeks, Prigent was sent to work in the German officers' canteen, scrubbing floors, peeling potatoes. Later he worked in a quarry breaking stones, then digging slit trenches around Braye Bay. Eventually, along with other workers, he was shipped back to Jersey. It may sound as though he was able to get away with things. However, I believe that may just be the bravado of youth talking. Certainly he was beaten on numerous occasions and on one was hit in the face with the butt of a guard's rifle and lost his front teeth (he didn't get them fixed properly until after the war):

> 'One night I got out of my bunk too slow. I lifted my arms to yawn and stretch and they thought I was going to hit the guard. Then he hit me in the face with the butt of his rifle and took my teeth out . . . If you were dragging your feet when you marched to work, and most of us did drag our feet because we were all exhausted and starved, they used to come along with a whip and whip you to make you march faster. If you were working too slow in

the stone quarry they used to come along and shout at you and whip you . . . Some of the prisoners, if they had been caught doing something wrong during the day at roll call they were brought out in front of us. They were whipped and kicked around the square where we stood. Then, when they collapsed, the guards used to carry them to a wooden tool shed. You never saw those chaps at roll call again . . . You thought, "in a couple of days time they'll be back," but people just used to disappear.'

Slave Labourers

'Very little distinction seems to have been made by the Germans between Russian war prisoners and forced labour mobilised in the towns and in the villages from the civil population in occupied territory. They have all been treated with the same brutality, undernourished, a very large proportion worked to death and many beaten to death.'

That is how MI19 (RPS) report 2292 on 'Forced Labour — Prison Atrocities' dated 25 July 1944 begins. It was compiled from the experiences of 14 Red Army soldiers and Russian civilians, all of whom without exception told of 'torture, starvation and very hard work'. However, they also said that the Germans had slack control over both POWs and forced labour, not only when they were still in occupied Russian territory but also after they were taken to France and the Channel Islands.

'In Alderney, Jersey and Cherbourg, many prisoners succeeded in escaping four or five times and to keep in hiding for months on end in semi-demolished houses in Cherbourg, with French farmers in the villages or with English people on the islands. Whilst they were in hiding they were treated well and on no occasion were they ever denounced. When recaptured, particularly in France and the islands, the prisoners were given very hard sentences. In addition to the beatings on recapture they would be sentenced to 25 to 50 lashes a month and to three months' solitary confinement in one of the prison dungeons on 200 grammes (less than half a pound) of bread a day and no other food. Stealing was a further method of staying alive. This consisted of digging up a few potatoes and eating them raw or sneaking away to the shore to find mussels or winkles. Occasionally a German foodstore would be raided and food stolen. Those who did not steal, died, which accounts for the large proportion of deaths (over 50% in Alderney, 40% in Jersey).[2]

'Why the Germans should have allowed such a high proportion of workers doing essential work for them to die was answered by the informants as follows: "We were treated worse than cattle. Our term of usefulness was generally accepted by the Germans as being six

Below: Summer 1942 and OT workers, with their uniformed OT overseer, work on the foundations of a gun platform on the Atlantic Wall. *Bundesarchiv*

months. After that we were expended. They tried to get out of us every ounce of labour and energy they could on as little food as possible. If we managed to carry on for a another few months well and good, and if not all went to schedule."'

This explanation is not altogether complete for, though it is true that when a Russian prisoner fell ill hardly any medical assistance was given to him, beyond placing him in a separate barrack and excusing him from work, when 800 workmen on Alderney and 600 on Jersey were too exhausted to work, they were all sent away for a prolonged rest. At St Malo and at Cherbourg, exhausted Russian prisoners were given three to four months' improved food and no work to enable them to recover their strength. Thereupon they were sent back to work. Furthermore several of the informants were gashed or maimed by German guards. Some of these were taken to hospital for treatment and were operated on by German doctors. In at least three instances men were sent to Paris for a further operation, yet, whilst taking this amount of trouble over the injured, no measures were at any time taken against the guards who crippled the workers and caused this extra work to the German medical organisation.

'The explanation according to some of the informants is that the cases quoted are the exception and not the rule, and the fact that a few German doctors were sufficiently humane to take an interest in the Russian patients, does not affect the huge proportion of deaths. Moreover, if a short treatment can revitalise sturdy workers there is no reason why they should not be treated for a certain period so that they may be further exploited.'

Poor Equipment
Political prisoner Odd Nansen, whom we met in an earlier chapter up in the snows of northern Norway, remembers not being very impressed with the work of the OT volunteers:

'When one sees them at it, one realises that the result can be no great shakes, either for quantity or quality. After a closer look at their tools, one understands even more. Most things in the first place, they haven't got. There are no decent hammers. All they have are some things like Lilliputian sledgehammers. None of the axes have an edge and whetstones are unobtainable. There are no decent joiner's tools. Everything is the cheapest kind of Nuremberg trash, as we called it in the old days. It's ordered and delivered by the bundle. We saw it lying in open railway trucks in Trondheim and elsewhere. A percentage of it was ruined, rusty or smashed. There is a shortage of decent nails. They have only certain sizes which they have to make do with. But above all they are short of decent material. Round, crooked logs and the cheapest kind of boarding material are all that can be had. Those we have to fetch from old abortive snow-shelters that are being pulled down on other hills not far away. Presumably they are last winter's abortive attempts to keep the road open. This year they'll try again. I hardly think it will come off. According to report they're planning to build 21km of snow-roofs in all. An Oslo firm has it in hand. Perhaps we'll be put on it as well.
    'They're a melancholy-looking crowd. Spiritless and gloomy, lacklustre, gangling and crook-backed they go around, no they swarm around, to all appearance about as aimlessly as ants in and around an ant-heap, only a good deal slower in their movements. Perhaps they rather suggest another insect — in a gluepot. The Grini tempo was the speed of an express train compared with this. Grini efficiency might be set up as a pattern for these people.'[3]

Prisoners of War
Undoubtedly POWs of various nationalities were also used to supplement the labour pool, which was welcomed by some prisoners as they received extra rations. However, among the POWs who were required to work some were very badly treated, whilst others survived because of their inner discipline. One such group were French colonial troops — Senegalese, Moroccan, Tunisian and Algerian — some of whom had the advantage of receiving Red Cross parcels, containing cigarettes, which put them very high up, if not at the top, of the bartering ladder. 'In Jersey', records Michael Ginns, 'thanks to the tight discipline of the senior NCO, Sergeant Mohamed ben Mohamed, described as a "true soldier of France", all 115 of them survived to return to France in 1945.' These POWs had worked on the docks and in fatigue parties in ammunition and fuel dumps, rather than actually building fortifications, and that probably holds good for most POWs everywhere.

Work for All
The Germans were not averse to compelling local people to work on the Atlantic Wall, and Rommel advocated it in some cases. However, the Desert Fox was quick to point out that civilians worked better if they were paid promptly and in cash. This was not the case in the Netherlands, when Rotterdam and The Hague became a fortress area. In May 1944 a large number of the citizens of Rotterdam were forced to work at Hoek van Holland on the fortifications under the supervision of German soldiers. Thousands of people had been forced to move out of the densely inhabited coast zone and many of the buildings in the zone were deliberately wrecked. This caused great unrest, especially when rumours circulated that a 50km belt of fortifications was to be constructed in the coastal area. Fortunately this proved to be exaggerated, but the destruction and misery caused by the evacuations and the enforced labour were bad enough.[4]

Notes
1. MI19 dealt with refugees arriving in the UK. They were normally taken to the Royal Patriotic School (Battersea) for interrogation as one of its aims was to secure intelligence from such arrivals. Some of its interrogation reports are now held by the PRO.
2. Whilst Bunny Pantcheff's detailed survey of Alderney probably substantiates this claim as far as slave labourers on the island were concerned, I have yet to find documented evidence to substantiate it for Jersey.
3. Day after Day by Odd Nansen. 'Grini' was a labour camp in Norway.
4. See The Netherlands at War 1940–45 by Walter B. Maass

45

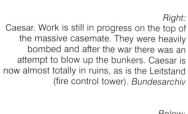

Right:
Caesar. Work is still in progress on the top of the massive casemate. They were heavily bombed and after the war there was an attempt to blow up the bunkers. Caesar is now almost totally in ruins, as is the Leitstand (fire control tower). *Bundesarchiv*

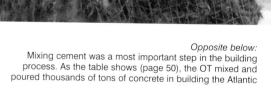

Below:
Massive cranes were needed to emplace such guns as this one at the Batterie Lindemann, Pas de Calais. The three 40.6cm guns were called Anton, Bruno and Caesar. *Bundesarchiv*

Opposite top:
Batterie Lindemann in all its glory. These impressive structures were 'opened' in 1942, despite not being fully completed and became a symbol of the strength of the Atlantic Wall, being used in much of the Nazi propaganda material. *Bundesarchiv*

Opposite below:
Mixing cement was a most important step in the building process. As the table shows (page 50), the OT mixed and poured thousands of tons of concrete in building the Atlantic Wall. *Bundesarchiv*

Below:
Camouflage netting being hoisted up to cover new constructions on the Atlantic Wall. Note the OT armband on the overseer's arm. *Bundesarchiv*

Below:
A 5-ton harbour works crane, from the Victoria Pier, Jersey, was hired by the German firm of Theodor Elsche to help in the construction of an anti-tank wall to the south of Le Braye Slip, St Ouen's Bay, Jersey, September 1941.
CIOS Jersey

Above:
Like ants on an ant heap, this mass of labourers is working on an earthpile, possibly the basis for a gun position.
CIOS Jersey

Right:
'A corner of a foreign field' — in this case the Russian Cemetery at Longy Common, Alderney, as it appeared in March 1945. The death rate among the Russian workers was very high in the early days of their enforced captivity. In 1963 the bodies were all exhumed and reburied in Normandy.
Alderney Society and Museum

The Types of Defensive Structures

Economy of Force

In a military culture so dedicated to the offensive, it may seem strange that the Germans were not averse to building defensive fortifications. However, they reasoned that by doing so they would be able to hold a particular line with a relatively smaller force than would otherwise be necessary. 'Economy of Force' was therefore a fundamental principle in designing fortifications. In other words, such fortifications existed not to protect their soldiers, but rather to enable them to fight more effectively and by doing so they were able to tie down fewer men to a static defence, so that the bulk of their forces could still manoeuvre. This principle was applied to a certain degree in designing the Wall, but the arguments over where the immediate counter-attack forces, that is to say the panzer manoeuvre force, would be located, led to major problems.

Characteristics of Fortifications

Design Principles

During the last year of the war, the USA produced a *Handbook on German Military Forces* (TM-E 30-451 dated 1 March 1945), which was issued to US troops who would be serving in North-West Europe. Chapter V of that manual dealt specifically with 'Fortifications and Defenses' and provided an excellent summary of the main types of such fortifications and defences as were found in the Atlantic Wall. Initially, however, it dealt with the Wehrmacht principles of design and construction. The basic considerations were fire effect, cover and concealment. Fire effect was top priority, whilst natural concealment was used as much as possible, by blending into the surrounding terrain. Where fire effect was not a consideration — for example with personnel or supply shelters — then fortifications would be completely below ground level, or as low as the local water-table permitted. In order to present as small a target as possible to high-angle fire and bombing, emplacements, pillboxes and casemates were built no larger than was necessary to allow crews to operate their guns. Nevertheless, when one considers the massive dimensions of some of the coastal artillery guns, then the size of such casemates was correspondingly enormous.

Below: The basis of all bunker design was the mesh of reinforcing rods, as can be seen in this typical example under construction. Note also that the pipework for the ventilation system as well as the chimney for the stove are fixed into position before the concrete is poured. CIOS Jersey

Construction

All permanent, fortress-type works and many field works were to be made of reinforced concrete. Steel bars were used for reinforcing, running in three dimensions so as to form 25–30cm cubes. Rod diameter varied from 10mm to 15mm, with the most common size being 12mm. Rods were hooked at each end. In this connection, see the table below that lists the amounts of concrete, rod steel and sheet steel used in the various structures.

Quantities of Basic Components Used

FORTIFICATION	CONCRETE (cubic metres)	ROD STEEL (tons)	SHEET STEEL (tons)
Casemate for 4.7cm Pak	830	40	6.2
Two-section bunker	660	33	6
Gun emplacement for 5cm gun with gun shield	535	23.5	3.2
Anti-tank gun bunker with cupola and observation post	66	27	4.1
Ammunition bunker	740	34	5.7
One-storey battalion command post	990	49	8.7
Two-storey regimental/battalion command post	1,480	68	9.1
Command post for supply company	850	43	9.6
Field artillery embrasure	1,330	63	15.6
Infantry-gun embrasure	385	17	4.1
Headquarters signals bunker	1,100	53	10
Section bunker with observation post	485	23	3.7
Armoured machine gun position	610	30	5.3
Six embrasures with tank cupola	1,730	83	7
Large medical bunker	1,360	50	20
120° embrasure with reserve room	1,080	52	11
Six-man bunker with ammunition magazine	500	23	6
15-man bunker	570	24	7
60° embrasure for field gun	495	20	5.4
Embrasure for 7.5cm gun	340	16	4.5[1]

Some field works were, however, built of masonry, bricks or timber. As the drawings show, steel was also used in concrete structures for beams, turrets, cupolas, gun shields, machine gun loopholes and doors. These were prefabricated and given code/model numbers so that they could be more easily ordered.

Above right: Lifting one of the heavy metal machine gun posts into position. They had six slots for all-round vision and weighed over 3 tons. Entry was via a door in the back of the upper half, just 50 x 58cm! A pedal-operated blower provided ventilation. The top half had armour up to 12cm thick, whilst the lower part was only 2cm thick, but was of course below ground level. *Bundesarchiv*

Right: Some bunkers remained unfinished when D-Day came. This one was photographed by a British Army cameraman 'somewhere in Normandy', 17 June 1944. *IWM — KX26734*

Right:
Excellent shot of a Tobruk complete with an MG34, on the Channel Islands. This was the most common type of Tobruk, designated Type 58c and also known as a Ringstand because of the all-round track on which to mount a machine gun. *IWM — HU29108*

Below:
The turret of a French Hotchkiss H 35 which has been fitted to the top of this position on the beaches of Le Grande Vey, France, is being inspected by a GI, 15 September 1944. *US Army*

Even the concrete works themselves were given a type number and were constructed from master plans prepared by the Army Ordnance Office. The normal thickness of concrete walls and roofs was 2m, but reduced thickness was to be found in smaller field works. The minimum thickness for walls and roofs in casemates was 2m or more, commensurate with the calibre of the gun (3m+ in some of the extra large casemates). Roofs over interior compartments in most structures were supported by steel I-beams encased within the concrete, the size of the beams depending upon the length of the span. Steel plates were then laid between the I-beams and rested on the lower flanges to form the ceiling. These plates prevented the inside of the roof from spalling if the structure took a direct hit from artillery fire or bombing. In some cases the roof was supported by reinforced concrete beams instead of steel I-beams, when it was necessary to save steel.

Types of Fortifications

In general terms, the Wall fortifications can be divided into the following categories: open emplacements, pillboxes and casemates, shelters and, lastly, observation posts (OP). Of course obstacles of all types, such as anti-tank ditches, 'dragon's teeth' and so on, including minefields, must also be included.

Open Emplacements

These were known under the generic name of the Tobruk Type. From their experience in North Africa, the Germans had derived a type of open, circular pit, lined with concrete, which they called a Tobruk. Subsequently Hitler's staff issued orders that Tobruk pits were to be used as defence works in the field, and instructions on how they should be built were distributed down to divisional level. Such a pit comprised a concrete weapon chamber built entirely underground, with a neck-like

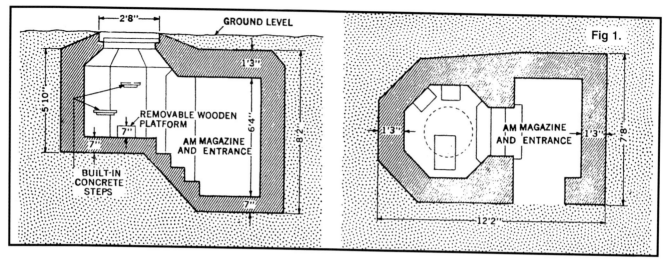

Above: A Ringstand. *Source: US Army training manual TM-E 30-451 dated 1 March 1945*

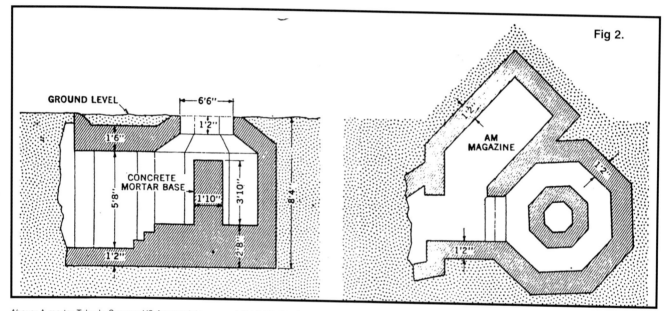

Above: A mortar Tobruk. *Source: US Army training manual TM-E 30-451 dated 1 March 1945*

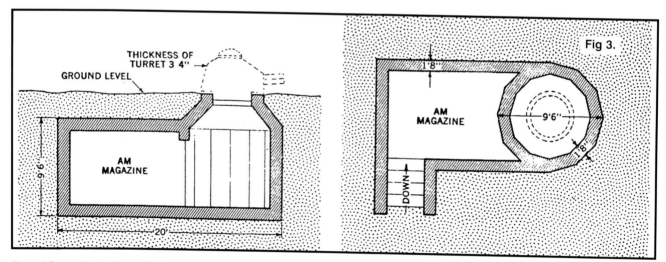

Above: A Panzerstellung. *Source: US Army training manual TM-E 30-451 dated 1 March 1945*

opening at the top. The concrete was generally reinforced and the pits varied in size depending upon the weapon to be mounted within them. However, the diameter of the neck was always kept as small as possible so as to reduce the risk of direct hits. A Tobruk did not have a concrete roof as this would have given away its position to the enemy, instead a board of irregular shape was used as a lid and camouflaged the circular opening (it also kept out the rain!).

The most common type of Tobruk was designated the Type 58c and known as a Ringstand — because of the rail around the inside of the neck, which provided a 360° track on which to mount a machine gun (see Figure 1). Note also the underground ammunition chamber and entrance also underground. Figure 2 shows a 50mm mortar emplacement (Type 61a), which had a larger Ringstand, a concrete base on which to mount the mortar and a separate ammunition chamber. Figure 3 shows a Panzerstellung, which used a Tobruk as a base on which to mount a tank turret — normally that of a captured French Renault 35, which mounted a 37mm anti-tank gun and a co-axial machine gun. The turret was bolted to a circular metal plate, which was rotated by hand along a 360° track, giving all-round traverse.

Pillboxes and Casemates

In accordance with German doctrine, although there were many concrete pillboxes and casemates in the Atlantic Wall, they were mainly supported by even more open field works. The pillboxes themselves had walls and roofs up to 2m thick, as did the casemates which housed the large calibre guns. They also normally had a stepped embrasure to prevent bullets ricocheting into the gun opening, whilst in some cases a steel gun shield would be added to close the opening. Some examples of pillboxes and casemates are shown in Figures 4, 5 and 6.

Above right: A Type 630 pillbox. *Source: US Army training manual TM-E 30-451 dated 1 March 1945*

Below right: A Type 685 casemate. *Source: US Army training manual TM-E 30-451 dated 1 March 1945*

Below: A Type 677 casemate. *Source: US Army training manual TM-E 30-451 dated 1 March 1945*

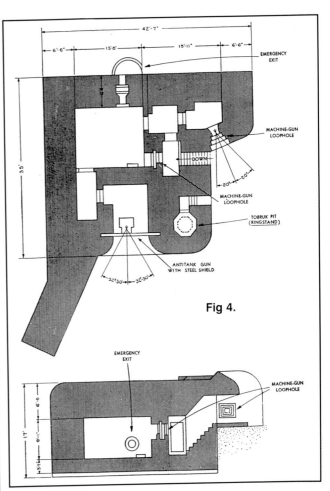

Fig 4.

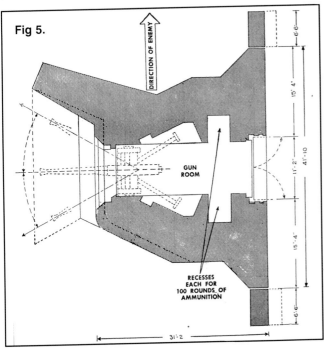

Fig 5.

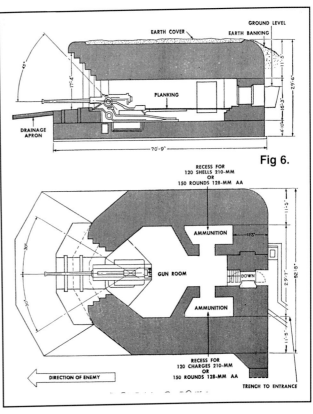

Fig 6.

The 600 Series

A new standard bunker design was created for the Atlantic Wall, namely the 600 series. These were supposedly bombproof, constructed of reinforced concrete, with walls between 2m and 3.5m thick. The series included designs for coastal artillery and below are descriptions of three examples of this series.

The *Type 630 pillbox* was designed to hold a light anti-tank gun, with a 2m concrete roof, sides and front wall, but the rear wall was some 8mm thinner. Close defence was provided by a machine gun firing through a loophole at the rear, whilst there was a second loophole at the bottom of the stairway from where a defender could fire at anyone trying to get in. A Tobruk pit (Ringstand) was built into the front wall as an OP/MG post. Of course there were many 'local designs' as well where the pillbox was specially modified to suit local conditions. Also there was an all-steel 'mobile' pillbox (weighing just over 3 tons!) that could be placed anywhere suitable. This was constructed in two halves, then welded together. The top half contained the aperture, armament, air vents and entrance door. The steel plate varied in thickness from 12cm near the aperture to 5cm on the sides and top of the top half, while the bottom half was only some 2cm thick, but

was designed to be dug in and thus well protected by the ground.

The *Type 685 casemate* was designed to hold guns of 21cm calibre. It had a 3.5m thick roof, but was of simple design, with a gun room (with recesses for ammunition) and possibly separate living quarters for the gun crew. The embrasure allowed for 60° traverse and 40° elevation for the weapon. There were a whole range of such casemates (e.g. Types 683, 684, 686, 688, 689, 690, 692 and 694) with differing amounts of traverse to suit the weapon housed and varying from 90° to 120°. Additional protection and camouflage could be added by banking up the sides and by covering the top with a layer of earth.

The *Type 677 casemate* was designed to enable the gun it housed to deliver flanking fire. To do this a wing wall was built on the side towards the enemy so as to shield the embrasure from enemy fire, the length of the wall depending on local conditions. The Type 677 was for an 8cm gun or larger.

Below: This Type 677 casemate at Courseulles is under new management, a Canadian triple 20mm Oerlikon AA mounting having taken up residence on top of the casemate which still houses an 8.8cm anti-tank gun. *Ken Bell, National Archives of Canada PA140856*

Above:
Is it a house or is it a gun emplacement? Largest of the guns on the Channel Islands were those of the Mirus Battery, which comprised four reconditioned 30.5cm guns off a World War 1 Russian battleship. These were located at St Saviour's, Guernsey. *IWM — HU 29057*

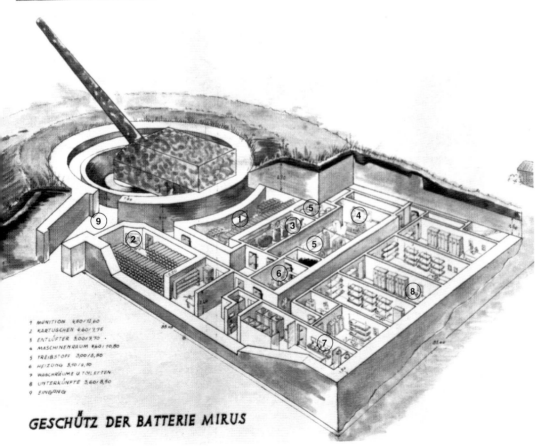

Left:
Plan of one of the Mirus Battery gun emplacements showing:
(1) ammunition;
(2) propelling charges;
(3) ventilator;
(4) generating room;
(5) fuel stores;
(6) heating;
(7) washroom/toilet;
(8) quarters;
(9) entrance.

1 MUNITION 4,60/12,60
2 KARTUSCHEN 4,60/7,75
3 ENTLÜFTER 3,00/2,70
4 MASCHINENRAUM 4,60/10,80
5 TREIBSTOFF 3,00/5,50
6 HEIZUNG 3,10/6,10
7 WASCHRÄUME U TOILETTEN
8 UNTERKÜNFTE 3,60/8,50
9 EINGANG

GESCHÜTZ DER BATTERIE MIRUS

Custom-built casemates

Whilst the two types shown in the drawings are but two of the many standard casemates, there were of course even more 'custom-built' casemates for such massive guns as those of the Mirus Battery in the Channel Islands and one can imagine how much labour, effort, steel and concrete went into their construction.

Camouflage

Pillboxes, casemates and the other works were all camouflaged, where possible, by banks of earth at the sides and on top. They might also be hidden by enclosing them in wooden buildings, with the gun being fired through false doors or windows, though such arrangements were never allowed to interfere with the gun's field of fire.

Shelters

It was clearly desirable to have adequate shelters for all troops manning the fortifications. Generally, these were built in rear of the fortified line to house the reserves and also in individual defensive positions to house the troops manning the installations. Some personnel shelters had room for two sections (roughly 20 men), but the norm was no more than 10 men in one shelter for obvious reasons. Personnel shelters could also be used as headquarters, command posts, medical stations or signal centres. However, the types provided specially for such purposes had differing designs, size and number of interior compartments and other modifications.[2]

One of the most common types of shelter was the *Type 621*, designed to hold an infantry Gruppe (squad/section) of 10 men. Built of reinforced concrete with a roof thickness of 2m, it was designed to be completely underground, with a covering of at least 30cm of earth on top. Seventeen steel I-beams, each 4m long, supported the ceiling above the interior compartment. Steel plates resting on the bottom flanges of the I-beams provided an all-steel ceiling. Shorter I-beams supported the ceiling over the doors and entrance stairs. A camouflaged 'flat-top' stretched over the trench at the rear, which provided access to the entrance stairs and concealed it from the air. The flat-top had a row of hooks cast into the roof along the rear side of the shelter to secure it. A Tobruk pit was built into one of the side wings for observation. There were two entrances/exits provided to enable the section to deploy rapidly. Each entrance was covered by a machine gun, firing through a loophole in the interior wall at the foot of the stairs. Both entrances converged into a gas lock which was sealed by three steel doors about 25mm thick, which all opened outwards. To make the chimney grenade-proof the vertical shaft was continued below the stovepipe and curved outwards into the space used for the emergency exit. Thus a grenade dropped into the chimney did not enter the shelter but fell outside the sidewall to explode harmlessly. Four ventilation shafts opened into the rear wall between the entrance stairs, two of which were dummies to mislead attackers trying to introduce smoke into the ventilating system to drive out the occupants. The blower was driven by an electric motor, but could be hand operated in a power failure. To communicate with those inside, there was a telephone at the head of the entrance stairs and both a telephone and speaking tube in the Tobruk. Also, a telephone cable, deeply buried, led to other nearby installations. Sometimes section shelters were adapted to include a steel turret for observation and/or an externally mounted machine gun on top of the Tobruk. However, it was laid down that troops were not to fight from their shelters but just to use them as protection when not engaged in combat.

Figure 9 shows a typical anti-tank gun shelter, designated as *Type 629*. The accommodation for the personnel was similar to that of other personnel shelters, but there was also a separate compartment for the gun and its ammunition. Double doors on this compartment enabled the gun to be rolled out and up a ramp (slope 1:6) to an open emplacement to the rear of the shelter from which it fired over the top of the shelter. It had two Tobruk pits, each with a machine gun to support the anti-tank

Top: This machine gun embrasure was on high ground near Dieppe, located so as to protect the entrance to its well-camouflaged bunker. *Ken Bell, National Archives of Canada*

Left: Painted with disruptive camouflage, this bunker in front of the eastern headland at Dieppe incorporates a separate entrance to a Tobruk Ringstand. *Ken Bell, National Archives of Canada PA183166*

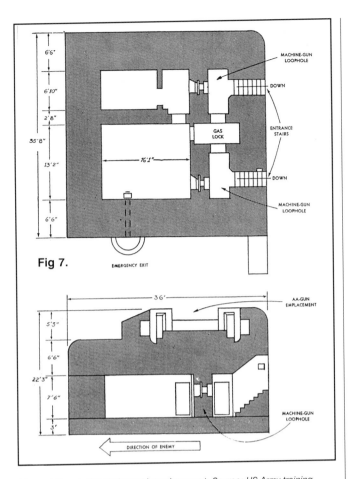

Fig 7.

Measurements shown: 6'6", 6'10", 2'8", 35'8", 13'2", 6'6", 16'1"

MACHINE-GUN LOOPHOLE

DOWN

GAS LOCK

ENTRANCE STAIRS

DOWN

MACHINE-GUN LOOPHOLE

EMERGENCY EXIT

Lower diagram measurements: 36', 5'3", 6'6", 22'3", 7'6", 3'

AA-GUN EMPLACEMENT

MACHINE-GUN LOOPHOLE

DIRECTION OF ENEMY

Above: A Type L 409 shelter and emplacement. *Source: US Army training manual TM-E 30-451 dated 1 March 1945*

Above: A slightly damaged Type 622 accommodation bunker at Carpiquet now housing Canadian troops. *Ken Bell, National Archives of Canada PA141708*

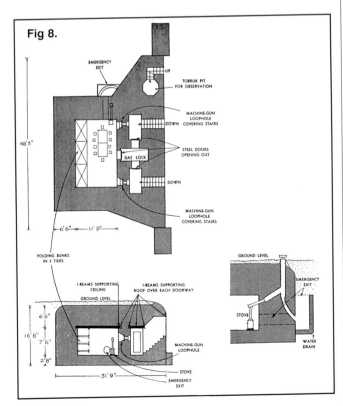

Fig 8.

EMERGENCY EXIT

UP

TOBRUK PIT FOR OBSERVATION

MACHINE-GUN LOOPHOLE COVERING STAIRS

DOWN

GAS LOCK

STEEL DOORS OPENING OUT

DOWN

MACHINE-GUN LOOPHOLE COVERING STAIRS

48'3"

6'6", 11'9"

FOLDING BUNKS IN 3 TIERS

I-BEAMS SUPPORTING CEILING

I-BEAMS SUPPORTING ROOF OVER EACH DOORWAY

GROUND LEVEL

6'0", 16'8", 7'6", 2'8"

MACHINE-GUN LOOPHOLE

STOVE

EMERGENCY EXIT

31'9"

GROUND LEVEL

EMERGENCY EXIT

STOVE

WATER DRAIN

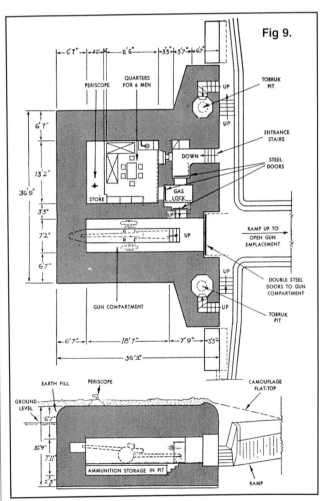

Fig 9.

Measurements: 6'7", 4'2", 11'6", 3'3", 3'7", 6'7", 6'7", 13'2", 3'3", 7'2", 6'7"

PERISCOPE

QUARTERS FOR 6 MEN

TOBRUK PIT

UP / UP

ENTRANCE STAIRS

DOWN

STEEL DOORS

GAS LOCK

UP

STORE

RAMP UP TO OPEN GUN EMPLACEMENT

36'9"

UP

GUN COMPARTMENT

DOUBLE STEEL DOORS TO GUN COMPARTMENT

TOBRUK PIT

UP

6'7", 18'7", 7'9", 3'3", 36'2"

EARTH FILL

PERISCOPE

CAMOUFLAGE FLAT-TOP

GROUND LEVEL

6'7", 16'9", 7'11", 2'3"

AMMUNITION STORAGE IN PIT

RAMP

Above: A Type 629 anti-tank gun shelter. *Source: US Army training manual TM-E 30-451 dated 1 March 1945*

Left: A Type 621 personnel shelter. *Source: US Army training manual TM-E 30-451 dated 1 March 1945*

gun, and they were connected by telephone and speaking tube to the gun crew's quarters. The shelter was also equipped with a periscope. Figure 7 shows a combined shelter and emplacement, designated as *Type L 409* (the L standing for Luftwaffe), which was a personnel shelter with an open gun emplacement on the roof. This type was for a light anti-aircraft gun and its crew, but there were other variations in the *L 400 series*, for example the *L 405* radar and the *L 411* searchlight, whilst the shelter below could be adapted for other uses, for example the *L 434* battalion command post or *L 407* ammunition magazine.

Finally there were **Supply Shelters**, designed to hold ammunition, rations and other supplies, and drinking water. These were normally entirely underground and would have walls 2m thick, just one entrance, no emergency exits, nor loopholes, nor Tobruks.

Observation Posts
A typical observation post (OP) is shown at Figure 10, of the kind used for Army coastal artillery — *Type 636*. It had separate rooms for observation, plotting, radar, officers' quarters and other ranks' quarters. A Giant Würzburg radar set

was mounted on the roof, while there were at least two machine gun loopholes covering the rear entrance (one in the exterior wall, one in the interior wall at the foot of the stairs). The quarters were for two officers and nine men, but as this was insufficient to cover all those who would be working in such a post, a further personnel shelter would be built nearby. Some of the coastal artillery observation posts built on the Channel Islands were far more elaborate and will be explained in more detail later.

Stützpunkt 37H
Not far from the village of Wassenaar on the Dutch coast, which lies between Scheveningen and Katwijk, the Germans built Strongpoint 37H (or Wassenaarse Slag in Dutch) on what they called the *freie Küste*, that is to say, the less well defended land between two larger strongpoints. The small strongpoint is typical of those built in areas of 'free coast' and is still largely intact — especially the subterranean passageways and command/observation post. It is open to the public in the summer. It was one of the few German coastal positions in Holland to see actual combat, when, on 28 February 1944, six Free French commandos came ashore to reconnoitre the strongpoint. It is still not clear exactly what happened, but probably one of them activated an alarm signal and they had to withdraw into the sea. Their subsequent rendezvous with a British MTB went disastrously wrong and all were drowned. Their commander was Charles Trepel and a monument now recalls their brave action.

The strongpoint comprised three concrete bunkers (each 3m thick): No 8698 — a Type 612 Schartenstand für Lande und Sturmabwehrgeschütze ohne Nebenräume, armed with an 8cm Feldkanone 30(t); No 8699 — a Type 676 Kleinstschartenstand für 5cm KwK; No 8697 — a non-regular type armed with a 4.7cm Festungspak (t). For all round defence several Tobruk pits were added. Two of them of the 216 Type were armed with heavy machine guns. In the centre of the strongpoint was a command post/observation post, with a covered observation tower. The strongpoint commander had his own bunker, which housed himself and a messenger.

This post had a 120-man garrison which on 24 May 1944 comprised one officer, three NCOs and 19 men of the 31st Jäger Regiment (Luftwaffe); three NCOs and 23 men of the Festung Stamm Abteilung (fortress troops) manning the artillery pieces (4.7cm Pak and the 5cm KwK); three NCOs and 12 men of VB3 Artillery Regiment 16 (VB — vorgeschobene Beobachtung [advanced observation]); and 56 men of 14 Company 31st Jäger Regiment, manning two mortars. These troops went to France in August 1944 and were replaced by an officer, seven NCOs and 43 men of No 1 Company, 12th Infantry Regiment, plus two NCOs and four men of the artillery from the 21st SS Regiment.

The troops lived in several concrete living bunkers, which were of lighter construction

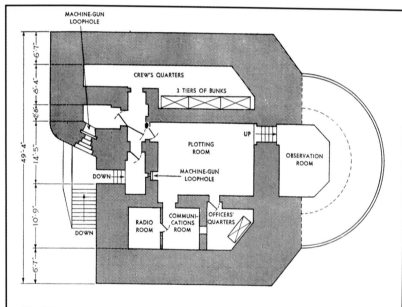

Fig 10.

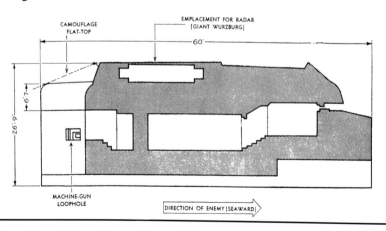

Above: A Type 636 observation post. *Source: US Army training manual TM-E 30-451 dated 1 March 1945*

Right:
Beach obstacles came in many forms — such as these basic stakes made from tree-trunks, some of which had Teller mines attached. These were on the Dieppe beach and still *in situ* when the Canadians arrived there for a second time. *Donald Grant, National Archives of Canada PA131224*

Left:
A single sentry walks between anti-tank tetrahedra which cover a gap in the sand dunes bordering a beach. Note the rifles of off-duty guards resting on some of the obstacles. *Bundesarchiv*

Right:
A 'Belgian Gate' (also known as 'Element C'), being dragged along the beach at low tide. These mobile obstacles were some 3m high and 3m wide. *Bundesarchiv*

with a *Tagesraum* (daytime living room) added. There were also toilets, store rooms, water storage facilities, a kitchen and bathroom (with the additional function of chemical treatment). Finally there was a searchlight position, with a separate storage building. All main bunkers, living quarters and most of the other buildings were connected by a subterranean passageway made of brickwork — a unique feature.

Obstacles

Some of the obstacles used on the Atlantic Wall — such as anti-tank ditches, concrete 'dragon's teeth' of various types, and barbed-wire fences — were standard German field engineering obstacles that could be found in other locations such as on the Westwall. However, the Atlantic Wall, as it covered the coast, had numerous obstacles that were unique to it, some of which came from the fertile, imaginative mind of Field Marshal Rommel. A selection of these obstacles is shown in the photographs accompanying this chapter and are listed in Chapter 7 in Rommel's report on the Wall. In general terms, obstacles were usually erected within main battle positions, covered by fire from open emplacements or pillboxes and could be either fixed or movable. They were generally made of steel and concrete, but Rommel also incorporated wooden obstacles.

Minefields

Minefields were normally laid out to a definite pattern, except in areas where the German commanders did not wish to undertake offensive action, where they might well be sewn irregularly. Within an anti-tank minefield there would generally also be some anti-personnel mines, so as to make the job of clearing a gap more hazardous. The reverse was also used, namely a row or two of anti-tank mines would be laid on the edge of an anti-personnel minefield, so that an AFV could not just drive through detonating the anti-personnel mines. Safe lanes would be left through minefields, so as to allow for patrolling, and these were varied from time to time. Mines would generally be laid close to or on roads, railways, airfields and at other important points. Hastily scattered mines might well be used on surfaced roads, when time did not permit digging them in. German mines were generally of excellent quality; for example, the Teller anti-tank mine (the basic Tmi 29 contained 4.5kg of TNT) and the Schuminen (universally known as S-mines) were lethal anti-personnel mines.

In his book *The History of Landmines*, Mike Croll cites the situation which pertained in Guernsey as being something of a 'microcosm of German mine warfare'. Here, postwar, the clearance of the small (approximately 90 sq km) island involved lifting a total of 115 minefields, containing a staggering 72,866 mines, including Teller mines, S-mines, Stockminen (stake mines) and locally made versions of the S-mine. He goes on to explain how:

'Large areas of the island were planted with "Rommel's Asparagus" using captured French 300lb shells and much of the coastline featured mined underwater obstacles. Along the cliffs 518 improvised mines and over 1,000 Rollbomben were used.'

These last were aircraft bombs placed at the top of cliffs and camouflaged, which could then be rolled down on top of anyone climbing up!

After his experience in North Africa, Rommel was a great advocate of the use of minefields and following his initial inspection of the Atlantic Wall told his chief engineer, General

Wilhelm Meise, that he wanted millions more mines laid (see Chapter 7).

How Good were these Defences?

It is interesting to see that the Germans clearly asked themselves this question even before they were put to the ultimate test by the Normandy invasion. From the autumn of 1943, the Fortress Engineer staffs were required to report to the inspector of western fortifications, Generalleutnant Rudolf Schmetzer, who had been in the job since 15 August 1940, on the results of all enemy bombs released over the fortified defence systems in their areas, then, later, on the results of heavy naval guns firing at these emplacements. Schmetzer was ordered to Paris from 2 June to 10 July 1944 to report on these investigations and the gist of his findings was produced in a written report which was translated and published for the US Army in 1947. The report was entitled: 'The effect of bombs and heavy naval guns on the fortified defence system of the Atlantic Wall.' Schmetzer had used not only the detailed reports which he had received, but he had also kept in touch with the OT, the chief naval fortress engineer staff and the staff at Luftflotte 3, and had carried out his own inspections of constructions with walls of reinforced concrete 2m thick or over. Here are some examples of the results his report listed.

Personnel Shelters

As far as Gruppe shelters were concerned, he cites the case of a normal shelter made of 'faultless quality' reinforced concrete 2m thick, occupied by a sergeant and eight artillerymen, which had received three direct hits during an air-raid. The first one hit one of the short walls (about 15sq m in size) and:

'At the explosion the whole construction rumbled and shook tremendously, so that bottles and other objects fell from the table. At the same time the electric lights went out, small bits of concrete fell down and the room was full of dust which made breathing somewhat difficult. A candle was lit. After a short time, when the dust had settled, minor damage could be observed, such as several very thin cracks in the wall and small pieces broken out of the supports carrying the iron roof girders immediately beneath the roof.

'About 5–10 minutes later, the second direct hit landed on the unsupported part of the roof, in distance only 50cm from the wall which had been hit before, producing the same results as the first direct hit. There were a few more cracks in the wall and they were slightly deeper, as were also the small pieces broken out from under the roof. To the men in the shelter, the damage appeared quite insignificant, now as before.

'After a further lapse of 10–15 minutes, the third direct hit landed, again on the roof, approximately 3m from where the second bomb had struck, about 1.5m from the short wall opposite and not much further from the long wall. The sergeant and three of the men, who were sitting with their backs towards the short wall which had been hit first of all, declared that everything had happened exactly as during the first two direct hits. They were convinced that the shelter had withstood the attack as before. It was only after the candle had again been lit and the dust had settled that they saw "The roof coming right down to the floor", and discovered four of their comrades dead under the debris, the fifth injured by a fragment of concrete and a large gaping hole in the roof.'

Intensive examination was carried out and it was found that all three direct hits had been made by bombs of 500kg in weight. The building was so badly damaged that it could not be repaired. Despite this, the general feeling was that the shelter had not done badly, having survived two direct hits. Receiving three direct hits on a structure with an exposed surface of less than 10m x 15m was considered 'somewhat unusual'.

Casemates

Another case cited the explosion of a heavy bomb (probably 250kg or heavier) which exploded in the air about 2m outside the open embrasure of a manned gun emplacement. The heavy armoured outer door at the rear of the embrasure was closed. While there were just a few deep scars on the brickwork caused by fragments, the blast had a devastating effect inside the casemate:

'The gun mount was heavily damaged, although the barrel was still intact. The crew, 11 men, who had thrown themselves flat on the ground were dead — burst lungs. One of them — presumably the only man not lying on the floor — had been hurled upwards and was hanging under the roof with the cloth of his jacket and trousers caught between the roof and the wall . . . The armoured door had been torn out. Its lower wing was lying 30m to the rear of the structure and the upper wing 50m behind it. The gun embrasure remained fully serviceable, the gun ready to fire after its mount had been exchanged.'

Clearly the strong air pressure was to blame, especially as it 'rebounded' in the enclosed space. Whilst the chance of an 'in the air' explosion was infrequent, a hit on the concrete slab in front of the gun emplacement would have had much the same effect. The danger from the blast and fragmentation could only have been lessened had the large open embrasure been smaller. Also, the fact that the casemate was tightly closed in the rear enhanced the danger from blast. Perhaps this could have been lessened had the large gun door been open — but this would have presented a risk to the rear of the casemate from bomb splinters, which would have meant erecting an earth parapet, not too steeply sloped, in front of the open door.

Another case was that of a coastal battery which had been under constant heavy air attack, resulting in penetration under two of its gun emplacements, followed by penetration by a naval armour piercing shell of the largest calibre through one of them. It was an Army coastal battery of six guns (17cm or 20cm cannon), north-east of the mouth of the Orne river on the Butte de Houlgate. The battery was comprised of six static guns — that is to say, guns on gun mounts which were in turn on a concrete base — four of which were unprotected, whilst the fifth and sixth guns on the left wing of the site were in concrete emplacements, constructed in the usual manner. All shelters were of 2m thick reinforced concrete. Schmetzer considered that this particular battery had been subjected to the heaviest bombing attacks: 'to a degree probably unequalled in the entire Atlantic Wall area'. When he inspected the battery on 24 June 1944, he found:

'The entire battery terrain was full of bomb craters, some of which had undoubtedly been caused by 1,000kg bombs. During the entire period, the total casualties in dead, wounded and sick amounted to only 25% (the battery had never been relieved), which must be attributed to some extent to the fact that there was a sufficient number of shelters which were strong enough and that the air raid

precautions system functioned extremely well. In spite of numerous direct hits, not one of the strong shelters for gun crews, ammunition, command and observation posts was put out of action or even seriously damaged.

'Of the four guns which were unprotected, one was still located, quite intact, in its old place. The barrel and gun mount did show several scratches caused by shell splinters, but the gun was only put out of action for two hours because of minor damage that was repaired then and there.

'The three remaining guns had all been slightly damaged (the exact dates of the particular damage were not known), to an extent which made it impossible for them to be repaired in their firing positions. They were dismantled and brought to rearward positions, where they were repaired in the Ordnance Depot. After two to four days at the most, they were again in working order and brought up to a new firing position. Although they fired frequently from there, they were neither spotted by the enemy nor hit by any more bombs, nor fired at — one of the reasons for the few serious losses suffered by the battery.

'On the other hand, both concrete gun emplacements were out of action. They had only been completed just before the invasion and showed signs of somewhat hasty construction. Their adaptation to the terrain, their protection by earth parapets and camouflage were faulty and the concrete did not appear to be completely flawless . . . Each emplacement was badly damaged in several places by bombs which had penetrated beneath it and by close hits — large cracks, various big fragments broken out of the rear walls, front walls and foundation slabs. The two gun mounts were unserviceable but the barrels remained intact . . . the concrete gun emplacement of the sixth gun had been fired at by the battleship Nelson with 10 very heavy AP shells (44.5cm calibre) . . . At the time of firing, a direct hit resulted in complete penetration of the shell through the emplacement . . . It only exploded about 40 minutes later in the shelled terrain behind the emplacement. Consequently, it must have been fired with an adjustable delayed action fuse.'

Schmetzer's conclusions were most interesting and are worth quoting in full:

'The four guns standing open without protective constructions withstood the numerous heavy bombing attacks far better than the concrete gun emplacements which the Führer had expected to have so much power of resistance. These emplacements were to be a standard type for guns of the most various types and calibres, immaterial whether they were used on gun carriages, so that they could be pulled out of the emplacement quickly to perform other tasks, or mounted on pivots as static guns. Their thick concrete protection was to assure the guns' readiness for action even after the heaviest bombing attack or artillery fire. They certainly did not fulfil their task. Their format, with the large embrasure, as well as their rear, with the door, were particularly exposed to splinters, blast and shelling, also to the danger of bombs penetrating beneath the foundation. Since the lower edge of the structures was often only sunk into the ground two metres — or three metres at the utmost — and the walls at the front and rear also could not be adequately covered with earth, a protection of these two walls by means of protective walls sunk to an appropriate depth had been demanded on

principle. On account of the increased amount of work and material involved, the OT declined to carry out this reinforcement arguing that they could build more emplacements of this type in the short time available, which would be according to the Führer's intentions. Added to that was the impossibility to fit these high structures which towered over the terrain, unobtrusively into the ground or to camouflage them sufficiently. Without considerably increased forces, means, time and special installations which were no longer available owing to the circumstances ruling at the time, a solution could not be found to eliminate these serious weaknesses.'

These are but three extracts from Schmetzer's report which contained many other examples of the results of bombing and shelling against the Atlantic Wall. In 1947, captured Generalleutnant Max Pemsel commented upon Schmetzer's report thus:

'A very accurate report by an expert for specialists on the question of the resistance capacity of the fortified defence installations. The heavy fortified defence installations of smaller size have proved their worth as shelters for men and ammunition and also as observation posts. As far as defensive installations were concerned, the little Tobruks were particularly popular.

'The large embrasures for guns have proved disadvantageous — as had been anticipated. Wherever the guns were not in embrasures but were well covered and camouflaged they remained undamaged for a long time. Their great advantage was that they offered only a small target, had a great mobility and were able to fire in all directions. Time, labour and material for the construction of the embrasures could have been saved. As the guns in the embrasures were to be as flexible as possible, the embrasures were too large and offered a good target to Naval Artillery. The more the embrasures were turned away from the sea, the greater the extent to which a wide seaward field of fire was sacrificed.'[3]

Marinepeilstände
Amongst all the types of structure built for the Wall, some of the most amazing were the tall, reinforced concrete, observation towers built on the Channel Islands, a number of which still remain today. A staggering 22 were planned, although only nine were eventually built, seven of which are still standing. These futuristic towers had multiple observation slots facing out to sea — on the average this was five on the islands, whereas the norm for those observation towers built elsewhere on the Wall was just two. The reason for this was that each slot dealt with a single coastal battery, so more slots made control much easier.

Other Major Structures
As well as the structures which were integral parts of the Atlantic Wall defences, other strange new structures also began appearing, for example:

'The Fifteenth Army had to defend the coastal sector between Ostend and west of Le Havre. About the summer of 1943 it was reported to von Rundstedt that huge structures were being erected in its area by the Todt Organisation, the object of which was unknown to it. The structures were set up so secretly that not even the Commander-in-Chief of the Fifteenth Army dared enter

Above: One of the Marinepeilstände (naval observation and direction finding towers) on the Channel Islands. This one is at Mannez Garenne, Alderney, near the lighthouse. *Martin Pocock*

the building area. It was natural that the Army should raise a protest about building going on in its area without being informed about it. It further reacted against these objects because they only invited enemy bombing attacks and thus endangered troops in the vicinity.'[4]

Not even von Rundstedt and his staff had any idea either, and so they quizzed OKW who, after expressing some surprise that they had not been informed, promised to rectify the situation but only orally, so tight was the secrecy. The massive new buildings were of course the sites for the new V-weapons, which would not be ready for use against the UK for some time, so it was essential to keep any knowledge of them away from the Allies. Somewhat later Hitler ordered that von Rundstedt should be included in briefings regarding the tactical employment of these weapons and a special staff was put under his orders, which, according to Günther Blumentritt was given the misleading title of 'General Headquarters for Special Employment'.

Despite all their precautions, the construction of such massive structures did not go unnoticed by Allied agents and they soon became targets for the Allied Air Forces.

'After some nasty experiences Western Command proposed that the field emplacements of the V-1 should be built more simply and naturally, in order not to be so noticeable. Hitler agreed, and the construction of the emplacements for these weapons was begun in a new form. From 80 to 100 such positions were erected up to the beginning of the invasion in 1944, between Calais and Le Havre.'[5]

Notes
1. Source *Die Organisation Todt*, Franz W. Seidler.
2. See, for example, the Naval Signal Headquarters built in Guernsey and mentioned in Chapter 12.
3. *World War II German Military Studies*, Volume 12.
4. Blumentritt, *Von Rundstedt — the Soldier and the Man*.
5. Ibid.

Chapter 6

First Attacks — Operations 'Chariot' and 'Jubilee'

How Much did the British Know?

In his book *Resistance*, M. R. D. Foot, who also wrote the official history *SOE in France*, mentions the following spectacular coup:

'It hardly ever happened that a resister was able to get direct evidence of Axis intentions; though now and again this could be done. The locus classicus was the theft, by an alert French house decorator, of the plan for the Atlantic Wall; which was in London before a single block-house described in it was built.'

Foot goes on to say that he could testify as to the invaluable nature of these plans, saying that he had used a 'well thumbed copy when helping Combined Operations headquarters to plan raids on the Channel coast'. Henri Michel in his book *The Shadow War — Resistance in Europe 1939–45* also mentions this spectacular theft, but adds a caveat that there could be no certainty that: 'these were the authoritative plans, that they would not subsequently be changed or that the Allies would realise their importance and make good use of them'. Certainly it would appear that they did. Indeed General Omar Bradley went so far as to say later that: 'securing the blueprint of the German Atlantic Wall, was an incredible and brilliant feat — so valuable that the landing operation succeeded with the minimum loss of men and material'.

The full story of this remarkable theft is told by Richard Collier in his book *Ten Thousand Eyes*, in which he explains how, in May 1942, Rene Duchet, a Caen house-painter and at that time an embryo French spy, saw an announcement that the local Organisation Todt was inviting bids from painters and decorators to refurbish its offices. He applied, ensuring that his bid was much lower than anyone else's would be, and was given the job. During his first interview with Bauleiter Hugo Schnedderer, he noticed a pile of maps and documents on the office desk and was amazed to be left on his own while the Bauleiter spoke to one of his staff. On the top of the pile was a map on which it said in large red letters: *Sonderzeichungen — Streng Geheim* meaning 'Special Blueprint — Top Secret'. Ignoring the horrendous risk of being caught red-handed, Duchet took the map and stuffed it behind a mirror on the office wall, from whence he was later able to retrieve it during his redecoration of the offices. He was greatly helped by the fact that Schnedderer was suddenly posted elsewhere and the map was not missed. Some weeks later, the precious blueprint was taken, in a biscuit tin, across the Channel by fishing boat and later arrived in London. Duchet went on with his wartime spying and eventually was in charge of all part-time agents in the area. After the war, Commandant Duchet of the Deuxième Bureau was awarded the Medal of Freedom by the Americans (the highest honour a civilian can attain), whilst the French gave him not only the Medal of the Resistance but also the Croix de Guerre. 'A model of tenacity and Lorraine patriotism' is how the citation for this last award read. Sadly he died a few years after the end of the war.

This was of course just one of the many feats of bravery performed by civilians in the occupied countries, which materially assisted in the success of 'Overlord'. All over Normandy, for example, there were volunteer agents of an organisation known as Centurie, who, from late 1942, painstakingly collected information on German defences, installations and troop deployments. Their constant stream of information was assembled in Caen, then sent by courier to an inconspicuous backstreet area of Paris, where it was collated and prepared for collection by RAF pilots, using the old fashioned looking but nevertheless highly effective Westland Lysander aircraft, from predesignated fields outside the city at the dead of night. It was then flown over to London, where it was carefully logged onto a master map of the Normandy coastline. Without doubt such information would prove immensely useful to the invading forces. William B. Breuer, for example, in his book *Hitler's Fortress Cherbourg*, makes the point that:

'While the man with the rifle and machine gun bore the brunt of the ordeal, as is always the case in war, many factors were involved in the seizure of crucial Cherbourg. The work of the Centurie underground in Normandy provided American commanders with a tremendous advantage — knowing in precise detail German defenses along and behind the Atlantic Wall.'

St Nazaire — 'Bill Pritchard's Idea'

'The idea started towards the end of 1941 I think, and was put up to Lord Louis Mountbatten by Bill Pritchard who was really the man who had the idea and Bob Montgomery, who is alive and who was on the raid. Bill Pritchard was killed on the raid. They had come out of St Nazaire in 1940 and seen how much we'd left behind there, undamaged. And they felt that we should go back and do something about it.'

That is ex-commando Sir Roland Swayne's explanation of the origin of the daring raid which took place on the night of 27–28 March 1942 against the French port of St Nazaire, which lies on France's Atlantic coast some 240km south of Brest. Swayne had been a member of the commandos for some time and had already taken part in earlier raids in the Channel Islands. At the time of the run-up to Operation 'Chariot' — as the St Nazaire raid was code-named — he was serving in No 1 Commando and was selected to take a detachment of 12 men to join No 2 Commando, to be trained as a demolition group.

Above: Target for Operation 'Chariot' was the massive prewar dry dock — known as the Normandie Dock after the liner. The prewar liner was over 1,000ft long, displaced 86,495 tons and made its maiden voyage on 29 May 1935. She was built by Chantiers de L'Atlantique-Penhet at St Nazaire. *IWM — HU53265*

Above: The *Normandie* was far away in New York when St Nazaire was raided, but the enemy vessel that could have used its dry dock was the 41,000-ton German battleship *Tirpitz*, which had to operate out of Norway instead. It was bombed by the RAF on numerous occasions and finally sunk off Tromsö on 12 November 1944. *IWM — HU2256*

'We did our training blowing up docks . . . and practised blowing up pumping stations and locks in Leith, Rosyth and Edinburgh,'

he told an IWM interviewer in 1988, when he made a sound recording of his wartime memories (Accession No 10231/3). Then they moved to Wales and practised blowing up Pontypool, Newport and Cardiff.

'We learnt how to lower sacks of explosive against the lock gates at places where they would do the most damage. And we learnt how to deal with these big metal caissons, empty narrow chambers that slot into the locks to close the locks. And also pumping machinery, the impeller pumps and machinery required to empty a lock and to transfer water in the lock system.'

Clearly the 'powers that be' were after doing a lot more than just blowing up the kit that the BEF had left behind in 1940. In fact St Nazaire was now an important U-boat base, with seven submarine pens, and even more to the point, its port area contained a massive prewar dry dock (the Normandie Dock) capable of holding one of the largest German battleships, the *Tirpitz*, should it ever decide to come to operate in the Atlantic. It had been decided that, by using an old US World War 1 destroyer, now known as HMS *Campbeltown*, loaded with 3 tons of high explosives, a raiding party of commandos would ram, then blow up the lock gates of the Normandie Dock,

whilst also dealing with other port facilities. This should put the dock out of commission for a long time. However, it was a daunting task, both for the 257 commandos and for the 345 sailors who would have to get them there.

German Forces

As this book is primarily about the Atlantic Wall, it is relevant to go into some detail about the German garrison of this important port and submarine base, which would later be classified as a Festung (Fortress) in January 1944. In 1942 the defences were considerable and all under the command and control of the Kriegsmarine. In overall command was the Kommandant Loire, Kapitän-zur-See Zuckschwerdt, whose HQ was at La Baule, further up the coast. Under his command was a coastal artillery battalion, a brigade of flak artillery and certain minor forces under the St Nazaire Harbour Commander. The coastal artillery was 280 MAA (Marine Artillerie Abteilung) under the command of Korvettenkapitän Edo Dieckmann, whose HQ was at Chemoulin Point. The battalion had a total of 28 guns under command varying in calibre from 7.5cm to 15cm, 17cm and a railway-mounted battery of 24cm guns. All these guns would fire during the raid, but the railway guns took so long to traverse that they managed to fire only a few rounds. 22 Marine Flak Brigade was under command of Kapitän-zur-See C.C. Mecke, with its HQ at St Marc. He had

Below: HMS *Campbeltown* had its bridge stripped and armoured during a refit prior to the raid. Splinter matting was also put in place. *IWM — HU53259*

three battalions all close to St Nazaire: 703rd Battalion (Korvettenkapitän Thiessen); 809th Battalion (Korvettenkapitän Burhenne); and 705th Battalion (Korvettenkapitän Koch). Their guns were dual-purpose (that is suitable for both the AA and ground role), and mainly of 2cm, 3.7cm or 4cm calibres, although there were some heavy flak batteries, but these were unable to engage ground targets. Many of these guns were mounted on top of flak towers, on rooftops or on AA mountings on the tops of concrete bunkers. To assist in acquiring targets for the coastal artillery and for general scanning, there were two radar stations, one at Le Croisic and the other at St Marc, whilst the flak guns had other radar stations, but only for airborne targets. Korvettenkapitän Kellermann was the Hafenkommandant, and in addition to harbour guard companies, he also commanded a number of harbour defence boats, and was in fact on a patrol near the mouth of the estuary on the night of the raid. In addition to these permanent defences were the crews of the numerous ships and submarines that happened to be in the harbour at the time. An approximate total of all available manpower was in excess of 5,000, plus even more along the sides of the estuary. There was even a small barrage balloon unit. 'Such was the citadel' comments C. E. Lucas Phillips in his book on the raid (see Bibliography), 'that was to be assaulted by an old destroyer and by 257 soldiers, carried into battle by light motor launches.'

The demolition teams having been trained as completely as possible, they and the rest of the commandos who would take part in the raid were taken to Falmouth and put on board various ships in the harbour. There was no going ashore from then on and, having assembled on the first evening, Colonel Augustus Newman, who was to lead the commando force, outlined the purpose of the raid and gave out the various teams' tasks.

Sir Roland Swayne's task was, with eight men, to blow up the southern locks on the new harbour entrance. His recollection was as follows:

> 'I think there were two locks we had to blow up and a swing bridge. I had eight men and a detachment under John Venderwerve, of No 2 Commando with four soldiers armed with tommy guns to protect us while we did this. There were three lock gates . . . There was Bradley, who was to blow up the gates at the top end of the lock, someone called Philip Walton who was to blow up the middle one and then there was the pumping station. I can't remember who was to blow up that . . . but the whole thing was beautifully planned. Equipment was good, we all had very well thought out loads of explosive to carry and the arming was very good. We had Tommy Guns and Remington Colts [revolvers] . . . you could actually kill somebody at 50 or 100 yards' range with a Remington — well perhaps not 100 yards but certainly 50, if you knew how to shoot with it.'

As the table below shows, a large number of the commandos on the raid would travel in two groups of Motor Launches (MLs), that would follow HMS *Campbeltown*. The old American flush-decked destroyer had first entered service in the US Navy towards the end of the Great War and was one of 50 such 'gift horses' to be transferred to the Royal Navy in 1940. She already had 18 months of arduous convoy duties under her belt before being selected for Operation 'Chariot'. *Campbeltown* was given a thorough refit before the raid, between 10 and 19 March, being radically altered to look like a German *Moewe* ('Seagull') class torpedo boat. She was also fitted with large metal plates on deck behind which some of the commandos would have to lie, whilst her bridge was stripped and armoured. On the raid she would be commanded by Lieutenant-Commander Stephen Beattie.

Commando Boatloading and Targets
There were in fact 17 motor launches as the list shows, whilst below are also shown details of the commandos' targets and who did what.

Group One (seven MLs). Under command Captain Hodgson. In port ML column, to land at the Old Mole.
1a. Demolition (Lieutenant Swayne and eight other ranks [OR]) — the two most southerly lock gates and the swing bridge in the Southern Entrance. (Protection: Lieutenant Venderwerve and four OR).
1b. Demolition (Captain Bradley and six OR) — central lock gate in southern entrance.
1c. Demolition (Lieutenant Walton and four OR) — northern lock gate and lifting bridge of southern entrance. (Protection: 2nd Lieutenant Watson and 4 OR).
1d. (two MLs) Demolition (Lieutenant Wilson, 2nd Lieutenant Basset-Wilson and Lieutenant Bonvin and 12 OR) — boiler house, impounding station and hydraulic power station in old town. (Protection: Lieutenant Houghton and four OR).
1e. Assault (Captain Hodgson, Lieutenant Oughtred and 12 OR) — destroy gun positions on East Jetty and form protective post at landward end.
1f. (Control) Captain Pritchard and demolition control party for this group.

Group Two (six MLs). Under command Captain Burn. In starboard ML column, to land at the Old Entrance.
2a. Demolition (Lieutenant Woodcock and eight OR) — two lock gates and swing bridge at northern end of submarine basin. (Protection: Lieutenant Jenkins and four OR).
2b. Lieutenant-Colonel Newman's HQ party.
2c. Demolition (Lieutenant Pennington and 4 OR) — destroy swing bridge at northern end of submarine base. (Protection: Lieutenant Jenkins and 4 OR).
2d. Assault (Captain Burn, Lieutenant Peyton and 12 OR) — destroy gun positions on towers adjacent to bridge and form protective block. A further emergency task also detailed.
2e. (two MLs) Assault (Captain Hooper and Troop Sergeant-Major Haines and 26 OR) — special task party to destroy two gun positions north of Old Mole if occupied, silence any ships in the dry dock and come into HQ reserve.

Group Three (four MLs). Under command Major Copland with Captain Montgomery for demolition control in HMS *Campbeltown*.
3a. Demolition (Lieutenant Burtenshaw and six OR) — to destroy outer caisson should *Campbeltown* not succeed. Lieutenant Chant and 4 OR to destroy adjacent winding hut. (Protection: Lieutenant Hopwood).
3b. Demolition (Lieutenant Brett and six OR) — to destroy inner caisson; Lieutenant Purdon and four OR to destroy its adjacent winding hut. (Protection: Lieutenant Denison).
3c. Assault (Lieutenant Roderick, Lieutenant Stutchbury and 12 OR) — destroy four gun positions immediately east of outer caisson, destroy any guards in the area of the underground oil tanks and form protective block; drop incendiaries down ventilators of oil tanks if opportunity offered.

3d. Assault (Captain Roy, Lieutenant Proctor and 12 OR) — destroy gun positions on roof of pumping house, form bridgehead at bridge to cover withdrawal of parties to the northward and engage any hostile vessels in submarine basin.

Bomber support programme.
Phase 1: 10 Whitleys from 4 Group to attack area of Normandie Dock from 23.30–00.30hrs.

Phase 2: 25 Whitleys from 4 Group to attack same target area from 00.30–01.20hrs.

Phase 3: 25 Wellingtons from 1 Group to attack northern end of Penhouet Basin and adjacent slips, 1,600m north of Old Entrance from 01.20–04.00hrs.

The raiders set sail from Falmouth on 26 March, under the overall command of Commander Robert Ryder, RN, on a roundabout route, with a two destroyer escort, down through the Bay of Biscay, quite far to the south of the mouth of the Loire, but then they doubled back again to the north-east until they rendezvoused with a submarine which was the 'beacon' they had to contact, near the river estuary.

As Sir Roland Swayne recalled:

'*From that point we were on our own. We navigated up the estuary and then on up the river behind the Campbeltown and that all worked absolutely perfectly . . . we went up the northern channel of the Loire which was well away from the coastal batteries on the southern shore, and nothing happened at all until we were quite close in, when the shooting started. We were in ML 14 in the column which was very near the end and we saw everything developing in front of us — not that you could see much at night, but you could see the tracer. And it was a wonderful firework display.*'

Achtung Landegefahr!
On the shore, Kapitän-zur-See Mecke, the local flak brigade commander, who would later be awarded the Knight's Cross, had been puzzled by the way enemy aircraft were behaving. They seemed to be dropping very few bombs, despite the number of aircraft involved and this raised his suspicions that something was wrong. Accordingly, at around midnight he sent a signal to all command posts: 'The conduct of the enemy aircraft is inexplicable and indicates suspicion of parachute landings.' By 01.00hrs, most of the British aircraft had

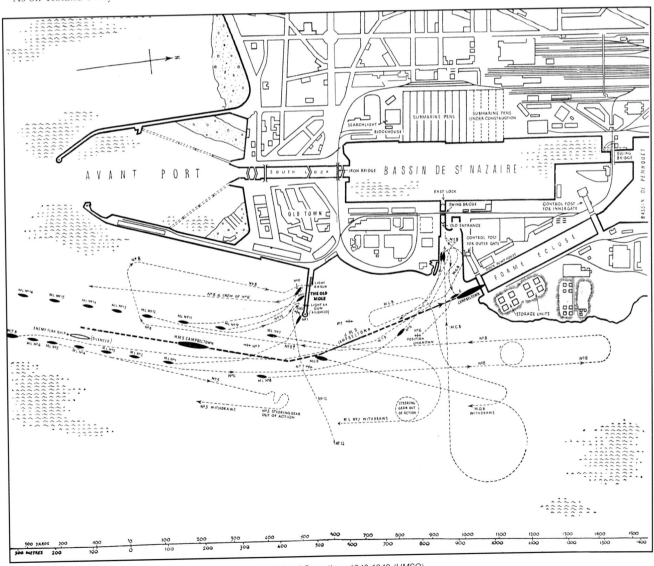

Above: Operation 'Chariot' — the raid on St Nazaire. *Source: Combined Operations 1940-1942 (HMSO)*

disappeared and those which remained in the area were flying beyond the effective range of his guns. He had already ordered a cease-fire to his guns and the switching off of all searchlights, but nevertheless had given the order for increased alertness and continual observation, especially seawards.

Acting on this order or, as he says in his own words, 'because he was bored with looking at the night sky', Korvettenkapitän Burhenne, who commanded 809th Naval Flak Battalion and had his headquarters on the east bank of the river, was looking seawards and saw through his binoculars a number of small ships moving at a moderate speed towards the port. When he reported this to the naval headquarters he was told not to be stupid and that his job was to look into the sky not the river. However, he immediately reported what he had seen to Mecke. Then at about 01.15hrs a lookout at the naval station near St Marc reported the sighting of some 17 vessels at extreme range. One of Mecke's staff immediately telephoned the Harbourmaster to find out if any German ships were expected and was told 'No'. This prompted Mecke to send an urgent signal to all concerned: 'Achtung Landegefahr' ('Beware Landing').

'On receipt of this codeword, the machinery for repelling an invasion in accordance with Emergency Orders was put in force throughout the command. More particularly, all anti-aircraft guns switched to the defence of the shores and all available troops and crews of minesweepers, harbour defence boats and tankers in St Nazaire, many of whom were in their air-raid shelters, from which they were promptly routed out, were pressed into becoming infantry as Stosstruppen (thrust troops). The most important of these were the spare hands of Mecke's own battalions — the watch off duty, the clerks, instructors, storemen and so on.

'At the same time the commander of the coast-defence guns, Korvettenkapitän Dieckmann, who had become restless at the sound of engines and who had come out immediately at his headquarters at Chemoulin on receipt of the sighting report at 1.15, gave the order to his batteries: "Stand by to attack naval targets." Why the searchlights had not already been switched on is not explained. According to the signals log, five minutes elapsed before Mecke's order to illuminate was put into effect. Those five minutes were of priceless value to the dim shapes moving steadily onwards under the misty moon.'[1]

Meanwhile the convoy was getting nearer and nearer, and on the bridge of the leading gunboat, Commander Ryder could not believe their luck. Then, at 01.22hrs a large searchlight came on and soon the whole force was illuminated. At once they were challenged by two signal stations, but thanks to a well-rehearsed plan and to the fact that they knew both the call sign of one of the local German torpedo boats and the colours of the current German Very light recognition signal, they managed to gain a few more precious minutes. The Germans were fooled completely. Not for one moment did they imagine that a British force would take such risks. However, it gradually became obvious that had they been a genuine German force they would have stopped when challenged. Every enemy gun that could be brought to bear on the British force began to fire, whilst the attackers, having run up the White Ensign, replied strongly, having held their fire to the very last moment.

Those commandos on board the Campbeltown had been lying down behind their protection shields. One of them recalled that when the destroyer hit the dock gates at about 01.30hrs on the 28th, he was holding on tight and hardly felt the shock. He landed on the road which ran on the top of the lock gates, was wounded by a grenade, but saw the pump-house just outside the dry dock blown to pieces and then heard the scuttling charges on the Campbeltown go up. Another demolition party in the second ML landed on the Old Mole to blow the inner gate of the South Lock, but having landed successfully, they came under heavy fire, so decided to try to approach their objective via a different route, but were again unsuccessful. However, they were one of very few hold-ups and undoubtedly, the early part of the raid, the demolition phase, went very well and most of the primary targets had soon been successfully dealt with. They returned to the Old Mole 'a bit peeved' at having to leave intact the lock gates they had hoped to destroy, met up with Colonel Newman's HQ group and together waited to be picked up by the MLs, but there was no sign of them — as most of them had already been sunk. However, this had been anticipated and it had been agreed that should things 'get sticky' then they should try to get out of St Nazaire and fight their way into the open country. Eventually Colonel Newman issued three orders: first to try to get back to England, second not to surrender until they ran out of ammunition and third not to surrender at all if they could help it.

Mecke's flak guns and Dieckmann's coastal-defence guns were now freely engaging the MLs. The enemy fire on Roland Swayne's ML, for example, increased as it came abreast the Old Mole, the enemy infantry located there finding it very easy to engage the MLs at point-blank range, and soon there were burning vessels everywhere. After making no progress against this storm of fire, the skipper of Swayne's ML reluctantly decided that it was too hazardous to continue and turned the ship around. Naturally this did not please the commandos and there was a lot of grumbling, as they felt they should carry on. But their grumbles were in vain, there was no way through the curtain of enemy fire and their ML had to break off the engagement and head back down river. However, en route for home they had the misfortune to meet up with some German naval vessels and, after a savage fire fight, they were all killed or captured, the survivors being brought back to St Nazaire. Despite this setback the rest of the raid had gone well.

Raid over, only a very few of the raiding party had managed to escape. A large number of those who landed were killed or captured, whilst all but two of the MLs were sunk, so the naval losses were equally high. The Germans were naturally amazed that such a raid should have taken place with apparently little motive. However, the pièce de résistance was yet to come.

'At 11.35 on 28 March 1942, at St Nazaire, France, the air was suddenly shattered by a thunderous explosion in the bows of the old destroyer lodged in the caisson of Normandie lock. The forward half of the ship and a large number of unfortunate German soldiers inspecting her, were vaporised. The caisson was breached and what remained of the old destroyer was washed into the lock by the resulting inrush of water, effectively eliminating St Nazaire as a repair facility for Tirpitz. So ended the career of HMS Campbeltown, the former USS Buchanan (DD.131).'[2]

Those ashore heard the terrific explosion and said to each other: 'There goes the Campbeltown.' The number of German soldiers and sightseers blown up with the vessel was estimated at about 400, including some 40 senior officers. Then two days later, at about 16.30hrs on the 30th, there were yet more explosions, as delayed-action torpedoes also detonated — pandemonium

Above: HMS *Campbeltown* as she is best remembered, when she was wedged into the lock gates at St Nazaire, just before exploding. *IWM — HU2242*

again broke loose, with everyone trying to get out of the port area. There was such a crowd at the exit bridge that the German sentries opened fire and killed some 280 French workmen and even some of their own OT workers, whose khaki uniforms were mistaken for British battledress. The Germans had to close the port for some days and evacuate the entire population of the old town, so the raid had many repercussions. Churchill commented that the Germans treated the prisoners they took 'with respect', but had inflicted severe reprisals on the brave French population who had: 'on the spur of the moment rushed from every quarter to the aid of what they hoped was the vanguard of liberation'.[3]

German Reaction

Throughout France news of the raid caused an upsurge of French patriotism, whilst it is said to have infuriated Adolf Hitler. The loss of the Normandie Dock was bad enough, but even worse was the knowledge that the commandos had been able to penetrate German defences so easily. He ordered von Rundstedt personally to conduct an immediate inquiry. This took place at St Nazaire on 31 March. Von Rundstedt reported that there was no fault to find with the German conduct of the action and that no blame could be laid at anyone's door for the British landing. However, that did not satisfy the Führer, who demanded that someone's head must roll. This led to General Alfred Jodl, Director of Operations at OKW and Hitler's chief military adviser, visiting von Rundstedt three days later, 'to examine in more detail the failure to repel the enemy'. The outcome was yet another row between the Heer and the Kriegsmarine on who was responsible for what, which did no good for inter-service co-operation on the Atlantic Wall. As C. E. Lucas Phillips said in his book *The Greatest Raid of All*:

'This probing into naval affairs, or the manner in which it was done, lit the fires of wrath in Grand Admiral Raeder, the Commander-in-Chief. There seemed to be no one at Hitler's headquarters, he complained, in a position to present a correct picture of events and as a result the Army officers of Supreme Command formed a judgement wholly false and detrimental to the Navy. In very much sharper terms Raeder wrote personally to Field Marshal Keitel: "I have heard with the greatest displeasure of your signal to CinC West on the subject of the St Nazaire enquiry and the questionnaire that has been drafted at your express wish. I have not been informed at any stage of the proceedings, although the greater part of the questions are within my province and are my personal responsibility. You have not once informed me of the instructions you were issuing. This procedure is against all military custom. I must therefore insist on an explanation and apology from you." As far as official records go, he does not seem to have received that apology.'

A Deed of Glory

In all some 83 decorations were awarded to Allied participants in Operation 'Chariot', who lost 144 killed and over 200 captured. Of the decorations, five Victoria Crosses were won, three by the Royal Navy: Commander Robert Ryder, Lieutenant-Commander Stephen Beattie and Able Seaman William Savage; and two by the Army: Lieutenant-Colonel Augustus Newman and Sergeant Thomas Durrant. It had been a remarkable raid and a wake-up call to the German defenders that the Allies were likely to strike anywhere along their uncompleted defence line. Fittingly Lord Louis Mountbatten, wrote to Lieutenant-Colonel Newman, VC, on his release from POW camp in 1945 thus:

'Having been associated with practically all combined operations, from two-man raids to the planning of Normandy, I have no hesitation in saying that the finest and most profitable of the lot was your raid on St Nazaire.'

A YEAR AGO TO-NIGHT: A V.C.'S DRAWINGS OF THE ST. NAZAIRE RAID.

Above: Impressions of the St Nazaire raid, drawn from memory by Commander R. E. D. Ryder VC, RN, that appeared in the *Illustrated London News* on 27 March 1943, on the anniversary of the operation. *IWM — HU53261* Dieppe

This was a fitting epitaph for an operation which Winston Churchill described as 'a Deed of Glory'.

Operation 'Jubilee' — a Glorious Disaster

If 'Chariot' was a success for the Allies as far as breaking through the enemy defences was concerned, then 'Jubilee', which followed some five months later on 19 August 1942, has to be classed as a spectacular failure. Far larger than any other previous raid, it involved landing some 5,000 British and Canadian troops at the French Channel port of Dieppe, with the aim of capturing the port and the headlands around it, then holding the area for some hours whilst the landing force obtained at first hand all the information they could about the state of preparedness of the enemy defences. As the official PR booklet, *Combined Operations 1940–42*, published by the Ministry of Information during the war, put it:

'*To mount a raid on a much larger scale than that which had been carried out on St Nazaire would not only harass the enemy, which is, it cannot be too often repeated, the primary object of raiding; it would also be a means of*

providing the Allied General Staffs with very important and, indeed, essential information concerning his defences in the West.'[4]

Plans for the raid, which was initially called Operation 'Rutter', began in April and on 13 May the outline plan was approved by the Chiefs of Staff Committee. It called for the raid to be launched on 2 July, but bad weather and German air attacks on the assembled troops forced first a postponement until 8 July, then a cancellation. C-in-C South-East Command (one General Bernard Law Montgomery), who had been supervising the plans, was strongly of the opinion that it should not be remounted. However, after discussions between Winston Churchill, the Chief of the Imperial General Staff and Lord Louis Mountbatten, the Chief of Combined Operations, it was agreed that, whilst the assault on Dieppe, now code-named 'Jubilee', could be remounted within a month, it would be impossible to plan another new large-scale operation that summer, therefore it should go ahead. Undoubtedly, pressure from Stalin for the Allies to open a Second Front played a major role in this decision, which was, of course, a huge security gamble since much of the briefing of those taking part had already begun.[5]

Dieppe was not chosen at random, but rather carefully selected after a close study of a number of French ports. It was considered that the Dieppe defences represented a fair sample of what the Allies would be up against anywhere along the northern coast of France, thus a major raid would test their strength and preparedness. A certain amount of information was naturally already known from, for example, air photographs, whilst one of the earlier commando raids had in fact been on one of two heavy coast defence batteries at Berneval to the east of Dieppe. Clearly this battery and the one to the west of Dieppe at Varengeville-sur-Mer, would both have to be dealt with as part of the overall attack.

Allied Forces

The main assault would be undertaken by a large force of Canadians, many of whom had been waiting for at least two years to see some action and, despite being both ill-prepared and badly equipped for such a raid, they were willing and eager to take part. In total there were six Canadian infantry regiments from 4th and 6th Infantry Brigades of 2nd Infantry Division: the Royal Regiment of Canada, the Essex Scottish Regiment and the Royal Hamilton Light Infantry, all Ontario regiments which made up 4th Infantry Brigade; and the South Saskatchewan Regiment, the Queen's Own Cameron Highlanders of Canada and the Fusiliers Mont Royal making up 6th Infantry Brigade. They would be supported by the 14th Canadian Army Tank Battalion (Calgary Regiment) from the First Canadian Army, who were manning the new British heavy tank — the Infantry Tank Mark IV (A22), appropriately named the Churchill.[6] The new tank would not show its true worth until the following year in Tunisia, being, in 1942, still very mechanically unreliable, having been produced in haste under the threat of invasion in 1940–41.

The entire assault would consist of eight landings at or near Dieppe, the two outer ones being at Berneval to the east of the port and the other at Varengeville near the mouth of the River Saane to the west. These would be undertaken by No 3 and No 4 Commandos respectively, with the aim of destroying the coastal batteries. In addition to the Canadian and British forces already described, there were some Free French commandos and some American Rangers. The entire force would travel in

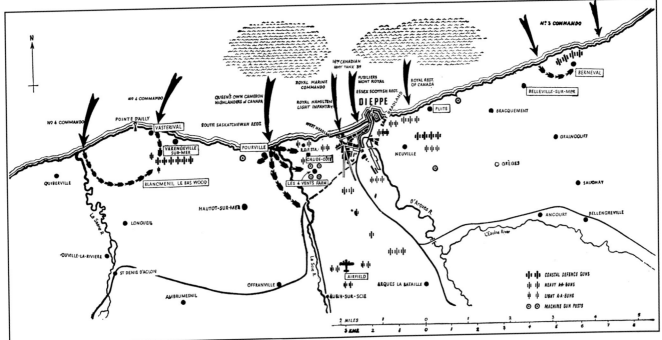

Above: Operation 'Jubilee' — showing the area of operations for the Dieppe raid. *Source: Combined Operations 1940-1942 (HMSO)*

over 200 vessels, with two minesweeping flotillas in the van, eight escort destroyers (including one Polish), a gunboat and a sloop to guard the ships carrying troops. HQ ship was the destroyer HMS *Calpe*, with a second destroyer HMS *Fernie* as the reserve HQ ship. Those landing were under the overall command of Major-General John Roberts, MC, GOC 2nd Canadian Infantry Division, with brigade commanders being Brigadier Sherwood Lett, MC, (4th Infantry Brigade) and Brigadier William Southam (6th Infantry Brigade). Roberts had his HQ on board HMS *Calpe*.

German Forces

Despite the fact that the area between Dieppe and Le Havre on the mouth of the Seine was possibly one of the most threatened areas of the Atlantic Wall, the troops manning the defences were, like most of the coastal defence divisions, fairly low category troops. The area belonged to the Fifteenth Army (Generaloberst Curt Haase, who would be replaced on 30 November 1942), whose three Corps — LXXXI, LXXXII and LXXXIV, covered the coast from the Scheldt to Caen. The first named of these, commanded by General der Panzertruppen Adolf Kuntzen (HQ Rouen) was directly responsible for the Dieppe area, with the 302nd Static Infantry Division actually being located in and around Dieppe. Formed in late 1940, in Schwerin, (Wehrkreise II) the 302nd Infantry Division was to become universally known as the 'Dieppe Division' after its stout defence of the town. Its commander was Generalmajor Conrad Haase (who was not related to the Army commander).[7] The 302nd Infantry Division had some 80km of coastline to guard and it would be hard pressed to do so effectively, as its infantry regiments (570th, 571st and 572nd Grenadier Regiments) were each minus at least a complete company. These deficiencies were partly made up in July 1942, when each regiment was assigned a 14th Company, but the reinforcements were, in the main, half-trained recruits and did not even compare with those whose empty spaces they

filled who had inevitably gone to the ever-demanding Russian Front. In his book *Dieppe 1942 — the Jubilee Disaster* Ronald Atkin explains that a large number of these replacements, who arrived just before the raid, were *Volksdeutsch* (ethnic Germans, living outside the normal borders of Germany) or out-and-out foreigners. As evidence he cites the fact that of the four prisoners brought back to England from the main beaches at Dieppe, only one was a true German, the other three coming from Poland. Two of these had been given the alternative of a concentration camp or joining the Wehrmacht and had only arrived with 200 others in Dieppe on 10 August after a six-day journey from Germany, having been soldiers for just three weeks.

Whatever the quality of the men, clearly it was difficult to keep the garrison focused and instantly ready for any emergency, hour after hour, day after day, month after month. The army commander issued orders calling for the highest degree of watchfulness when the tides and moon were favourable for a landing. One of these periods was 10–19 August. The order he issued was to prove amazingly apposite. It read:

'The troops must realise that it will be a very sticky business. Bombs and naval guns, sea weapons and Commandos, assault boats and parachutists, airborne troops and hostile civilians, sabotage and murder will have to be coped with. Steady nerves will be required if we do not want to go under.

'Fear does not exist. When the hail of fire pours down upon the troops, they must wipe their eyes and ears, clutch their weapons harder and defend themselves as never before.

'US or THEM! That must be the slogan of all.

'The German Army has in the past received all kinds of tasks from the Führer and has always carried them out. The Army will carry out this task too. My soldiers won't be the worst. I have looked into your eyes. You are German men. You will willingly and bravely do your duty. And thus remain victorious.

'Long live our people, our Fatherland and our Führer.'[8]

In line with the other static infantry divisions manning the Atlantic Wall, much of the division's weaponry comprised captured small arms, for which some types of ammunition were in short supply. However, the artillery was relatively strong, with three heavy and four lighter batteries located in a semi-circle around Dieppe.

'The town's seafront was guarded by a complicated array of pillboxes and machine gun nests and gun sites, but these defences were positioned mainly to draw the attention of landing parties. The main firepower was concentrated on the heights above the town. An old French tank had been cemented into the sea wall near the west jetty as a static defence position. "This was the only tank we had in Dieppe," Linder recalled.'[9]

Although there were only some 1,500 men garrisoning Dieppe under the command of Oberstleutnant Hermann Bartelt of 571st Regiment, there were plenty of reserves some distance away. These totalled about 6,000 men, whilst 10th Panzer Division was resting and refitting about 90km away after being withdrawn from Russia. Once again, there was intense rivalry between the three services, which, as in St Nazaire, would bring problems, especially as regards the vulnerable siting of the heavy coastal battery at Varengeville outside the defence perimeter.

Organisation Todt

In the autumn of the previous year, the OT had sent working parties to build the mass of concrete constructions that were beginning to spring up all along the Atlantic coast, with the two headlands being turned into strongpoints. The beach was not yet mined, nor were there many beach obstacles. However, the exits up re-entrants and gullies were blocked with booby-trapped wire entanglements.

The Assault Force Departs

Led by three minesweepers, which would clear a path through a suspected enemy minefield, the force formed up into its agreed order of sailing, with the two Commandos on the outer flanks. Time passed and first light drew ever closer without any enemy reaction, but then about seven miles from the French coast, at about 03.50hrs, some of the landing craft ran into a small enemy force of armed trawlers, and surprise was lost. This interception was entirely fortuitous for the Germans, the small group of German vessels (five commandeered coastal motor vessels, an armed minesweeper and two submarine chasers) being on its way from Boulogne to Dieppe. The German ships opened fire, especially at the gunboat that was leading that particular group of landing craft. It was badly damaged and there were many casualties on board, but they continued to attack the enemy, sinking one of the trawlers and severely damaging others. However, the landing craft, which were carrying No 3 Commando — whose objective was to capture the battery at Berneval — were now scattered and clearly all hope of surprise was lost.

Nevertheless, those who managed to land at Yellow Beach, including a party of some 40 US Rangers, fought with great courage. Part of the commando force worked its way around the battery and caused so many casualties that the German gunners turned one of the guns around and engaged them at point-blank range. Fortunately the gun would not depress sufficiently, so the shells went harmlessly over their heads to burst 'somewhere in France'. For nearly two hours the commandos continued to harass the gun battery, so that it was

unable to bring its heavy guns to bear upon the Canadians during the most crucial period of the operation. Then ammunition began to run low and it became very clear that they would never be able to capture the battery, so those who were still able, returned to the beach, waded out to their landing craft and re-embarked.

Ten miles to the south-west, on Orange Beach, No 4 Commando was engaged in a similar battle. Led by Lieutenant-Colonel Lord Lovat, the 250-strong force was scheduled to land at two points, one close to the village of Vasterival, the other 1.5km away some 600m from the mouth of the River Saane. The first party was under the command of Major Derek Mills-Roberts and in a graphic account of the action that took place from the moment they reached the enemy shore, he recalled:

'We were in a mile when the lighthouse (the main landmark) suddenly doused and flak lit up the sky. The tracer rose from all angles along the high cliffs as a squadron of Brewster Buffaloes roared inshore at low level. Surprise might have been lost and haste was now essential; we moved in at top speed . . . we landed on a narrow beach. It seemed like stealing round to the back door where a noisy party is in progress.'

They landed swiftly and found the gullies up which they hoped to get up the cliffs. Both were choked with thick wire, but fortunately they were able to blow a hole through the thick wire using Bangalore torpedoes[10] and managed to reach the villas which made up the seaside village without being spotted.

However, it would be nearly an hour before Lord Lovat and his party were in position for the final assault. The battery they had come to knock out had begun firing, so it was vital they move in. At about 05.50hrs, they opened up with small arms and their little 2in mortar. The third bomb from the mortar fell right in the middle of a pile of shells and charges which were stacked alongside the guns ready for use. There was a blinding explosion and the battery was completely wrecked and did not fire again despite the desperate efforts of the gun crews to put out the fire, under intense sniper fire from the commandos. At 06.20hrs Lord Lovat put in his assault and captured the guns — all six being subsequently blown up. The commandos then withdrew to the beach, carrying their wounded.

The official report after the raid read:

'At daybreak No 4 Commando, consisting of 252 all ranks, including Allied personnel, assaulted the six-gun battery covering the West approaches to the port of Dieppe. The position was defended by an approximately equal number of Germans with all the advantages of concrete, wire and land mines, concealed machine gun posts, mortars, dual purpose flak guns mounted in a high tower and full knowledge of the ground. They had had two years to perfect these defences and when the time came they fought with the greatest determination. Yet within 100 minutes of the landings, the position was overrun, the battery and all its works were totally destroyed and at least 150 Germans left dead or wounded in the path of the raiders and the scene of the fighting. Prisoners were also taken. British casualties numbered 45 all ranks, of whom 12 were back on duty within two months. Operation 'Cauldron' is a classic example of the use of well trained infantry, bold leadership and the thoroughness of the plan of attack and its swift execution.'

Above: Wounded men climb onto a destroyer whilst the Operation 'Jubilee' action takes place. *IWM — A11227*

The Canadians Attack

So there had been both success and failure on the flanks of the assault and it would be the same with the main assault by the Canadians. On the inner left flank at Puits (Blue Beach) was the Royal Regiment of Canada, whilst on the inner right (on Green Beach) the South Saskatchewan Regiment to be followed by the Cameron Highlanders of Canada. In the centre (on Red and White beaches) was the rest of the assaulting force, including the tanks of the Calgary Regiment.

The leading wave of the Royal Regiment of Canada reached their beach at first light and began taking heavy casualties from the moment they landed. As the Canadian artillery FOO (Forward Observation Officer) who was with the battalion to direct fire from the destroyer HMS *Garth* put it:

'Owing to the heavy and sustained fire of the enemy, the Royal Regiment of Canada was changed in five minutes from an assault battalion on the offensive to something less than two companies on the defensive, pinned down by fire from positions they could not discover.'

The battalion was now also under heavy mortar fire and unable to make contact with the Essex Scottish on its right. Despite covering fire from the two naval support craft which were with the assault group (which continued until all their guns were silenced), shelling from the destroyer *Garth* and an attack by cannon-firing Hawker Hurricanes, it was soon obvious that the landing had failed and several unsuccessful attempts were made to withdraw.

On the other side of Dieppe, the South Saskatchewan battalion had landed at Pourville, encountering very little opposition whilst getting ashore. However, resistance soon stiffened. Nevertheless the battalion made steady progress, fighting with great tenacity, capturing some of its objectives but not Les Quatre Vents farm which remained very active.

It was followed some 40 minutes later by the Queen's Own Cameron Highlanders of Canada:

'It was broad daylight, and as they swept in a piper began to play "The Hundred Pipers" and continued to do so during the landing.'

This battalion's objective was the airfield at St Aubin, about 5km from Pourville and it pressed on up the valley of the River Scie. Whilst the men engaged in forcing a crossing over the river it became clear that something had gone wrong with the centre assault force, as the tanks they should have met there did not appear. Nevertheless, they continued to press forward vigorously, inflicting heavy casualties on the enemy but suffering considerable losses themselves.

Eventually the battalion was forced to withdraw and soon discovered that the enemy had recaptured the all-important high ground west of Pourville, so was able to dominate the beach from which it and the South Saskatchewans would have to withdraw. The landing craft came in at about 10.45hrs, despite heavy mortar fire which hit and capsized at least one. To reach them the Canadians had to cross 200m of open ground, then swim through 150m of water, as the state of the tide made

Above: Two of a series of German photographs taken after the Dieppe raid, showing captured Canadian and British soldiers. *IWM — HU1892 and 1897*

Above:
Knocked-out Churchill tanks
surrounded by dead bodies make for
a macabre beach scene after the
Dieppe raid. *IWM — HU1809A*

Right:
After the raid, the wounded are
unloaded at Portsmouth.
IWM — H22637

Above: There was even a handful of Germans taken prisoner, whilst the Canadians lost 3,367 killed, wounded or missing — more than in their entire 20-month campaign in Italy. *IWM — H22597*

the promenade from the beach. However, they managed to get a small demolition party through the wire which festooned the seawall, who blew up various pillboxes with Bangalore Torpedoes, and destroyed the Casino and various other defences including a 4in gun.

Meanwhile the tanks had begun to arrive in 10 tank landing craft (LCT), accompanied by sappers who were to demolish any anti-tank obstacles on the beach. They were landed in three waves as follows:

Wave 1

LCT1 — Landed all its three tanks, one of which reached the promenade 80m beyond the sea wall.
LCT2 — Landed its three tanks at the east end of the beach all of which got up to the promenade.
LCT3 — Lost one tank at sea but landed the other two which remained on the beach. The one lost at sea was the one equipped with flame-throwing equipment.

Wave 2

LCT4, 5 and *6* — All landed three tanks each, four of which reached the promenade.

Wave 3

LCT7 — Landed its three tanks, all reaching the promenade.
LCT8 — Carried RHQ. First tank off bellied in shale, blocking exit. LCT backed off and looked for another landing site. Here CO's tank was lost in deep water coming ashore. Third tank did not land.
LCT9 and *10* — Both landed their tanks, four of which reached the promenade.

They were heavily engaged and all craft received countless direct hits, but nevertheless all but two of the 30-strong tank force were successfully landed. The CO's tank was dropped into 2m of water when the ramp chains were cut by enemy fire, just as it was going through the exit door. The CO (Lieutenant-Colonel Andrews) and his crew baled out safely, but he was killed on the beach. Several tanks remained on the beach, their tracks having been damaged by enemy fire, but a large number managed to get over the seawall and did considerable damage to the enemy until they had expended all their ammunition.

By about 06.30 it was clear that the situation was not going as well as had been hoped. There was no word from the Royal Regiment at Puits or from No 3 Commando at Berneval, though both No 4 Commando's action at Varengeville and the two-battalion landing at Pourville had gone reasonably well. The Force Commander then decided it was time to use his reserve, the Fusiliers Mont Royal, giving them the task of reinforcing the Essex Scottish so they could capture the vital eastern headland. Accordingly, they set off in their landing craft at about 07.00hrs, lost two craft going in to the beach and then came under heavy fire on landing. Some were able to shelter behind stranded tanks, whilst their CO was wounded and half of his men were swept along by a strong tide well to the west end of the beach, near the Casino, where they were cut off on a small stretch of shingle and, after taking over 100 casualties, were forced to surrender. Other small parties penetrated deep into the town, but were stopped by superior enemy forces. One of these groups was taken prisoner and forced to undress down to their underwear, then left in charge of a single German guard. They managed to overpower him and made off in their pants and vests! Few of them managed to escape, however.

it impossible for the landing craft to come any closer without being beached. By noon most of the troops had been re-embarked apart from a small rearguard under Lieutenant-Colonel Cecil Merritt (CO of the Saskatchewans), who would later be awarded the Victoria Cross for this action.

In the centre, the assault on Dieppe itself was to be delivered by the Essex Scottish Regiment and the Royal Hamilton Light Infantry. They would land on the seafront, where the beach stretched for 1.5km, from the western breakwater to the cliffs at the Vieux Château and the Casino. Then there was a seawall, a road (Boulevard Maréchal Foch) and ornamental gardens, another road and then houses, which the Germans had fortified. Once the two regiments had secured the beach, then the tanks would land and then push on to hold the town whilst numerous demolitions were laid and blown. If the landing was a success, then the tanks and infantry would exploit to capture a supposed German Army HQ at Arques-la-Bataille (this intelligence proved to be incorrect, the HQ having moved well before the raid took place). The landing was to be covered by a short but intense naval bombardment from the destroyers, followed by some 60 Spitfires and Hurricanes strafing the houses, and three squadrons of Bostons and Blenheims dropping smoke bombs on the headland above the harbour. Close in covering fire was again provided by special naval craft, all of which suffered direct hits, one being sunk.

The two infantry regiments leapt out of their landing craft and stormed forward. However, just as at Puits, they came under heavy fire from all directions — both frontal and enfilade. Some of the enemy guns in the houses had been silenced by the covering barrage, but not all of them, whilst to the east, once the aerial smoke had begun to clear, the mass of artillery in the caves which were all over the face of the headland began to fire with great effect. The Essex Scottish, being the nearer, took most of the casualties from this fire and could not penetrate any further than the seawall which divided

The town was shrouded in smoke and the vital headlands had still not been taken, though there were successes in other areas. Roberts decided to use the Royal Marine Commando (CO Lieutenant-Colonel 'Tiger' Phillips) to reinforce the Royal Hamilton Light Infantry, to capture the western headland. However, once again the enemy fire was murderous and few of those who reached shore were unwounded, so once again the assault was thwarted.

It was by now becoming clear that Dieppe could not be captured and the force would have to be withdrawn if that were possible. The main withdrawal from the central beaches began about 11.00hrs, when a curtain of smoke was laid between the two headlands by aircraft. It was carried out under continual enemy fire, with some troops managing to get on board vessels that were not sinking, whilst others were not so lucky, this being a random extract from an account by one of the lucky ones:

'I made my way out to an LCA [Landing Craft Assault], but the first one I came to was hit and I was knocked off it. I was picked up by another which was over-crowded and sinking, but another craft came alongside and took off most of the men, leaving the rest of us to bale out until we attracted the attention of a further ship which stopped and took us on board.'

Soon further rescue and evacuation was impossible. Just after 13.00 the *Calpe* closed to within 2km of the shore, when it came under machine gun fire from German posts on the Dieppe breakwater. No signs of troops or landing craft could be seen apart from derelicts. Roberts received a message from Brigadier Southam's HQ ashore to say that he was having to surrender. The expedition then returned to England, some of the ships not getting home until past midnight.

The Results

The butcher's bill was considerable. Of the 5,000 Canadian troops engaged, 3,367 were killed in action, wounded or missing. This figure included 906 killed or died of wounds. Thus, although Mountbatten was able to tell the War Cabinet that two-thirds of the force had returned safely, his statement hid the truth. As Ronald Atkin says:

'In nine hours at Dieppe, the Canadian Army lost more men than in the 20 months of the Italian campaign. The 2nd Division was practically wiped out and its battle worthiness reduced drastically for many months. Not since the Somme in 1916 had a Canadian formation suffered such losses.'

On top of these figures, the Commandos lost 270 and the Navy 550, whilst the loss of weapons and equipment was considerable, in particular almost all the new Churchill heavy tanks (27 were landed and stayed on shore, two were lost at sea and just one remained on board an LCT).

Another important loss was that of Brigadier Southam's copy of the orders for Operation 'Jubilee', which contained the instructions about tying up prisoners to prevent them from destroying important documents. This was to lead to the tit-for-tat binding of both British and German POWs. Granted, it was stopped very swiftly by the British, but the unfortunate Allied POWs had to put up with being shackled for some time.

On the German side of course there was jubilation. 'The enemy has been battered to destruction. He has suffered heavy,

gruesome losses,' wrote von Rundstedt in his report on the action. Hitler was delighted and not only asked for his thanks and appreciation to be passed on to all ranks but also granted additional rations for the wounded. Total German casualties were just over 600, which included a handful of prisoners taken and very little equipment lost. It had been a complete reversal of the St Nazaire raid and must have given the Germans the belief that perhaps their Atlantic Wall was not so bad after all.

Commando VC winner Captain (later Colonel) Patrick Porteous was in no doubt about Dieppe saying:

'It was the biggest disaster that ever happened and the people that planned it should be shot. It was impossible for it to have succeeded — the Intelligence wasn't good enough. The plan depended entirely on total surprise, the slightest variation on that and the whole thing collapsed. It was only mounted to raise morale in Russia, and in England too when we'd been forced back in the Western Desert, and to give the Canadians something to do — they'd been hanging around so long getting bored.'

From the point of view of the planners for the Second Front, the raid was to prove a source of valuable information. Churchill said that the raid had justified the heavy casualties and 'shed revealing light on many shortcomings'. Probably the most significant remark was made by von Rundstedt, when he said at the end of his comments on the landing: 'He will not do it like this a second time!'

Notes
1. *The Greatest Raid of All* by C. E. Lucas Phillips.
2. *The Destroyer Campbeltown* by Al Ross.
3. *Hinge of Fate*, Volume IV of Winston Churchill's *History of the Second World War*.
4. *Combined Operations 1940–42*.
5. In his *History of the Second World War* Churchill makes the point that a postwar examination of German records did not show that there was any leakage and thus any special warning of the coming attack. However, the German assessment of that particular sector had led to heightened defence measures all along that part of the coast.
6. The 38-ton A22 initially had a 3in howitzer in its front hull and a 2-pounder gun in its turret (Churchill I and II), but these were replaced in the next model (known as Churchill III) by a 6-pounder in a welded turret. Churchill Is and IIs, plus some IIIs, were used by the Canadians at Dieppe, and one tank was equipped with a flame-thrower.
7. To differentiate between the two Generals Haase, the army commander was known as 'Der Grosse Haase' and 302nd Division commander as 'Der Kleine Haase'. 'Kleine' made all his officers swear to defend their positions 'to the death' and then himself swore that he would die rather than retreat or surrender.
8. *Dieppe 1942* by Ronald Atkin
9. *Ibid.*
10. Bangalore torpedoes are explosive devices contained in long metal tubes, which can be joined together to produce any desired length and are mainly used for blowing gaps in barbed-wire barriers, but can be used for other demolitions, such as blowing up pillboxes.

Enter Rommel

Special Inspector Rommel

It was now time for one of Germany's most famous soldiers to play his part in the saga of the Atlantic Wall. Feldmarschall Erwin Johannes Eugen Rommel had made his name in North Africa as the Desert Fox, a legendary panzer leader and military hero, by his brilliant leadership, his outstanding tactical ability and his realisation that showmanship was equally important to becoming a successful commander. He was someone who was admired — even almost revered — by the enemy as well as by his own troops. Despite sickness and eventual defeat in North Africa he was still one of the brightest stars of the Wehrmacht. On leaving North Africa, he had been earmarked by Hitler for a new high post, this time in Italy. However, this post as C-in-C Army Group B, was kept secret from everyone — even from Luftwaffe Feldmarschall Albert Kesselring who was then C-in-C Southern Italy. Differences of opinion on how the battle in Italy should be fought were bound to occur between them and ultimately the Führer decided to give Kesselring complete charge in Italy and to find Rommel and his burgeoning new HQ another task. This must have come as a bitter disappointment to Rommel, who nevertheless wrote philosophically to his wife: 'I'll take it as it comes.' OKW was actually all in favour of

disbanding Army Group B, but as von Rundstedt's chief of staff, Günther Blumentritt, explained, Hitler had other ideas:

> 'Against this Hitler ordered its revival. He knew that in 1944 something vital would occur in the west or on some other front and on that account wished to hold this valuable staff in reserve. But in order to keep Rommel and his staff employed until a responsible position could be found for him somewhere, Hitler decided to entrust him with the inspection of western defences.'[1]

He gave Rommel certain instructions based on his Führer Directive 51 (see Chapter 2), the exact details of which Rommel was never able to discover, although OKW did later confirm to OB West (von Rundstedt) their outline content. Basically Hitler's aims in appointing Rommel were threefold:

Below: Field Marshal Erwin Rommel is greeted by his Führer with whom he had something of a 'love-hate' relationship. Hitler appointed him the inspector of coastal defence and gave him plenty of freedom, initially. However, it would all end in tears. *IWM — HU40165*

- So that Rommel could familiarise himself with that sector of the Western Front which would undoubtedly prove to be the decisive one, namely the Channel coast area.
- To have Rommel take all necessary steps to rectify any shortcomings in the Atlantic Wall defences, making full use of the OT and other resources.
- To avail himself of Rommel's experience in fighting the Allies, in particular the British.

Rommel had authority to report directly to Hitler, which inevitably led to friction, not so much between the two field marshals or between their two headquarters — OB West and Army Group B — but rather in departmental circles and in their relations with the Luftwaffe's Third Air Fleet and the Kriegsmarine's Naval Fleet West, both of whom had their own distinct lines of communication up to OKW.

So Rommel took off from Villafranca airfield on 21 November 1943 bound for the close *bocage* country of Normandy through which his 'road to fame' had passed in the heady days of 1940, when he was proving his abilities as a panzer divisional commander and where he would shortly end his military career. Now he was Die Inspekteur der Küstenverteidigung (Inspector of Coastal Defence) and would prove to everyone that he had an inbuilt sixth sense when it came to spotting the unspottable, plus a talent for inventing obstacles second to none and, above all, the ability to impress almost anyone with his enthusiasm and sheer common sense.

The Inspection Team Assembles

Rommel had begun assembling his inspection team whilst he was still in Italy. Acting on the advice of his then chief of staff, Generalmajor Alfred Gause — one of his trusted *Afrikaners* — he requested the assignment of Vizeadmiral Friedrich Oskar Ruge as the team's Naval Liaison Officer (Marineverbindungsoffizier). Postwar Ruge became Inspector of the Bundesmarine from 1956 until he retired in 1961. He was a jovial Swabian and, as Rommel also hailed from Swabia, there was an immediate rapport and he soon became a firm and trusted friend to whom Rommel could talk frankly. He had entered the Navy in 1914, served in the Baltic and led destroyer raids on Britain. In 1920 he had begun specialising in mine warfare and also established a reputation as a military writer. Ruge arrived on 30 November.

'I reported in this irregular attire,' he wrote later, referring to his warm and unmilitary muffler, 'but it seemed unimportant, since Rommel was apparently less interested in the uniform than in the man inside it. Rommel appeared smaller than I had imagined him, rather serious, full of energy and very natural.'[2]

Soon after his arrival, Rommel sent Ruge off to see the Kriegsmarine staff in Berlin and to collect as much background material as he could that would help them with their task — such items as tide tables, maps and charts, shipping details and other information. He would return to rejoin the team whilst they were en route — actually rejoining Rommel in northern Jutland on 2 December. It was indeed fortunate that Ruge had a detailed personal knowledge of the coast, because much of the material that he so painstakingly collected was destroyed in an air-raid whilst he was still in Berlin.

A special train had been arranged for the team, with spacious compartments and a 'parlour car' which Ruge reckoned had been designed for a Balkan potentate. There was also a large briefing room and a dining car. The team boarded the train on 1 December at Munich railway station, bound for Copenhagen where the inspection tour would begin with a visit to General Hermann von Hannecken, who was commanding all the German forces in Denmark (he was C-in-C there from 27 September 1942 to 27 January 1945). Rommel met him on the evening of 3 December and began his tour the next morning at Esbjerg on the west coast of Jutland. They spent 10 days in Denmark, in which short time Rommel realised that the much vaunted Atlantic Wall was a hollow sham and that a vast amount of work would be needed if a determined enemy assault was to be defeated. He was soon to discover that this applied to most of the rest of these supposedly impregnable defences. Rommel also realised that they were planning to fight the main battles too far back from the coast. He had already decided upon his main strategy, namely that the Allies must be defeated on the beaches before they could gain a proper foothold, and he would propound this message over and over again. In his logical way he reasoned that mobile warfare — of which he was a master — would be impossible against an enemy with total air superiority and a vast preponderance of mechanised weapons — tanks, guns, vehicles — at their disposal.

'I consider therefore that an attempt must be made, using every possible expedient, to beat off the enemy landing on the coast and to fight the battle in the more or less strongly fortified coastal strip.'

He told his chief engineer officer, General Wilhelm Meise, much the same:

'When the invasion begins our own supply lines won't be able to bring forward any aircraft, gasoline, rockets, tanks, guns or shells because of enemy air attacks. That alone will rule out any sweeping land battles. Our only possible chance will be at the beaches — that's where the enemy is always weakest.'

He would hold this view throughout his period of command of Army Group B, despite the attempts of others who wanted to fight the battle differently. It was fortunate indeed for the Allies that Rommel's logical approach was not followed to the letter.

After concluding that Denmark showed (in Ruge's words): 'how overtaxed the Wehrmacht was — a handful of modestly trained and equipped static divisions had to defend hundreds of kilometres of excellent landing beach,' most of the team moved to Rommel's new headquarters at Fontainebleau, whilst the Desert Fox flew to southern Germany for a few days' leave, then rejoined them on 18 December. The new HQ was a small, luxurious château which had once belonged to Madame de Pompadour.

The following day he visited von Rundstedt in Paris, writing to his wife afterwards that: 'R is very charming and I think everything will go well.' There was undoubtedly a certain amount of mutual respect between them — von Rundstedt was, at 68, Germany's most senior soldier, with Rommel, a mere 52, its youngest field marshal. Although he perhaps saw the younger man as a threat, von Rundstedt was quite happy to let Rommel do all the work. Rommel's new chief of staff, who took over from Gause, the brilliant General Hans Speidel, put it succinctly:

'Rundstedt's character, personality and mobility were failing and, at a time when supreme efforts were

Above: Field Marshal Gerd von Rundstedt, who, as C-in-C West, was Rommel's immediate superior. However, he was happy to let the younger, more energetic, Desert Fox do all the work. *IWM — MH10132*

Above: Rommel, his field marshal's baton tucked under his arm, is seen here with his brilliant chief of staff, General Hans Speidel. *Author's collection*

Above: Field Marshal Günther von Kluge, seen here walking past the famous restaurant La Mère Poulard on Mont St Michel. Von Kluge took over from von Rundstedt as C-in-C West on 3 July 1944. He did not like Rommel, whom he said was 'independent and disobedient', giving him a severe dressing down when they first met. Rommel refused to accept this and, once Kluge was appraised of the true situation, he changed his opinion. Von Kluge would poison himself on 18 August 1944 when accused of being implicated in the bomb plot against Hitler. *J. P. Benamou Collection*

demanded, Rundstedt remained unknown to the soldier at the front, while Rommel ceaselessly exerted his remarkable powers of leadership on the soldiers personally, sparing himself not at all.'[3]

Whilst his main headquarters staff began to settle into Maison Pompadour at Fontainebleau, Rommel and his inspection team continued their tour. The week before Christmas they were in the most important area, namely the Channel coast, and Rommel was again extremely disturbed by all he saw — the lack of proper defences, the relatively poor quality of many of the troops who would have the task of meeting the coming invasion, and the lack of a coherent command structure. He did not break for Christmas, but continued his tours and reports. 'Out on the move a lot,' he wrote to his son Manfred, 'and raising plenty of dust wherever I go.' To his wife Lucie he wrote: 'I'm going to throw myself into this new job with everything I've got and I'm going to see it turns out a success.' So he went everywhere and saw everything — including Luftwaffe and Kriegsmarine units and their headquarters as well as those of the Heer, also the secret V-weapon sites (he visited one on Christmas Day!); nowhere was excluded. His staff were appalled at the pressure under which he worked — and of course he made them work just as hard.

'I want mines!'

One of his favourite topics was the laying of mines and the planning of defensive minefields, of which he had gained much expertise in North Africa, for example in his preparations for the Battle of El Alamein. Now he wanted to lay many, many more.

'I want anti-personnel mines, anti-tank mines, anti-paratroop mines' he told Meise,

'I want mines to sink ships and mines to sink landing craft. I want some minefields designed so that our infantry can cross them but not enemy tanks. I want mines that detonate when a wire is tripped; mines that explode when a wire is cut; mines that can be remotely controlled and mines that will explode when a beam of light is interrupted. Some of them must be encased in a nonferrous metal, so that the enemy's mine detectors won't register them.'

And as he talked he drew diagrams to illustrate his thoughts. His ideal defence line would be an impenetrable mixture of minefields and bunkers up to 10km wide — like his Alamein line but at least 50 times longer. 'Quite apart from Rommel's greatness as a soldier,' wrote Meise later, 'in my view he was the greatest engineer of World War 2. There was nothing I could teach him. He was my master.'[4]

Everywhere he went he imparted the 'Rommel Magic' and the ordinary soldiers, who probably had never seen a field marshal before in their lives, were impressed by the interest he took in their individual jobs. Anyone he discovered to be 'living the soft life' swiftly found themselves on the receiving end of his wrath — irrespective of rank. One example was Generaloberst Hans von Salmuth, commander of the Fifteenth Army, who protested when Rommel told him that he wanted his troops to lay more mines than ever before. Salmuth told him he wanted 'fresh, well-trained soldiers not physical wrecks,' then patronisingly went on: 'stick around a bit and you'll soon see that you can't do everything at once. If anybody tells you different, then he is just trying to flatter you or he's a pig idiot.' Once Rommel's staff were out of earshot the furious Desert Fox gave Salmuth a tongue lashing that left him red-faced and speechless. 'He's quite a roughneck that one,' beamed Rommel to Ruge as they started their journey back to Fontainebleau, 'that's the only language he understands.' From then on Salmuth was 'pro-Rommel' and warmed to the Field Marshal's ideas. In a report from the Fifteenth Army files which is quoted in David Irving's brilliant book on Rommel (see Bibliography):

'Field Marshal Rommel's view is that our defence forces must be concentrated much closer to the coast. Our reserves are to be brought right forward and thrown into an immediate counter-attack. If the British once get a foothold on dry land, they can't be thrown out again.'

Rommel explained his plan for laying mines all the way along the coast. There were over 600,000 mines waiting to be laid, Rommel told Salmuth, whilst even dummy minefields had proved their worth in North Africa. Rommel and Salmuth toured the Fifteenth Army sector and visited everywhere,

Below: On one of his early visits to what he considered to be the most important part of the Atlantic Wall, namely the Channel coast, Rommel is seen here (fourth from right) at the Batterie Saltzwedel neu/Tirpitz at Raversijde near Ostend, 21 December 1943. The battery commander Kapitänleutnant R. Hoppe (saluting) is greeting General der Infanterie Freiherr von und zu Werner Gilsa, who was then commanding LXXXIX Corps. *Raversijde*

driving like a whirlwind through the French towns and villages in a Horch car, frequently to the shouts of 'C'est Rommel!' from the local populace.

During December and January Rommel continued his inspections, covering mile after mile of coast in tireless reconnaissance; turning out coastal battalion after coastal battalion for inspection, march-past and pre-emptory interrogation; quizzing commanders, from generals down to corporals, finding out their views and laying down his own priorities. He was convinced that, in most places where a landing was possible, there should be several parallel minefields, each some kilometres wide, forming a defensive zone up to 8km in depth and requiring many millions of mines. These minefields would be covered from fortified strongpoints, sometimes including stationary tanks, and requiring considerable constructional effort. Dummy positions were to be built in order to deceive the invader, whilst fictitious staffs, movement tables, orders and so forth, would be co-ordinated into an army group deception programme — not unlike what the Allies were doing on the other side of the Channel. In the sea itself would be four belts of underwater obstacles, one in 2m of water, one at low tide, one at half tide and one at mean high tide. Against airborne attack Rommel ordered the erection of stakes (soon known as 'Rommel's asparagus'). Everywhere he went he produced new ideas from his ever-fertile imagination.

Rommel continued his duties as 'Special Inspector' for some months — he did not visit the western and southern coastlines in France until February 1944 — then set about writing his report. In general he had been very disturbed by almost everything he had seen. He had found the Army forces to be 'barely adequate' for a vigorous defence, whilst the Navy and Air Force were both too weak to be able to provide tangible help. There was a lack of proper defensive plans, except for the fortresses. Everywhere there was a lack of mobility and of basic defensive weapons such as minefields. 'I have ordered all the troops to ram stakes into the beaches as a barrier against landing craft,' he noted in his diary on 15 January 1944, the day on which he was given tactical command of all troops on the coast opposite Great Britain. He also made an educated guess as to where the enemy landings were most likely to take place — namely in the Pas de Calais area, because of the presence there of the V-rocket sites. He later retracted this guess. He also put in his report that the enemy would precede any seaborne landings with severe aerial bombing, sea bombardments and airborne landings, all of which came true. He also said that he did not think the coastal defences were strong enough to withstand the Allied attack and that an immediate and decisive counter-attack would have to be launched and that this was the main reason for keeping mobile troops — panzers and panzergrenadiers — close to the coast. This was to be the main bone of contention with von Rundstedt and his advisors.

Below: January 1944, first inspection of the Normandy beaches by Field Marshal Rommel (left). *J. P. Benamou Collection*

Rommel's Report

Completed and signed on 22 April, Rommel's eventual report was both long and detailed, containing many comments and instructions for everyone involved in manning the Atlantic Wall. To save space I will try to paraphrase the most important points he raises. He began with some praise — the carrot perhaps before the stick — when he said that:

'Almost without exception unusual progress has been made in all defence group sectors in accordance with the seriousness of the situation. I expressed my satisfaction to the commanders and troops of all available forces and their clever employment of a great part of the civilian population.'

However, he went on to say that: 'Here and there I have noticed units that do not seem to have recognised the urgency of the situation and who do not even follow instructions.'

Rommel then listed examples, such as his instruction that all mines laid on the beaches had to be live all the time, but that he had found this order has been countermanded in some locations. 'I do not intend to issue unnecessary orders every day,' he said,

'I give orders only when and if necessary. I expect, however, that my orders will be executed at once and to the letter, and that no unit under my command makes changes, or even gives orders to the contrary, or delays execution through unnecessary red tape. On the contrary, I expect that all my orders will be followed immediately and precisely and that the carrying out of orders will be supervised.'

Then he listed various conclusions he had reached, which comprised, in essence, an engineering treatise on obstacles of all types.

Beach Defences

Beach Defences In general these 'K' obstacles ('K'=*Küste* [coast]) needed to be 'dense and effective' so that they would not only delay the enemy but also destroy him in the water. Rommel mentioned items such as the 'Nutcracker' Mine I–III, the concrete shell for the Teller mine (to reduce the shock of other explosions such as shell fire setting off the mines in sympathy) and the concrete obstacles known as tetrahedra. The first of these were, according to experiments, very effective against landing craft and amphibious vehicles, including tanks. The concrete shells also protected against the penetration by seawater and the pressure of the waves which could cause the charge to detonate. Little by little, the density of mines on the beaches had to be brought up to one per metre.

Factories for concrete In every sector the factories making concrete structures needed to liaise with the OT, so as to produce the special mixtures of concrete, which the OT already knew about.

Concrete Foundations for Czech obstacles (*Tschechenigel*) These improved the obstacles considerably by raising them up and thus preventing them from becoming choked up with sand — a major threat to beach defences. Where concrete was unavailable Rommel said brushwood mats were to be used and had already proved very effective.

Tetrahedra Steel tetrahedra (*beton tetrader*) were better than the lighter concrete ones. They were also particularly valuable in locations where it was impossible to drive in stakes — such as on cliffs and in shallow water, operated by pulleys mounted on anchored boats or floats operated with the use of horses. Mines could be fixed to their front that would explode on contact so as to destroy enemy vessels as well as merely stopping them.

Ram logs (*Hemmelbalker*) These had proved very effective even against large boats, but must have a slope of 30°–40°. Installing saw-like/chisel-like blades to protrude a few inches would help to cut open the bottom of a ship. Mined logs should be carefully and systematically placed at 20m intervals and at great depth.

Belgian Gates (*Rollböcke* and *Hemmküen* — also called 'Element C') Like the Czech obstacles, these could be very effective against boats. 'Some units,' commented Rommel, 'even installed mines on *Rollböcke* which I advise strongly.' He also told units to alter the placing of their movable 'K' obstacles as often as possible on the beach, but commented that: 'most units, however, have been slack in this respect'.

Defences Against Airborne Troops

Above: Rommel and his 'asparagus' — anti-paratroop and anti-glider-assault stakes, which he had caused to be erected in as many open, vulnerable places as possible. *IWM — HU3066*

Rommel explained that he had been ordered to take charge of defences against airborne troops. He especially thanked 348th Infantry Division (in the Dieppe area) for the way it had installed — and was continuing to install — 'strong obstacles against airborne troops in the sector between land and sea in such a quick and thorough manner'. The division had managed to employ civilians (including women who sang at their work!) principally because it paid them immediately and in cash. The placing of logs and the wiring of open fields was of the greatest importance, because, as Rommel explained:

'The time seems to be near when the coast cannot be penetrated from the sea by amphibious units on account of the strength of the "K" obstacles and the fortress-like defences. Only by using numerous airborne troops as reinforcements will a sea-borne assault have any chance of succeeding.'

He then explained the threat posed by these airborne and glider-borne troops, and ordered

'The thorough fencing-in of the area between land and sea is to be accomplished as quickly as possible by all divisions.'

Mining

Rommel expressed his worries that in many places mining of the coastal band of 300–10,000m had not been completed with real

minefields or even covered by dummy ones, which he said could be used where mines were in short supply. He also made the point that there could be no mines in areas where farmers were ploughing or cattle grazing. Areas of major minefields were not to be taken up without Army permission, whilst a broad minefield was to be laid around all fortress-like installations. Both the Americans and the British disliked entering potential minefields, and Rommel commented that even their experts could not tell a dummy minefield from a real one without properly checking it over. Engineers were not needed for the construction of dummy minefields except for their planning. All officers had to be able to construct dummy minefields.

Camouflage of Defence Positions
He commented that he had seen very well-constructed battle installations in the middle of green fields, yet the camouflage nets were the old-style black ones, which allowed enemy bombers to recognise them from a great height. The old nets must therefore be newly sprayed to fit in with their surroundings — or used on dummy installations.

Use of Smokescreens
The use of artificial smoke during enemy attacks was highly recommended, but using burning leaves or straw for makeshift smoke could, Rommel said, be just as effective, especially because artificial smoke was so scarce. It could also be used to draw the enemy's attention to dummy installations.

Tearing Down and Mining Beach Houses
There had been too much tearing down of houses. Rommel argued that the enemy would most likely shoot at such houses, villages and towns, if they were visible from the sea. Therefore they should only be taken down if it was necessary to create a field of fire, otherwise it was better to leave them as targets for

Above: This well-known, but striking, photograph of Rommel and party striding along a French beach between rows of obstacles encapsulates perfectly the energy and determination with which he did his job as inspector of fortifications. *Bundesarchiv*

the enemy. Mining such houses had proved unsatisfactory, and it was more effective to use mines on the beach or in minefields. Every bomb dropped or shell fired at these houses was one less to be used against the defenders.

Reinforcements
Commanders had to make use of every single man in the short time left before the enemy came and any member of the civilian population as well. He quoted an example in one company where only 13 men out of 180 were working on the beach and the rest were occupied in the bivouac area in which they had lived for over a year. Nothing had been done to protect their front lines.

Co-operation Between Infantry and Artillery
This was essential and he mentioned a highly professional demonstration that he had watched when 'all arms had interacted with great speed and professionalism'. Such co-operation was to be encouraged, especially with the coastal naval batteries.

Conclusion
Rommel closed his report by re-emphasising that the German forces needed swiftly to bring all their defences up to such a standard that they would hold up against the strongest attacks.

'Our defences, together with the sea, represent one of the strongest defence lines in history', he said.

'The enemy must be annihilated before he reaches our main battlefield . . . From week to week the Atlantic Wall

Chapter 8
Layout and Manning — Before D-Day

Fighting Strengths

Before looking at the make-up of the length of the Atlantic Wall from the North Cape to the Spanish border, we should try to get some idea of the size of the forces involved, so as to gauge what the Allies faced as they began their final preparations for the invasion. In his book *The Last Year of the German Army* historian James Lucas gives details of the strengths of the various German army groups as at 1 June 1944. In each case he shows both the total strength of the army group and the strength of the actual fighting troops at the sharp end. Amongst the figures given in the table are the following that are relevant to this study:

ARMY GROUP	RATION STRENGTH	BAYONET STRENGTH
West	348,888	190,538
Norway	105,439	42,265
Denmark	27,590	16,296[1]

How many of these troops were actually manning the Wall is not easy to estimate, though Generalleutnant Hans Speidel in his book *We Defended Normandy* says that there were approximately 60 static infantry divisions, manning the entire 5,000km of the 'Atlantic Front'. The strength of an average static division was then probably under 10,000 men rather than the normal 'war establishment' figure for an infantry division of 17,000 plus, which works out at 600,000 troops or 120 troops per kilometre. However, applying Lucas's 'bayonet strength' principle then roughly half of these would be supporting troops, so this figure can be cut in half to 60 fighting men. This is, of course, only an approximation, as the concentration varied enormously, for example between fortresses where there were large garrisons (10,000 in Boulogne, 25,000 in the Channel Islands and 35,000 in Brest) and hazardous landing areas with high cliffs or dangerous tides, which made a potential major landing well nigh impossible and thus needed much smaller garrisons.

In addition to the Army, both the Navy and the Air Force had major bases and units spread within Occupied Europe, including along the area of the Atlantic Wall. However, it was the naval coastal artillery — Marine Artillerie (MA) — and the Air Force anti-aircraft units — the flak arm — which were most concerned with defence of the Wall.

Naval Artillery

It is true to say that much of the responsibility for providing large static artillery batteries along the Wall rested on the Kriegsmarine. In many cases, it was one of the primary tasks of the senior naval commander in the area to co-ordinate the fire of all the coastal guns whilst the enemy was at sea, the Army not taking over until the enemy had landed. This led to

Above: An alert looking soldier stands in front of one of the many gun positions along the French section of the Atlantic Wall. The casemate houses a 105mm K 331/332(f) ex-French field gun. Note that he is wearing short lace-up ankle boots (*Schnürschuhe*) and canvas gaiters rather than the more usual black leather marching boots (*Marschstiefel*) — commonly called 'jackboots'. He is carrying a black leather map-case around his chest, and his standard issue 1884/98 bayonet on his belt, whilst his 7.92mm Karabiner 98k is slung. *Bundesarchiv*

disagreements as to the tactical principles in siting guns and observation posts which were never resolved before the invasion.

The Flak Arm

At the beginning of the war nearly a million men, that is to say almost two-thirds of the total Luftwaffe manpower was serving in the flak arm (flak being an abbreviation for Fliegerabwehrkanone — that is anti-aircraft gun). Its size increased so that by summer 1944 there were some million and a quarter men and women, that is to say nearly half of the

Above: The crew of a flak gun site relax. This gun was part of a battery of light AA guns, protecting the radar at Arromanches. Note the 'kills board' showing seven aircraft shot down. This photo was taken in 1943.
J. P. Benamou Collection

Luftwaffe, so employed. Basic flak units were of four types — heavy, light, mixed and searchlight — and they were to be found all along the Wall, sometimes with the dual purpose of being able to engage naval targets as well as aircraft. Of course, as with the Army, many sailors and airmen were in a supporting role; for example, Hans Speidel says that there were more than 300,000 Luftwaffe personnel making up the ground staff of the Air Force in the West alone, which worked out to 100 ground staff for every airman. Bitterly he ascribes this position to the 'ambition of Göring to create a special force of his own — a peculiar urge that seizes the grandees of any revolution'.

Vital Areas
There were 36 potentially vital areas on the Atlantic Wall. Reading from north to south these were:

Norway (3) — Narvik, Bergen and Trondheim.
Denmark (4) — Frederikshavn, Hanstholm, Ålborg and Esbjerg.
Germany (10) — Sylt, Helgoland, Brunsbüttel, Cuxhaven, Wesermünde, Wilhelmshaven, Wangerooge, Norderney, Emden and Borkum.
The Netherlands (4) — Den Helder, Ijmuiden, Hoek van Holland and Vlissingen.
France (12) — Dunkerque (Dunkirk), Calais, Boulogne, Le Havre, Cherbourg, St Malo, Brest, Lorient, St Nazaire, La Rochelle and both sides of the mouth of the Gironde.

Channel Islands (3) — Alderney, Guernsey and Jersey.
Most of these locations were heavily fortified by June 1944, 11 of them having been declared by Hitler to be fortresses (Festungen) on 19 January 1942. These were:
The Netherlands (2) — Ijmuiden and Hoek van Holland.
France (9) — Dunkerque, Boulogne and Le Havre in the Fifteenth Army sector along the Channel; Cherbourg, St Malo, Brest, Lorient and St Nazaire in the Seventh Army sector along the Atlantic coast; Gironde estuary in the First Army sector.

To these OKW added the Channel Islands, Calais and La Pallice–La Rochelle. The fates of these Festungen will be covered in a later chapter.

Super-Heavy Guns
Amongst the mass of coastal artillery with gun emplacements built into the Wall were an amazing number of guns of calibres between 28cm and 40.6cm. Many of these were naval turrets, and a few were rail guns. They were the following:

Norway — 11 locations with a total of 35 guns.
Denmark — two locations with a total of eight guns.
North-West Germany and the Frisian Islands — four locations with 12 guns.
Belgium — two locations with eight guns.
France — Dunkerque to Le Havre — 11 locations with 30 guns.
— West Normandy to the Seine — two locations with four guns.
— Brittany and Western France — four locations with 13 guns.
Channel Islands — one location with four guns.
Total = 37 locations with a total of 114 guns.

Norway

In June 1944 the German Army of Occupation in Norway was known as AOK Norwegen (Army Group Norway), even though it was only of single Army strength. Nevertheless, by then there was roughly one German soldier for every 10 Norwegians so the garrison was considerable. The commander from 1940 until December 1944 was Generaloberst Nikolaus von Falkenhorst, with Generalleutnant Rudolf Bamler as his chief of staff (1942–February 1944) who then handed over to Generalmajor Eugen Theilacker. Subordinate formations in June 1944 were XXXIII, LXX and LXXI Corps with 89th Infantry Division (the 'Horseshoe Division') in reserve. This division had been created in 1944 from personnel in the reinforced regiments of the Replacement Army and trained in Norway from March–June 1944, returning to central Europe about the time of the Normandy invasion. It was ordered first to the Rouen–Le Havre area, then on to Normandy in late June where it suffered heavy casualties. Its place as army group reserve was taken by the Norway Panzer Brigade.

As already mentioned, the protection of Norway had been given top priority because it was difficult to bring in reinforcements and to defend the large number of potential landing sites/ports and so on. Even so, the occupation forces were able to protect properly only the entrances to the fjords and the islands off the coast. The interiors of the fjords were only thinly defended, in some places just by field works without any troops, whilst strongpoints protected the military bases and main access routes into the interior. The following were designated as defensive areas: Narvik, Lofoten islands, Langøy, Tromsö, Bodö, Mo, Vega, Rorvik, Trondheim, Kristiansund, Ålesund, Solund, Bergen, Stavanger, Flekkefjord, Kristiansand, Arendal, Tönsberg and Oslo. The three most important were Narvik in the north, which was given top priority, then Bergen in the south with its vital air and sea bases, and finally Trondheim, because of its submarine pens.

There were some 225 artillery batteries of all types around the coast, containing a total of approximately 1,000 heavy and medium guns — over 40 of which were 24cm or larger in calibre. Good examples of these super-heavies were one of the batteries defending the approaches to Narvik, the four 40.6cm naval turret of the Battery Trondenes, and the 28cm triple gun turret at Fort Austrått, Lundahugen, Orland, guarding the far reaches of Trondheim Fjord. This turret was originally the stern gun turret of the German battleship *Gneisenau*. In addition to the gun batteries there were 15 torpedo batteries of various sizes (one to four tubes) protected by concrete bunkers.

In summary, over 280 large fortifications were built around the Norwegian coast, plus thousands of smaller fortifications and positions. Unlike in Denmark, the fortifications and defensive positions were solidly built on and into rock, so many of them have survived to the present day.

Army Forces

On 12 April 1945 the German Order of Battle showed the following troops in Norway, under command of the Twentieth Mountain Army:

Below: A good shot of troops manning beach positions, with anti-tank walls, wooden beach obstacles, wire and probably also a belt of mines. This photograph gives an excellent idea of the height of the wall. *J. P. Benamou Collection and Bundesarchiv*

KEY

1. Sønderby Battery
2. Roland Battery
3. Vester Vedsted Battery
4. Sønderho Battery
5. Pælebjerg Battery
6. Vesterhavsbad Battery
7. Grådyb (Gneisenau) and 3rd Flak Battery
8. Gammelby (Esbjerg 4th Flak Battery)
9. Gjessing (Esbjerg 5th Flak Battery)
10. Femhøje (Esbjerg 2nd Flak Battery)
11. Vogelnest (Tirpitz)
12. Oxby Battery
13. Blaavand Battery
14. Vrøgum Battery
15. Børsmose Battery
16. Dyreby Battery
17. Nymindegab Battery
18. Stauning Battery
19. Søndervig (Kryle) Battery
20. Bjerghuse (Nørre Fjand) Battery
21. Skalstrup Battery
22. Tørring Battery
23. Thyborøn Battery
24. Agger Battery
25. Lyngby Battery
26. Klitmøller Battery
27. Hansted 5th Flak Battery
28. Hansted 1st Battery
29. Hansted 2nd Battery and 2nd Flak Battery
30. Hansted 4th Flak Battery
31. Hansted 3rd Flak Battery
32. Vigsø Battery
33. Bulbjerg Battery
34. Svinkløv Battery
35. Faarupklit Battery
36. Løkken Battery
37. Hirsthals West Battery
38. Hirsthals East Battery
39. Tversted Battery
40. Skagen Battery
41. Aalbæk Battery
42. Aalbæk New Battery
43. Frederikshavn North Battery (Flak)
44. Frederikshavn Harbour Battery
45. Frederikshavn South Battery and Flak Battery
46. Sæby Battery
47. Asaa Battery
48. Hals Battery
49. Tofte Battery
50. Helberskov Battery
51. Udbyhøj Battery
52. Fjellerup Battery
53. Emmedsbo Battery
54. Grenaa Battery
55. Karholm Battery
56. Helgenæs Battery
57. Aakrogen Battery
58. Silistria Battery
59. Skaade Battery
60. Abelshoved Battery
61. Trelde Næs Battery
62. Røjle Battery
63. Midtskov Battery
64. Fynshoved Battery
65. Halskov Battery
66. Røsnæs Battery
67. Alleshave Battery
68. Ordrup Næs Battery
69. Sjællands Odde and Yolerby Batteries
70. Ebbelykke Battery
71. Spodsbjerg Battery
72. Salgaardshøj Battery
73. Hesbjerg Battery
74. Hornbæk Battery
75. Helsingør Battery
76. Nivaa Battery
77. Gedser Battery
78. Dueodde Battery

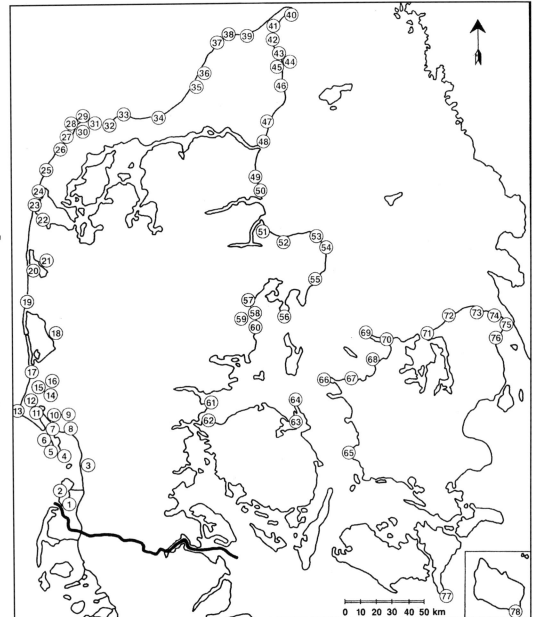

Above: Map of the coastal batteries, Denmark. *Source: Europa Nostra Bulletin 51*

XIX Mountain Corps — 6th Mountain Division, 388th Grenadier Brigade, 270th Division amalgamated with 193 Grenadier Brigade, Corps Reserve: Bicycle Reconnaissance Brigade Norway.

LXXI Corps — 503rd Grenadier Brigade, 140th Division, 139th Mountain Brigade, 210th Division amalgamated with Fortress Brigade Lofoten, 230th Division.

XXXIII Corps — 14th Luftwaffe Field Division, 102nd Division, 295th Division.

LXX Corps — 280th Division, 274th Division, 613rd Division HQ.

XXXVI Mountain Corps — Finnland MG Ski Brigade, Panzer Brigade Norway.

Army Reserve — 7th Mountain Division.[2]

Naval Artillery

There were also numerous naval artillery units located in Norway: a total of 14 naval artillery detachments (MAA 501–507 and 510–516); plus 10 naval AA detachments (701, 702, 706, 709, 710, 714, 715, 801, 802 and 822).

Denmark

Swiftly occupying the country in the spring of 1940, the Germans immediately began to fortify the coastline, so as to maintain communications with their troops in Norway. Befehlshaber der deutsches Truppen in Dänemark (Bef d. dtsch. Tr. I. Dänemark — Head of the Occupation Forces in Denmark) was Generalleutnant Hermann von Hannecken (from 27 September 1942 until 27 January 1945 when he handed over to Generaloberst Georg Lindemann who surrendered Armee Lindemann (the remnants of the German troops in Denmark) at the end of the war. Von Hannecken had specific orders to bolster coastal defences against a possible invasion.

As with Norway, the opinion of the Germans was that any invasion would be on the flanks of one or more of the harbours that the Allies would have to capture. Coastal defences were therefore reinforced in these places and thinned out elsewhere along the open coast. It was also necessary to fortify the land-bridges that led inland from the countless small fishing villages, through the dunes and then over the boggy areas behind them. A major expansion began in 1943, when the Army and Navy began a systematic extension of coastal defences from the German border up to Skagen and round to Frederikshavn. Along this line infantry strongpoints and other field defences were built in long chains. The key points in the defence were: Frederikshavn, Skagen, Lökken, Hanstholm and the western entrance to Limfjord, Sondervig, Blävand and Esbjerg, with Hanstholm and Esbjerg being the strongest. In total there were 78 batteries with some 300-plus guns of varying calibres, two of the largest being the 38cm guns at Oksby and Esbjerg. There were also, as in Norway, some torpedo batteries in concrete shelters.

At the time of D-Day the Danish invasion defences were still incomplete and that summer and autumn the Kriegsmarine warned of the potential danger of an attack in the Skagerrak and Kattegat, which could then penetrate into the Baltic. This would isolate Norway and have a serious effect upon submarine warfare, especially if Sweden joined in on the Allied side. Accordingly, a series of batteries was built in the east of Jutland and on the coasts of Funen and Zealand. Most of these were just basic field works containing few concrete structures. However, it was felt that without them more troops would be needed to defend Denmark (remember the German principle of 'Economy

of Force' mentioned in Chapter 5), whilst it would be highly dangerous to open up such an inviting route into Germany.

'The German works in Denmark exhibit great variety of design and construction varying in size from the small flanking positions that are found along most of Jutland's west coast to the large fort-like structures that were placed around Esbjerg, Hanstholm and Frederikshavn. The flanking positions normally consist of three bunkers while the three fortified towns just mentioned consist of around 1,300, 700 and 300 respectively. In all the Germans built more than 7,000 bunkers in Denmark. The number of fortified groups or areas is also very large. For instance, the combined number of just the coast defence batteries, anti-aircraft batteries and radar stations comes to more than 150. In addition there are infantry strongpoints of various sizes, flanking positions, various technical installations etc., in all more than 300 fortified areas.'[3]

After the war nearly all the bunkers — apart from a few taken over by the Danish military — were stripped of their equipment and covered over.

On 12 April 1944, the following troops were in Denmark:

Army Area 'Denmark' — 160th Division, 233rd Division.
Army Reserve — HQ 616th (North Jutland) Division.

Naval Artillery

There were nine naval artillery detachments, four naval AA detachments and two naval artillery arsenals in Denmark.

Germany

The small length of North Sea coastline of Germany, stretching from the Danish border to the Dutch border, contained most of the main German ports and naval bases, such as Hamburg, Bremerhaven, Wilhelmshaven and Cuxhaven, all of which were heavily garrisoned, protected and difficult to capture. This was made even more difficult by the fortification of the off-shore East Frisian Islands, which were garrisoned and protected with numerous gun batteries. The area of the German Bight, for example, had some 50 gun batteries, which included at least 12 heavy guns of 24cm calibre or over.

Naval Artillery

The naval artillery presence was considerable, and was divided under two headquarters until late 1944. These were the Naval Command North Sea and Coastal Command German Bight (later known as the Admiral German Bight). Under their command were numerous naval and AA artillery regiments and detachments, plus port protection flotillas and other units. As an example of the considerable numbers involved, here are the units listed as under command of Naval Command North Sea:

Borkum Island — a port protection flotilla, one naval artillery detachment and one naval AA detachment.
Emden (covering the five most northerly Dutch provinces) — a naval AA regiment with six naval AA detachments, plus two reserve AA detachments and a naval motor transport detachment.
Norderney — one naval artillery detachment and one naval AA detachment.
Wangerooge — two naval artillery detachments, one naval AA detachment and one training detachment for AA guns.
Wilhelmshaven — a port protection flotilla, a naval AA

regiment (later renamed 2 Marineflak Brigade), with seven naval AA detachments, including two AA floating batteries on the *Medusa* and *Niobe*, one naval artillery detachment and other units.

Wesermünde (Bremerhaven) — two naval AA detachments.

Helgoland — one naval artillery detachment, one naval AA detachment.

Cuxhaven — a port protection flotilla, one naval AA detachment and one naval artillery reserve detachment.

Brunsbüttel — naval AA regiment with four AA detachments.

Sylt — five naval AA detachments, reduced to three by the end of 1943.

Army Group B

Before continuing with this survey of the Atlantic Wall country by country, we must first mention the organisation of the military that was responsible for the remainder of the Wall. On 15 January 1944 Rommel's Armeegruppe B (Army Group B) officially took over responsibility for the Atlantic and Channel coasts, north of the Loire river, even though he did not visit the western and southern coastlines until the following month. This was the area in which Hitler was convinced the Allies would land. As we have already seen, the Army, Navy and Air Force all had their own separate lines of communication up to the OKW, so there was no centralised control under a supreme commander in the West.

Army Group B commanded:

On the Channel coast — Seventh Army (General Friedrich Dollmann), with an area of responsibility covering from Brittany to the River Seine.

On the Channel and North Sea coasts — Fifteenth Army (General Hans von Salmuth) covering from the River Seine to the River Scheldt.

On the North Sea coast — LXXXVIII Corps (General Hans Reinhardt) covering from the River Scheldt to the Dutch/German border.

The Atlantic coast of south-west France was under the control of General Kurt von der Chevallerie's First Army, which, together with France's Mediterranean coast, came under Army Group G (General Johannes Blaskowitz). The composition of First Army in May 1944 was LXXX Corps and LXXXVI Corps, plus 11th Panzer Division in reserve.

Within the area from the Spanish/French border to the island of Schiermonnikoog in the West Frisians, some 15,000 bunkers were to have been built. However, by June 1944 only about two-thirds (10,300) had been completed, with a further 800 still under construction.[4]

The Netherlands

The commander of all German troops in the Netherlands (Fortress Holland) was Luftwaffe General Friedrich Christiansen, known as 'Krischan', one of the very few Air Force officers who became a theatre/country commander. In fact, Rommel's Armeegruppe B dealt direct with General Hans Reinhardt's LXXXVIII Corps (374th and 719th Infantry Divisions and 16th Luftwaffe Field Division), which was responsible for the 'Wall' from the River Scheldt to the Dutch/German border. In addition, one of the divisions of Fifteenth Army was stationed in the Netherlands, namely 70th Infantry Division, which had been formed on Walcheren in 1944. It was given the nickname of the 'Whitebread Division' because so many of its soldiers had stomach problems, they

needed special rations. Nevertheless they would fight extremely bravely when attacked by the British and Canadians in November 1944 (see Chapter 10).

In the north, the coastline was protected by the West Frisian and Wadden Islands, which masked the Waddenzee and Ijsselmeer, making it difficult to get to the city of Amsterdam. Den Helder at the northern end of the North Holland peninsula was declared a fortress on 8 July 1942 so was heavily fortified. It had long been a naval base, whilst just to its east was Den Oever at the western end of the Ijsselmeer Barrier Dam which had been completed in 1932. At that time defensive works, including road blocks, had been built, plus nearly 20 bunkers, earthworks and such like at Kornwerderzand. The Germans constructed three additional bunkers here and also more to guard the eastern end of the dam.

Further down the coast Ijmuiden had also been declared a fortress as had the Hoek van Holland so there were many fortifications. Between the Hoek and Rotterdam, the island of Rozenburg had some formidable coastal batteries defending the seaway to Rotterdam. Finally there was the island of Walcheren — on which Vlissingen (Flushing) had been given fortress status — and the area of Zeeuws-Vlaanderen. For the civilian population, the worst consequence was the growing number of forced evacuations, such as that of most of the inhabitants of Walcheren. The German fixed defences on Walcheren were formidable, with 18 major coastal batteries, supplemented inshore with field artillery weapons and anti-tank guns. Many of the farm houses had been made into strongpoints with all the usual field defences, including minefields and flame-throwers. At Vlissingen there were torpedo batteries. The garrison was 10,000 men strong. Backing up the land garrison was a flotilla of some 85 small warships, again mainly based at Vlissingen. The Walcheren fortifications and the other defences held the key to the opening up of the Scheldt estuary which would unlock the major port of Antwerp.

The forced evacuations of civilians from the coastal areas continued, being especially serious in the densely inhabited coastal zone around Rotterdam and The Hague. Thousands of civilians had to move and many buildings were demolished. This caused great unrest, especially as the rumours were that a 50km belt of fortifications was to be constructed in the coastal area. Fortunately this turned out to be an exaggeration. The local inhabitants were, however, forced to work in helping to build fortifications.

Over 60 sites had batteries where coastal artillery guns were located, of varying calibres up to 24cm.

Naval Artillery

There were seven naval artillery detachments (201–206 and 607) and six naval AA detachments (246, 703, 808, 810, 813 and 816), plus two port protection flotillas, four river flotillas and a boom defence flotilla (Netzsperrflotille) stationed in the Netherlands.

Belgium

As in the Netherlands, the Atlantic Wall on the Belgian coast comprised many bunkers and field works, backing up the 37 battery sites along the 65km of North Sea coast. The great port of Antwerp and other ports such as Blankenberge, Zeebrugge, Ostend and Nieuport (there were a total of 15 in all) were all protected by permanent fortifications and became 'Defensive Areas' (Verteidigungsbereich — VB) whilst the areas in between got much less attention. This, for example, reduced the number of bunkers built in Flanders to 160 (from a planned 399). In the

Right:
Inside one of the infantry Gruppe bunkers, designed to hold a squad/section of 10 men. Note the racks for their rifles, steel helmets and personal equipment, the two-tier bunks and the coal/wood-burning stove, also the electric light. Their only 'pin-up' appears to be Adolf Hitler! The bunker was at Zeebrugge. *Bundesarchiv*

Below:
This bunker was clearly for work not relaxation. It was probably a coastal artillery control post. Its location was Calais and the photo was taken in July 1943. *Bundesarchiv*

Top: Loading an ex-Czech 4.7cm Pak 36(t) inside a casemate. The anti-tank gun is mounted co-axially with an MG37(t), both having been acquired from the Czech Army. *IWM — HU29046*

Above: Fortunately for the Allies, this was the sort of tank in the front line, that is to say, 'on the beaches', namely a static French Somua S-35, located close to the French/Belgian border, presumably guarding a minefield gap. In its day this cavalry medium tank was one of the best with an all cast turret and hull. However, by 1944 its 47mm gun was no match for Allied tanks. *Ken Bell, National Archives of Canada PA143907*

Left: One of the major bones of contention between Rommel and other senior commanders was who had control over the panzers — such as these PzKpfw V Panthers photographed near Bayeux. Had Rommel been able to get them down to engage the Allied landings, then things might have been very different. *Author's collection*

end only 50% of the anticipated total were ever built and the hinterland was protected merely by barriers and small infantry bases. Rommel's inspection tour (on 21 December 1943) highlighted the shortcomings in this area.

Naval Artillery

There was a naval artillery detachment at Ostend.

France

Being the largest country in Western Europe, with long sea coasts both on its northern Channel coastline and on its western coasts which were washed by the Atlantic, France was not only a major problem because of its size but also because certain parts of its coastline were clearly the most likely invasion locations, in view of their proximity to the probable Allied departure ports in the south of England. For convenience we will consider this part of the Wall in two areas: the Channel coast and the Atlantic coast.[5]

The Channel Coast

This was clearly an obvious target area. However, due to the fact that the Germans had no knowledge of the revolutionary prefabricated Mulberry Harbours, they concentrated their main efforts in the fortress areas as already listed. In Northern France, the fortresses of Dunkerque, Calais, Boulogne and Le Havre were all well protected, with the Pas de Calais area, encompassing Calais and Boulogne, having several heavy and super-heavy batteries, the best known being the following four heavy naval batteries:

- Batterie Lindemann — just to the south of Sangatte (now of illegal immigrant camp fame) near Cap Blanc Nez, with its Fire Control Tower (Marinepeilstand) and three massive naval turrets in casemates known as Anton, Bruno and Caesar, each containing a 40.6cm SKC/34 naval gun, making it one of the most powerful batteries on the whole Atlantic Wall.
- Batterie Grosser Kurfürst — was at Framzelle on Cap Gris-Nez, with four 28cm SKL/50 naval guns.
- Batterie Todt — slightly further down the coast at Haringzelles, with four 38cm SKC/34 naval guns.
- Batterie Friedrich August — slightly inland and south-east of Todt at La Tresorerie, with three 30.5cm SKL/50 naval guns.

These massive gun positions would all be captured by the Canadians.

In addition, there were other gun batteries in the area, some in casemates, others in open emplacements, plus bunkers, infantry strongpoints and other defences all along the coast, beginning at Bray-Dunes just across the border from Belgium, whilst inland there were more bunkers for radars and V-weapon sites. Dunkerque's defences circled the town and included a variety of flak batteries, then extended down to Loon-Plage some 5km along the coast. This particular fortress would be not be captured when neighbouring Calais and Boulogne were taken by the Allied advance in the summer of 1944 and it would have the doubtful distinction of being the last French town to be liberated on 10 May 1945. Calais was heavily bombed by the RAF in late September and then captured by the Canadians. In the Boulogne area at Wimereux (5km north) there was still a bunker from which, it is said, Hitler was to have watched Operation 'Sealion' in 1940. Festung Boulogne had been one of the first places to be designated as a fortress by the Führer and the town was ringed with gun batteries — both artillery and flak — infantry strongpoints and resistance nests. It had a

garrison of about 10,000 men who would fight tenaciously despite being mainly from second-class fortress units.

Below Boulogne was Dieppe, which had of course already been the subject of an Allied seaborne assault. Dieppe never received fortress status, but was nevertheless well protected — perhaps the Germans thought that, as the Allies had tried once before and thus knew the ground, it would be a likely invasion location. However, it was to be surrendered without a fight to the Canadians in September 1944. From Dieppe southwards, the high cliffs formed a natural barrier against any assault as far as Festung Le Havre which protected the mouth of the Orne river. It was one of the best-defended of the fortresses on the Atlantic Wall, with a total of 15 gun batteries (eight Navy, four Army and three Air Force Flak) with battery positions, radar bunkers, beach defences, fire control towers and so on, from Fécamp north of Le Havre down to Deauville and Riva Bella on the coast north-west of Caen. One of the heaviest batteries defending Le Havre was the 38cm naval gun at Le Grand Hameau, which had a range of some 22 miles, covering the mouth of the Orne river.

Lower Normandy

Next came that part of Normandy in which the Allies would eventually strike. The area from the Calvados coast to the Cotentin peninsula and Festung Cherbourg is well known and will be covered in more detail in later chapters. Suffice it now to highlight just two of the most important batteries, firstly the Merville battery (thought to be four 15cm guns) which was sited about half a mile inland, from where it could have done serious damage to the British landings on Sword Beach, so had to be taken out by an airborne assault in the early hours of D-Day. The second was the battery at Pointe du Hoc which was assaulted by the US 2nd Ranger Battalion on D-Day. The size of the guns was not massive — six 155mm French howitzers, four in open emplacements and two casemated — but their 23km range meant that they could reach both the Omaha and Utah Beach approaches effectively, so they had to be dealt with as a priority.

Cherbourg at the top of the Cotentin peninsula was another designated fortress, protected by a considerable number of heavy batteries and strongpoints from Framville to Gerville-Hague. It would take the Americans until 27 June before the port was captured, only for them to find that the port's facilities had been so completely destroyed that it could not be used for some time. The Cotentin peninsula itself was crowded with V-1 and V-2 installations, including assembly plants and launching sites, whilst in Upper Brittany was the fortress of St Malo, again ringed by defences and with a garrison of some 12,000, who once more would prove a tough nut to crack, the Citadel and the Isle of Cezembre holding out longest, even when shelled by British battleships.

The Atlantic Coast

On the Atlantic coast was France's oldest naval base — Brest — again heavily protected, as it was now the most important German naval base in France, being ringed by at least 20 coastal batteries and flak positions. Its massive garrison of some 35,000 was under the command of tough paratrooper General Bernhard Ramcke, who would hold out until 19 September 1944. Ramcke was awarded both the Swords and Diamonds to his Knight's Cross during the siege. The U-boat base at Lorient meant that it too was given fortress status, as was St Nazaire, so both were well defended. Both were 'sealed off' by the Americans and would be left until the end of the war without being assaulted, so as to reduce the number of unnecessary Allied casualties. Both fortresses were nevertheless regularly

Above: Batterie Kerbonn near Brest, photographed in 1941. The machine gun is covered, presumably to protect its working parts from the salt air. *Hans Sippli*

bombed. Finally there were the ports/naval bases of La Rochelle, La Pallice, Gironde, Bordeaux and Bayonne facing the Bay of Biscay. La Rochelle, together with the islands of Ré and Oleron, plus the U-boat base at La Pallice, made a formidable fortress with such gunpower as the Karolla battery on the Île de Ré, which comprised two of the gun turrets from the unfinished cruiser *Seydlitz*, both mounting two 20.3cm naval guns with a range in excess of 30km. It would be sealed off by American and Free French troops, then subjected to regular bombing raids until mid-April 1945, when the fortress would be finally taken.

Naval Artillery

The German naval organisation in France was enormous, with numerous naval artillery detachments and naval AA artillery detachments located at the ports and naval bases all along the coast from the Belgian border down to Spain. Some of those that still remain and can be visited will be covered in a later chapter.

The Channel Islands

Nowhere on the Atlantic Wall was there a greater concentration of German forces on the ground than in the Channel Islands, where 319th Infantry Division — the strongest division in the entire Heer — was located, together with numerous Kriegsmarine personnel, especially manning the naval batteries, and Luftwaffe personnel manning anti-aircraft guns. By way of example, here is the personnel strength on the three main islands just three months after D-Day, when the islands still expected to be invaded at any moment:

BRANCH OF SERVICE	GUERNSEY	JERSEY	ALDERNEY	TOTAL
Army — Infantry	4,150	3,900	800	8,850
Anti-tank	430	360	–	790
Tank	180	130	20	330
Artillery	520	820	70	1,410
Coast artillery	1,130	1,120	150	2,400
Engineers	90	360	10	460
Signals	180	120	70	370
Supply	720	1,150	200	2,070
Air Force	1,850	1,450	1,050	4,350
Navy	1,420	1,890	150	3,460
Construction Troops	310	150	150	610
Total	10,980	11,450	2,670	25,100

As far as large coastal batteries were concerned, there were a total of five on Alderney, 15 on Guernsey and eight on Jersey. The largest was Batterie Mirus of four 30.5cm guns on Guernsey, the guns being from the Imperial Russian Navy battleship *Imperator Alexandr Troti*. Also on the islands were the massive Marinepeilstände (observation towers), for fire control, some of which still remain complete today. In addition to coastal batteries and observation towers there were many smaller fortifications, because as will be remembered, the Channel Islands had one of Hitler's fortification orders all to themselves.

Army Group B

By the spring of 1944, Army Group B comprised:

Fifteenth Army — four Army Corps: LXXXI, LXXXII, LXXXIX and LXVII Reserve Corps.
Seventh Army — initially three Army Corps: XXV, LXXIV and LXXXIV, plus later II Parachute Corps.
LXXXVIII Corps — in the Netherlands.

As D-Day approached more reinforcements reached the divisions within these corps. Some were also refitted and regrouped, whilst others — mainly the reserve divisions — were still training. Another significant change was that, within the OB West area, the tank strength doubled — from 752 in early January 1944 to 1,403 by the end of April. There were in total 16 infantry and parachute divisions, 10 armoured and mechanised divisions, together with 25 coastal and seven reserve divisions, making up the 58 divisions in OB West. The panzer, mechanised and parachute divisions would clearly prove to be the most difficult opposition for the assaulting forces. However, it would be the coastal divisions that they would meet first, and, although they would be fighting from well-prepared defensive positions sited on ground which they knew well, in some cases their fighting ability was suspect. There appeared also to be little depth and no proper second line of defence once the coastal crust had been penetrated.

Fifteenth Army

Within the four army corps there were 14 infantry divisions and three Luftwaffe field divisions: six infantry and two

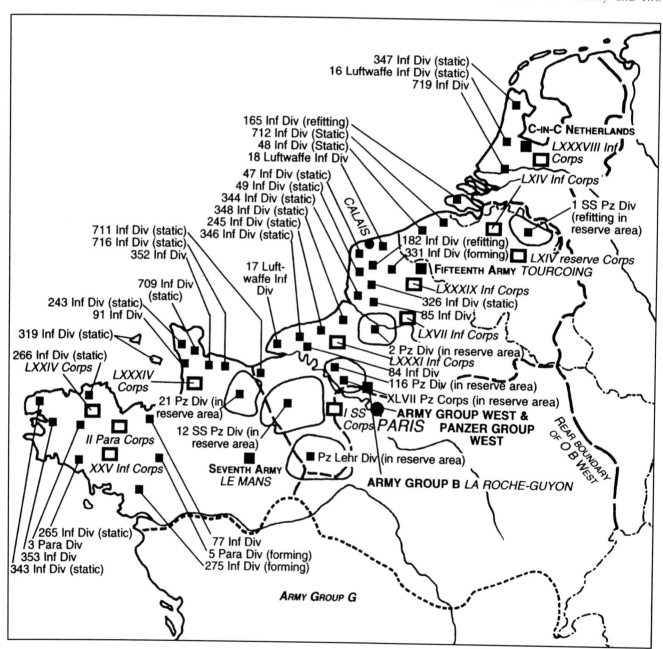

Above: Army Group B dispositions prior to D-Day.

Luftwaffe in the front line on the coast; eight infantry and one Luftwaffe in the hinterland. Generaloberst Hans von Salmuth, the army commander, was a highly experienced officer, who had initially received a monumental telling off from Rommel as we have seen, but thereafter was one of his strongest supporters. HQ Fifteenth Army was located at Tourcoing. The outline organisation of Fifteenth Army as at 6 June 1944 was:

LXXXI CORPS	LXXXII CORPS	LXXXIX CORPS	LXVII CORPS
84th Infantry Division	47th Infantry Division*	48th Infantry Division	49th Infantry Division*
245th Infantry Division	182th Infantry Division	165th Infantry Division	85th Infantry Division
346th Infantry Division	331st Infantry Division	712th Infantry Division	326th Infantry Division
348th Infantry Division*	18th Luftwaffe Field Division*	19th Luftwaffe Field Division	344th Infantry Division*
711th Infantry Division*			
17th Luftwaffe Field Division*			

Notes
* These were front-line divisions, the remainder being located initially in depth.

Not shown above is the sixteenth front-line infantry division of Fifteenth Army, the 70th Infantry Division, which was on Walcheren Island and has already been mentioned under 'Netherlands'.

Seventh Army

Rommel's other Army was the Seventh and within it were three, later four, army corps, containing a total of 15 divisions. The army commander was a highly experienced, but corpulent, artilleryman, Generaloberst Friedrich Dollmann, who disapproved of Hitler's methods. He would die of a heart attack in his HQ at Le Mans on 29 June 1944, just two days after the loss of Cherbourg for which Hitler had demanded his dismissal. However, both von Rundstedt and Rommel had refused to sack him and Dollmann died before he could hear of his Führer's demand. Rommel wished to promote General Erich Marcks, then the very able commander of LXXXIV Corps, who was immediately available within Seventh Army, but Hitler did not approve for political reasons. Instead he chose Obergruppenführer der Waffen-SS Paul Hausser, then commanding II SS Panzer Corps, to replace Dollmann.

It was to be the forward units of Marcks' LXXXIV Corps which would face the initial Allied onslaught. On 6 June 1944, the outline organisation of the Seventh Army was:

XXV Corps	LXXIV Corps	LXXXIV Corps	II PARACHUTE Corps
265th Infantry Division	77th Infantry Division	243rd Infantry Division	91st Air Landing Division‡
275th Infantry Division	266th Infantry Division	319th Infantry Division*	2nd Parachute Division‡
343rd Infantry Division	353rd Infantry Division	352nd Infantry Division	3rd Parachute Division
		709th Infantry Division	5th Parachute Division
		716th Infantry Division	

Notes
* In the Channel Islands
‡ Still forming

Manning the Wall

An Artilleryman

'*On the 5th of October 1943, at the age of 17 years and one month, I was called up for RAD labour service, then afterwards on 24 January 1944, I went to the 11th Replacement Battalion in Leipzig, where I was trained as an infantryman, but I was then sent to 275th Artillery Regiment at Redon in France. Redon, some 65km south-west of Rennes, was where I retrained as a gunner on the heavy field howitzer 18 [15cm schwere Feldhaubitze 18], then in the intelligence section and after that as an arithmetician with an artillery surveying squad. Having acquired all this knowledge, I was assigned to the 'VB' Vorgeschobner Beobachter[6] — an advanced observer, a lieutenant, at the Atlantic Wall.*'

That is how Harry Haendler began a letter to me about his job whilst on the Wall. He continued:

Above: An advanced artillery observation officer (a 'VB' see Harry Haendler's reminiscences) and his telephone operator, transmitting fire orders to the gun battery from their OP. The VB in the photo belonged to Elefant Batterie of 7./HKAR 1265 stationed in Guernsey. *Ludwig Spath via Guernsey Museums and Galleries*

'The bunker was underground, well equipped and protected by a 5cm Pak 38 L/60 anti-tank gun and a machine gun, which were part of an infantry base with a garrison of 15 men. They also used it as their living quarters. Our VB-Stand [advanced observer position] was in this bunker, but we artillerymen had our living quarters in a villa about 100 metres away, directly at the edge of the sea. We got our rations from the infantry, but the food was not particularly good, after all, we were in the fifth year of the war. However, life was agreeable for us artillerymen, as we could speak on an external line to our battery and could amuse ourselves on the beach. We also had to ram posts into the ground around the position which were then connected by wire — the "Rommel Asparagus" as they were called — to protect us from airborne troops landing. There were three of us in the VB-Stand — the lieutenant, a lance-corporal and myself.

'Our gun positions were located about 6–8km away in a gigantic concrete bunker. Our regiment was horse-drawn. We practised firing out to sea, observing the impact positions of the shells and making corrections. We didn't use moored targets. My job was to transmit the fire orders to the guns from our VB. Our Regiment was part of 275th Infantry Division and a few days after D-Day, on 10 July, we were transferred to Normandy, where I was wounded by a shell splinter through my nose during the Falaise battle.'

In his book *Hitler's Legions* Samuel Mitcham describes 275th Infantry Division as consisting of just 'the divisional staff, one regimental staff, one artillery unit (Harry Haendler's 275th Artillery Regiment), two battalions of "old men" and little else'. So the area in which they were located initially had to be bolstered with another regimental staff and one battalion from 343rd Infantry Division, together with two more battalions from the previously withdrawn 243rd Infantry Division. It also contained 27 companies of fortress cadre troops, seven 'Eastern' battalions, a Russian bicycle detachment, a Russian engineer company and a Russian cavalry regiment, the latter being on loan to the Normandy sector to help install minefields there — quite a mixture! They were sent to the fighting in Normandy to replace the exhausted Panzer Lehr Division, but were practically annihilated by the American breakout operation (Operation 'Cobra'), then reduced even further in the Falaise pocket and finally listed as 'destroyed' by the commander of Seventh Army. What was left of the division was then taken out of the line and rebuilt. It then went on fighting and took part later in the battle of Hürtgen Forest and finally ended the war in Czechoslovakia.

An Infantryman

'At the beginning of 1944, as a young soldier of 17 and a half, I joined the new 275th Division in Brittany. This division was raised in the area of St Nazaire and Redon, then deployed to protect the coast.'

That is how infantryman Roland Fischer began his reminiscences. He continued:

'At first I was assigned to a *Schützenkompanie* [rifle company] near Pontchâteau, but as signalmen were lacking I was later selected, with a comrade, and sent to Redon for training. This was also the headquarters of the division. During March and early April I was in the little town of Redon. Spring was beautiful then and we were always glad to get outside. Everything was turning green, but the great number of soldiers and the bad news from other fronts reminded us of the war. We were on the outskirts of the little town in separate shacks. Here we lived, ate and also had our lessons — in the morning signal training, in the afternoon infantry training. In addition we had lectures, cleaned our guns and our boots and mended our uniforms. Our lunch breaks were sometimes shortened as we had to dig trenches behind the shacks. By evening we were dead tired after all the physical strain. And, when at roll call, something was not tidy enough, then you had to do punishment drill on top of everything else. I had good comrades and we helped each other. My best friend from Plauen [Saxony] was afterwards killed in Normandy.

'The food was good. As most of us were under 18 we got some additional food. Artillery units were stationed near the town and there, on the outskirts, was a canteen. Sometimes in the evening I went there to buy something. Later I helped a Feldwebel [sergeant]. I got the meals for him and he always tipped me.

'Here at Redon, there was a divisional band, which sometimes played during the day. When the weather was fine and the windows open, we listened to the nice melodies. One day, during weapon training, I hadn't paid attention and gave wrong answers. I was sent out to run around the shacks. As I was a good runner that didn't bother me. I stopped at a corner and listened to the music. Finally I heard my name being called and ran back. When I was asked where I had been, I answered: "the song — La Paloma — sounded too sweet." Fortunately the NCO just smiled. Another time we had sharpshooting, which took place in a quarry outside the town. We had to march there. When it was my turn to fire I was lucky and was judged to be the best marksman, so the officer on duty allowed me to have some time off. I walked alone through Redon that morning. In time one got used to the duty rota. I like to think back to Redon, a pleasant little town with friendly people and I also remember the nice spring days of 1944.'

After Redon, Roland's company moved to the St Nazaire area, marching from Pontchâteau to Herbignac and then to a little village called Ferel. He was billeted in a school and had his first view of primitive country toilets:

'I was surprised. There was only a hole in the floor and a hook for paper. I asked someone: "Did they tear off the toilets?" He answered: "No, that's what they are like here in France, in the country."

'Now we had different training — cross-country route marches and fieldcraft mostly. The countryside was flat and criss-crossed with bushes. The weather was fine, most of us were young and cheerfully we sang the song of the infantry.'

It was from here that Roland had been sent back to Redon to train as a signaller and after six weeks he returned and was posted to the area around St Nazaire for more special training. This completed, he went back across the Loire and for a time was stationed in WN 67 (Widerstandnest 67) — a pocket of resistance:

'Everyday life was now quieter for us, we had lessons most of the time. The signal training took place as normal and when we had to encode messages I was quicker than the others. One day I had to report to an officer for a special task. I had no idea what I might have to do. I was given a message which I had to take to headquarters. I went there on my bike. I showed my pass and was allowed to enter a great quarry. This was the Signals HQ of St Nazaire. I was much surprised. After I had delivered the message I went back into the town and, as I had been given half a day's leave, I had a good look at the submarine bunker. It was just amazing especially when I stood in the big hall directly in front of a submarine. Friendly sailors smiled at me and I thought that they could go away to sea for weeks at a time — this seemed horrible to me.

'But now we went back across the Loire — by ship — I did not foresee that 30 years later a gigantic bridge would span the river. Now we were brought into action in the Atlantic Wall in the area of St Michel-Chef. In the bunker, there were three bunk beds, mine was the uppermost. It was like living in a submarine. We lived in cramped conditions, but a young man can quickly learn to cope with such circumstances. The village was still partly inhabited. Non-locals came there to do different jobs. Before entering the village they had to pass through a roadblock. This was our first task, we had to be sentries. So at the age of 17, I stood at the roadblock with a steel helmet and a rifle. The workers showed me their passes in the morning. I could only read their names and birthdays, all the rest was incomprehensible to me. I was controlled by a superior and had to report all military incidents.

'In the village, which had been a former health resort, there was a rather large shop for the inhabitants, workers and soldiers. All kinds of things could be bought there and from time to time I went there with a comrade. I got myself a German–French phrase book from which I learnt all the necessary words. I can still recall this well-thumbed booklet with lines under the terms I had tried to remember — greetings, talk, thanks, numbers, food, etc. We could walk on certain parts of the beach and once I was given a letter by an NCO, who then described the place where I had to hand in this letter. But I couldn't find it. Then a bit further on under some trees, I saw a house where a soldier was standing outside. I went in his direction and called to him. He shouted "Halt! There are mines!" He then approached me zig-zagging. I gave him the letter and learned that I had walked into a minefield. A week ago there had been an accident there — one soldier's leg had been blown off. I ran back trembling.

'One weekend I was detailed for staff guard. As the house was some 12km away I was given a bicycle. I had always liked cycling at home and so it was a nice change for me to ride through the beautiful countryside. Here among the bunkers we were trained as signallers and did guard duties. Now and then we got letters from home, from my mother, from friends in our village. This post and the lovely summer weather helped us to keep up our morale but what would happen? I often talked with comrades. Will the Allies attack France? There were so many rumours. But no one knew anything definite.

'Then, all of a sudden, the moment came. Early on the morning of the 6th of June 1944, the invasion of Normandy began. With us there was alarm everywhere, we had to be ready for possible action. Will they attack Brittany? For the time being nothing happened. The next day it was my 18th birthday. My sergeant came and congratulated me and gave me the day off . . .

'Then for some time I was transferred to another bunker, opposite the cemetery, where I had to work in a radio station with another soldier. He was from Danzig and often told me about his home. We would sit in the gathering dark and talk. I liked to eat cheese, but once when I looked at it closely I saw it was full of maggots — that made me lose my appetite! In front of the bunker there were several trenches. One evening, I was standing in one of them shaving, when I heard something rustling in a corner — it was a pack of rats. "What are you doing here? Be off!" I hissed at them and for the time being they ran away. I made haste to finish and as I went down into the bunker, the rabble of rats came round the corner again . . .

'Soon afterwards the alarm was given to our Regiment 985. We got our marching orders after the other two regiments — 983 and 984 had already left for Normandy. First of all we concentrated at Savonay to make final preparations. We, the signallers, went there with three infantry carts, I marched along the route with a horse. For three days we camped there in tents at the edge of a wood. Our equipment was checked and unserviceable items replaced. Unnecessary things were thrown away, the regimental library was broken up and whoever wanted to could get himself a few books. I was of course interested as I had grown up with books since my childhood. I filled my knapsack and bags with books. Soon after that our regiment marched towards Normandy. Horses pulled waggons with high loads. In between them the columns of soldiers marched. In front of our group was an older soldier. He began to sing "Fern bei Sedan" [Far away at Sedan] and we all joined in. Thus we marched into the night towards an uncertain fate.'

As already explained, Roland Fischer's division (275th Infantry Division) went into action in July, fighting in a battle in the area around St Lô, in the Department of Manche, to try to counter the American breakout (Operation 'Cobra'). Near Marigny his regiment was involved in a bitter engagement and he recalls there being a total of some 11,000 German casualties in that area. He was wounded and evacuated, but later in the autumn he was sent back to the Western Front again.

A Specialist Engineer

Gerard Koch was sent from Germany to the fortress 'Gironde South'. He was a member of a fortress engineer company (Festungspionierkompanie). He was in the construction platoon, but there were also some Goliathfahrer (Goliath drivers) attached. Goliath was a small remotely-controlled demolition tank, which was filled with high explosive. It could be used against tanks, pillboxes and such like. Gerhard was stationed at Soulac-sur-Mer and Motalivet was the southernmost point of their area. The garrison was withdrawn in July/August 1944.

A Naval Gunner

The last of these reminiscences of men who manned the Atlantic Wall comes from Hans Sippli, who lived — and still lives — in

Cuxhaven, where his father was a senior sergeant in the marine artillery, so he grew up in a naval atmosphere. He joined the Kriegsmarine between the wars and by the outbreak of war had completed several courses both as a recruit and as a naval artilleryman. He was a member of 4. Marineartillerieabteilung Standort Cuxhaven. Apart from an occasional 'Submarine Alarm!' which meant shooting into a designated grid square, they were not involved in any sea battles, but helped with the air defence (Flugabwehr) of Cuxhaven. Their first posting was to the island of Sylt. He did not remain a simple gunner for long, due to his previous training, and was rapidly promoted to MA-Gefreiter (lance-corporal of naval artillery). In May 1940 his battery left Sylt, moving first to the Netherlands then to Belgium, where he was stationed at the long mole of Zeebrugge. From there he went to Calais and in November 1942, he moved to Sète on the French Mediterranean coast: 'I felt odd walking around in the zone which had been unoccupied France until then,' he recalled.

'I attended a Schiessleiterlehrgang course at Toulon [learning how to direct the gunfire] by which time I was a MA-Oberfeldwebel mit Eignung zum Offizier [sergeant first class suited to become an officer] and was invited to attend a course for future officers, but instead I was captured on 23 August 1944.

'I found that performing one's duties in a fortress engaging targets out to sea (Seezielfestung) was boring. The battery had to be on the alert permanently and only two or three men could "go ashore" [leave the position] at a time. Even this was impossible when some of the crew were away in sick-bay or hospital. Besides, the forts were usually too far from the town to get there on foot. Senior officers and NCOs therefore had to take care that their men did not just become "zombies". It was definitely not enough just to know how to do one's job in the Leitstand [observation tower] so well that you could do it in your sleep, but it was also essential to keep up the men's morale by sports etc. As well as the occasional firing at targets moored to ships or towed by them, the instructors had to come up with more and more ideas.'

For a long time Hans was a Befehlsübermittler (that is one who transmits orders), a post known for short as a BUE. The BUE was connected to the Schiessleiter (the one who directs the fire) and who worked with another man who operated the range-finder (Entfernungsmessgerät). The orders were transmitted to the BUE who also got all the necessary information from the different artillery instruments, then worked out and passed on the appropriate fire orders to the guns. Finally, after getting the range of the target he would order 'Dauerfeuer' ('continuous bombardment').

The naval artillerymen wore grey uniforms when manning their guns. This was not the field grey of the Army but rather a grey-green colour with gold insignia rather than silver.

Below: This group of Atlantic Wall troops, from 736th Infantry Regiment of 716th Infantry Division which was located in the Caen area, are clearly *Osttruppen*, their Mongolian features being quite pronounced in some cases, whilst the officer with the pointer wears a shield on his sleeve which shows that his unit is from Turkistan. *J. P. Benamou Collection*

Life in Other Garrisons

'We know relatively little about how the German soldiers experienced their period of service at the fortified installations along the coast. Official documents allow us to describe the external framework of the soldiers' lives to a certain extent, but personal accounts by Germans stationed in Denmark during the Occupation are few and far between.'

That is how Jens Andersen opens a chapter about the daily life of German soldiers serving on the Danish part of the Atlantic Wall, in his book *The Atlantic Wall — from Agger to Bulbjerg*. He goes on to explain various aspects of their lives, commenting that in general terms there were often friendly relations between the local population and the soldiers, who were often invited into people's homes in small local communities, where it was 'difficult to regard the Germans as enemies — or to put it another way, the enemy had assumed a human face'. 'I did not have a single enemy here,' wrote Hermann Röndich, who was stationed at Lyngby,

'Every night, early in the morning or late in the evening I drove to Bedsted and back and I was never afraid . . . Our battery commandant, the Captain, was also very correct and proper in his behaviour. We had no problems or animosity with the population in Lyngby.'

Whilst relations with locals were generally good, the boredom and stress of being constantly ready for action in the more isolated defensive positions clearly affected some soldiers:

'The fact that so many soldiers were gathered together in one place with so little room and little chance of entertainment was bound to create tension and the men easily got on each other's nerves.'

In an interview in 1979, Heinrich Albrecht, who had commanded an Army coastal battery in Lyngby, gave an example of what he called men going 'bunker-mad' or 'dune-mad', explaining how one particular soldier had completely lost control of himself because of another man's snoring and had banged him over the head with a coffee pot, after which the whole crew of the bunker were suddenly at each other's throats. Albrecht had to fire a shot in the air from his pistol before he could get them to calm down. Those who could not compete with the boredom of course had an easy remedy — to volunteer for the Russian Front! Hardly surprisingly, most preferred the peaceful situation in the isolated gun sites to the dangers of front line service.

Foreign Visitors

Despite all its drawbacks and problems, Hitler was inordinately proud of his Wall and continually invited military missions from allied or neutral countries to inspect it, especially those fortifications built on the Channel coast. Von Rundstedt's chief of staff, Günther Blumentritt, says in his biography of his commander:

'In the west there was an increasing need to invite military missions from allied or neutral countries to inspect the Atlantic Wall. Hitler was very proud of his "Wall". One after another Turkish, Bulgarian, Hungarian, Finnish, Rumanian, Italian, Spanish and other missions arrived, with generals at their head.'

He goes on to say that von Rundstedt's international reputation imbued all these visitors with the desire at least to see him and, if possible, to talk to him. 'When the visitors arrived he was amiability itself and all foreign guests were charmed with him.' This was no mean feat as von Rundstedt had a very low opinion of the 'sacred' Atlantic Wall, openly describing it to his staff as being merely a 'propaganda bluff'.

Notes

1. Lucas, *The Last Year of the German Army*, using unit returns sent in to the Organisational Department of the Army High Command.
2. Lucas, *The Last Year of the German Army*
3. Extract from *Coast Fortifications in Denmark 1850–1945* by Peter Thorning Christensen
4. The area covered was of course not the *entire* Atlantic Wall — see page 36 for the total figures.
5. There was also the 'Southern Wall' built in southern France, to protect the areas Sète to Marseilles and Toulon to Nice. These have not been included in this survey, although, as will be seen from Hans Sippli's reminiscences, he did serve there for part of the time.
6. It was the Forward Observer, i.e. what the British Army calls a FOO or Forward Observation Officer, who acquired targets, passed details back to the gun positions and subsequently corrected their fire.
7. The leichter Ladungsträger (SdKfz 302) (E-Motor), to give its full title, weighed 0.37 tons and was just 1.5m long. As curator of the Tank Museum I had one which I used as a collecting box before we started to charge for admission. Children loved putting their money in it!

Above: 'Achtung Minen!' Troops at work laying a minefield. The tell-tale skull and crossbones sign was enough to make everyone careful, even if they couldn't understand the wording. *Bundesarchiv*

Right:
Army engineers mining a bridge over the canal at Troarn, south-east of Caen. *J. P. Benamou Collection*

Below left:
This is a Goliath (leichter Landunsträger) remotely controlled tracked demolition charge, still in its lair, being inspected by a British sergeant. Weighing around 0.4 tons, it was packed with explosive and was designed to blow up tanks or pillboxes or clear minefields. The remote control mechanism was, however, extremely delicate and many malfunctioned due to Allied shellfire. *IWM — B5115*

Below right:
An open, flanking emplacement for this 75mm field gun, on the French coast, gave it a good shoot along the beach, which was itself covered in rows of obstacles. *Bundesarchiv*

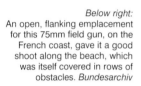

Right:
'Auf Wiedersehen Liebchen!' Members of the Wall garrison bid farewell to a painted lady in the make-believe window of this camouflaged building. *Bundesarchiv*

Below:
A 15.5cm Field Cannon 418(f) in an open mounting in northern France. As explained in Chapter 5, such guns were not subject to great damage when bombed — unlike those in concrete casemates — always provided the crew was properly protected. *Bundesarchiv*

Bottom:
A light anti-tank gun (probably a 4.2cm lePak 41), being manhandled out of its shelter and into its firing position. Photographed in northern France/Belgium during the early summer of 1943, it appears to be providing flank protection to a series of larger bunkers nearer the sea. *Bundesarchiv*

Chapter 9
D-Day — The Major Assault 'We Were Blind'

'The first indication that Normandy was threatened came in April 1944, from OKW. The sources of information were not known. Only then were reinforcements sent to Normandy. However, we did not know whether the invasion would take place only in Normandy or whether another would follow later in the Fifteenth Army sector. We knew that a large-scale exercise had been staged in England and that travel by diplomats and all leave had been cancelled. However, we did not know that the invasion was intended to be launched . . . for the following reasons:

(a) Our aerial reconnaissance did not get through and was able to bring back only scattered individual reports.
(b) On the sea, our E-boats and destroyers were too few to fulfil their mission.
(c) We had only five or six agents in England at the most.

Consequently we were "blind" and did not know what was going on more than a few miles beyond our coast.'[1]

The Waiting Game

Just prior to D-Day, Rommel had been doing his best to get the Führer to visit the Western Front, so that he could explain 'on the ground' the up-to-date situation and make him realise how short his Army Group was of both manpower and matériel. He also wanted to impress upon the Führer the vital need for Army Group B to be able to control the deployment of the panzer divisions in Geyr von Schweppenburg's Panzergruppe Oest. Rommel also wanted to acquire at least two more panzer divisions, a Luftwaffe flak corps and a Nebelwerfer brigade[2] for Normandy. However, when it became clear to him that Hitler would never come, Rommel decided to go to see him instead. He cleared this proposal with both von Rundstedt and Schmundt, the Führer's adjutant, and agreed a personal interview for 6 June. Interestingly it had been decided by OKW that the period 5–6 June would be an unlikely time for the Allies to contemplate any invasion, because the tides were unfavourable and none of the limited Luftwaffe reconnaissance reports had shown any obvious indication of pre-invasion action — but of course, as already explained, their capability was very limited. Rommel also wanted to go at this time for personal reasons as it was his wife's birthday on the 6th, so he could go to Berchtesgaden via his home in Herrlingen and see Lucie — admirable! However, as air travel had been banned for senior officers because of the danger from Allied aircraft, Rommel set off by car on the 5th and so was at home on the fateful night of 5/6 June.

On the other side of the Channel the Allies had been building up a massive Army in the United Kingdom, comprising many thousands of American, British, Canadian and other Allied troops with a vast array of state-of-the-art weapons, vehicles and equipment, backed up by a large number of Navy and Air

Force units, with an overall estimated total strength of more than three million men. Considerable lengths had been gone to, to keep Operation 'Overlord' as secret as possible, including the setting up of an entirely fictitious army group under the leadership of General George S. Patton. Operation 'Fortitude' was designed to convince the Germans that the actual main Allied landings would take place in the Pas de Calais area, opposite Dover, at the narrowest part of the English Channel. Patton was an integral part of the deception plan, because he had apparently 'disappeared' after the slapping incident in Sicily,[3] then reappeared in England. The Germans rated Patton as being by far the best Allied field commander at that time and found it totally illogical that he would be barred from army command for such a trivial reason. Thus he fitted the bill perfectly and the Germans believed that the network of dummy radio stations, dummy camps and storage depots and other facilities which had been built in south-east England and which their small number of recce aircraft had obviously seen, were in fact the main invasion force and aimed at the Pas de Calais area. The plan would work perfectly and the Germans would continue to expect a major landing in the Pas de Calais, whilst Patton would gleefully tell his Third Army troops in his own colourful way:

'I'm not supposed to be commanding this Army. I'm not even supposed to be in England. Let the first bastards to find out be the Goddamn Germans. I want them to look up and howl, "Ach! It's the Goddamn Third Army and that son-of-a-bitch Patton again!"'

Meanwhile, back in France, at HQ Fifteenth Army on the evening of 5 June, the headquarters radio intercept had, as normal, been carefully monitoring the BBC's coded broadcasts to the French resistance and had come to the conclusion that the invasion would take place at some time within the next 48 hours. Although the army commander, General von Salmuth, was not himself entirely convinced by his intelligence staff, he wisely put his army on full alert and authorised the sending of the following message to his corps headquarters and other relevant outstations, via the teleprinter link:

'Broadcast from BBC 21.15, June 5 has been processed. According to our available records it means: "Expect invasion within 48 hours starting 06.00 June 6."'[4]

This message was also sent to OB West, who passed it on to OKW.

Fifteenth Army did not, however, send the message on to HQ Seventh Army as they rightly expected Army Group B to do this. Further down the line within the Seventh Army sector, General Erich Marcks was in the command post of his LXXXIV Corps, where his staff had planned a small party to celebrate his 54th birthday. The party mood was, however, somewhat dampened because the intuitive, battlewise Marcks was very disturbed by enemy activity in his area and was not in the mood to celebrate. He was still there at 01.11hrs when the commander of 716th Infantry Division, Major-General Wilhelm Richter, suddenly reported on his field telephone link that enemy paratroops had landed east of the River Orne. A few minutes later, Marcks' chief of staff telephoned HQ Seventh Army and spoke to the army chief of staff, Generalmajor Max Pemsel, who passed on the information to General Speidel at Army Group B and then put Seventh Army on full alert. Pemsel later made further calls to Speidel in the early morning, to report seaborne landings.

At Rommel's HQ, Hans Speidel was in charge when the first reports came in about the paratroop landings near Caen and in

Below: The guns roar! The noise level must have been earsplitting both for those watching at sea and for those on the receiving end. A veritable storm of shells plastered the known enemy positions defending the landing beaches. The ferocity took the defenders by surprise, one gun emplacement after another being damaged or destroyed. *IWM — HU63686*

Below: This gun position clearly shows the effects of sustained naval gunfire. Note also the chalked sign 'clear of booby traps' near to the American military policeman and the pair of German 'jackboots' beside it. *IWM — EA27370*

the south-east of the Cotentin peninsula. Their strength and purpose were not immediately clear but he ordered all units to battle stations. Further reports of more paratroop landings followed between 03.00 and 04.00hrs. Speidel, however, remained sceptical about the landings, especially when Gummi-truppen (small size, but lifelike rubber models of paratroops dropped to cause confusion as they looked like real paratroops whilst they were descending) were being found. This reinforced his opinion that the Normandy assault was just a feint, designed to disguise the real landings that would come in the Pas de Calais area. Waves of Allied aircraft were now detected approaching the area and by 05.30hrs a heavy sea bombardment had begun. Coastal defences put into action their automatic defence measures and the codeword Operation 'Normandy' was sent out from HQ Army Group B and relayed down to field formations. Unfortunately for the defenders, the complete Allied air superiority prevented any visual confirmation of what was happening. Speidel rang Rommel at Herrlingen about 06.15hrs, explained the situation and told him what action he had taken. Rommel approved all the measures and told Speidel that he would return to La Roche-Guyon immediately. Cancelling his visit to Hitler, the Desert Fox was soon on the road, leaving home at about 10.30hrs with just his aide, Hauptmann Helmut Lang, and his driver Obergefreiter Daniel. Despite having to use side roads to avoid Allied aircraft, they were back safely at their headquarters by 20.00hrs.

As the reports of the Allied landings built up, von Rundstedt gradually came round to the conclusion that this was a major assault. Quite against his own standing orders, he began to release elements of Panzergruppe Oest and to move them forward. He even asked OKW to release more armour, but could not get an answer as Jodl was fast asleep and his staff did not dare wake Hitler, despite OBW's growing annoyance. Schmundt finally woke Hitler at about 09.00 and summoned Jodl and Keitel to give him a full briefing on the situation. Afterwards it was said that Hitler was quite happy about the invasion news, appearing eager to get to grips with the enemy. Still, however, no one could actually decide whether this was the real invasion or not. This pattern would continue throughout D-Day, with commanders at the sharp end taking the appropriate action, committing their forward troops to the battle, sending out reconnaissance to discover exactly what the enemy was doing, then inevitably requesting armoured support to help them deal with incursions that were too powerful for their limited resources. This was not easy even when permission had been given to release armour, due to the complete Allied air supremacy, which harried every daylight move.

The Allied Landings

The Allied seaborne landings had all taken place in the Seventh Army sector, British and Canadian troops having landed at three carefully selected beaches code-named Sword, Juno and Gold, all of which were located within the 716th Infantry Division's sector, roughly between Ouistreham in the east and Arromanches in the west. The American First Army had landed to the west in the 352nd Infantry Division's area between Vierville and Colleville — code-named Omaha Beach — then some 24km further west on Utah Beach around La Madeleine in the 709th Infantry Division area. The seaborne assault had been preceded by the dropping of airborne troops some four and a half hours before the first amphibious troops hit the beach, with the British 6th Airborne landing units to the east of the beachhead past Ouistreham, whilst in the west US 82nd and 101st Airborne Divisions landed north of Carentan around St Come-du-Mont and St Mère Église.

Left:
Troops carrying heavy weapons equipment wade through the surf in the Fox Red sector of Omaha Beach, where Company L of 16th Infantry found shelter before moving right to assault the F-1 strongpoint. *US Army via Real War Photos*

Right:
An old French 75mm field gun which was used part of the German defences on Omaha Beach area. The Canon de 75 mle 1897 was probably the most widely used light field gun ever produced. It even went on in worldwide service for many years postwar. *US Army via 1st Infantry Division Museum, Cantigny*

Left:
Bloody Omaha. Smoke from grass fires obscured the bluffs in a number of sectors, notably at Dog Red, as troops prepared to land. *US Army via Real War Photos*

Above:
Troops and civilian labourers
— presumably OT workers —
have been rounded up by two
GIs, one of whom is wounded,
on Omaha Beach. *US Army via
Real War Photos*

Left:
This captured enemy
blockhouse which protected
the E-1 draw (west side) has
become a temporary HQ for
the Engineer Special Brigade
Group. This unit operated
Omaha Beach as a port of
supply until December 1944.
Postwar, the blockhouse
became a battle monument.
US Army via Real War Photos

these 10 tanks — stand burning at the beach. The obstacle demolition squads have given up their activity. Debarkation from the landing boats has ceased; the boats keep farther seawards. The fire of our battle positions and artillery is well placed and has inflicted considerable casualties on the enemy. A great many wounded and dead lie on the beach. Some of our battle positions have ceased firing; they do not answer any longer when rung up on the telephone. Hard east of this pillbox, one group of enemy commandos (one company) has set foot on land and attacked Pillbox 76 from the south, but after being repelled with casualties it has withdrawn towards Gruchy.'[7]

The regimental commander then commented that he thought they had been successful in frustrating the enemy achieving a landing on a broad front, that the 'Moaning Minnies' at St Laurent had been most effective and that counter-measures were now being taken against enemy infiltrations in a couple of places. However, he also said that casualty figures were rising because of the continuous fire from naval guns and the off-shore landing craft, so he was in need of reinforcements. He also reported that the enemy had put in a strong commando operation against the main artillery battery position at nearby Pointe du Hoc, scaling the cliffs with rope ladders. He had sent an assault detachment of 40 men from St Pierre-du-Mont to retrieve the situation.

In fact as we now know, the landing on Omaha Beach was by far the least successful of any on D-Day, the troops of US V Corps being pinned down by the stiff resistance of 352nd Infantry Division and unable to make much progress. The enemy beach defences were certainly not dissimilar to those on Utah, but probably better co-ordinated, as the drawing of a typical area shows.

If the attacking troops were able to reach the shingle bank at the edge of the tidal sands, they would still have to cross the narrow shelf of flat beach in order to reach the low cliffs beyond. The defenders had made liberal use of wire and mines to slow up further movement beyond the shingle. Along most of the beach a row of concertina wire had been laid just to the landward side of the shingle; at the western end the wire was placed on top of the sea wall. Irregularly laid minefields — usually posted with warning signs — lay on the flat ground behind the wire and on the cliff slope and these included charges of TNT covered by rocks and set off by a tripwire. There were also some dummy minefields, though most were real. As the *Omaha Beachhead* recalls:

Below: German defences at Les Moulins, Omaha Beach. Source: US Army — American Forces in Action: Omaha Beach

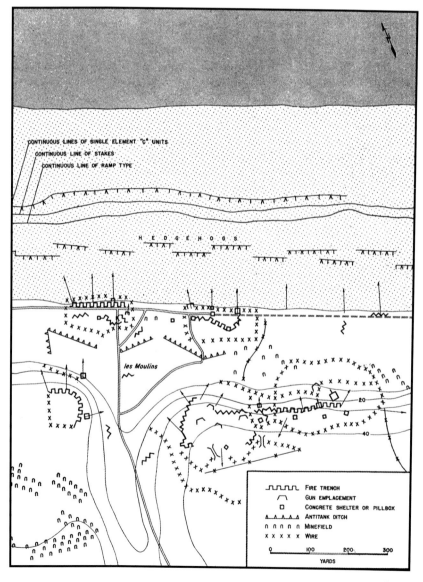

'Enemy firing positions were laid out to cover the tidal flat and beach shelf with direct fire, both plunging and grazing, from all types of weapons. Observation on the whole Omaha area and flanking fire from cliff positions at either end were aided by the crescent curve of the shoreline. The emplacements between Vierville and Pointe de la Percée were particularly dangerous because of their ability to deliver enfilade fire on a large stretch of the landing area. Each strongpoint was a complex system made up of elements including pillboxes, gun casemates, open positions for light guns and firing trenches surrounded by minefields and wire [see sketchmap]. The elements were connected with each other and with underground quarters and magazines by deep trenches or by tunnels. Most of the strongpoints protecting Omaha were situated near the entrance to the draws [gullies], which were further protected by antitank ditches and roadblocks. In some cases the elements of a strongpoint were echeloned from the north edge of the beach flat, with weapons sited for both grazing and plunging fire on every yard of approach to the draw. In June, the Germans were still in process of completing or strengthening several strongpoints . . .

'While machine guns were the basic weapons in all emplacements, there were over 60 light artillery pieces of various types. Eight concrete casemates and four open field positions were designed for guns of calibre from 75mm to 88mm; 35 pillboxes were occupied by lighter guns; and there were about 18 antitank guns (37mm to 75mm). The heavier guns were sited to give lateral fire along the beach, with traverse limited by thick concrete wing-walls which concealed the flash of these guns and made them hard to spot from the sea. Mortar positions were sometimes included in the strongpoints but were more frequently placed behind the bluffs. About 40 rocket pits were later found, located several hundred yards inland on the high ground and each fitted to fire four x 32cm rockets.

'The considerable areas between the strongpoints were supposed to be protected by their flanking fires, by minefields scattered on the beach flat and the slopes of the bluff, and by machine gun emplacements along the crest. While the line of defence was not continuous, no areas of the beach were left uncovered in the pattern of defensive fires. Nearly all weapons, machine guns as well as artillery pieces, were sited primarily to give lateral fires down the length of the beach, and the defence of a given sector usually depended as much on the flanking fire from neighbouring positions as on the emplacements in the sector itself.'

The account goes on to state that the Omaha sector was not strongly defended as far as coastal batteries of heavier guns were concerned. However, it makes a specific point of mentioning the battery of what was believed to be six French 155mm howitzers, partly mounted in casemates, at Pointe du Hoc, some 5,000m to the west.

'This position was regarded as the most dangerous in the American zone, for the guns of that calibre could cover not only the V and VII Corps landing beaches, but also both transport areas.'

There were other dangerous batteries, including some in the British landing zone (for example at Port-en-Bessin) which could also be a threat to the landings, but Pointe du Hoc was the most important and would have to be 'taken out' by a special Ranger force.

Someone who vividly remembers the beach defences at Omaha is Lieutenant Tony Carter of Wareham who was a member of the crew of the *Prins Leopold*, one of four Belgian cross-Channel steamers requisitioned by the Admiralty for service in Combined Operations as assault landing ships and fitted to carry seven LCA in davits, one of which he commanded on the run in. They had already taken part in the Dieppe raid, then Sicily, and now would carry the American Rangers to Pointe du Hoc, as will be recounted later. However, this is what he had to say about the beach defences:

'I still have quite a clear picture of these defences, although I cannot guarantee the accuracy of a memory that is over half a century old! The principal part of the defence consisted of rows of posts running out from somewhere below the high water mark, at right angles to the beach, in straight lines and angled at about 30° to the vertical, pointing to seaward. It was possible to turn an LCA round between the rows of posts, so the rows must

have been placed some 40 feet apart. Many of these posts had Teller mines wired to their tops. As we were coming in at low water, these were all above our heads. I am unable to remember seeing such posts, or their remains, on any of the other beaches that we visited in the weeks immediately after D-Day, but I expect they would have been systematically moved as quickly as possible. At the end of each of the avenues formed by the posts was a device we referred to as the 'five-barred gate' or 'Element C/Belgian Gate' as it was known officially. This was of course rather like a very large five-barred gate and it was also littered with Teller mines. We could not guess from the RAF photos that we were shown, whether there would be room to get an LCA round it and into an avenue. In the event, of course, we did, so I think this device must have been placed a little way out from the last posts in the avenues and I can remember having to carry out a sort of letter "S" manoeuvre to get in. That makes me think that the planners of the operation must have had a pretty good idea that this was possible, or there would have been some provision made for its destruction. When I returned to the beach, some 20 minutes after the initial landing, there was certainly no Element C and there was an LCI [Landing Craft Infantry] on the beach, so I imagine that she must have charged the device and destroyed it on her way in. I am unable to hazard a guess at the number of posts in each row, or their distance apart, although I am sure that no craft could have passed laterally between them. As for the length of each avenue, I could make a wild guess and say: "70-80 metres" but that could be very inaccurate.'

Landing on Omaha

'The landing craft came in under the comforting thunder of the tremendous fire support from naval guns as well as tank and artillery pieces firing from the LCTs. Up to within a few hundred yards of the water's edge there was every reason to hope that the enemy shore defences might have been neutralised. Then, many of the leading craft began to come under fire from automatic weapons and artillery, which increased in volume as they approached touchdown. It was evident at H-Hour that the enemy fortifications had not been knocked out.'

Undoubtedly many gun positions and strongpoints had survived the early fire, because rough seas, difficulties in observation in the smoke and dust, together with well-concealed emplacements, all made accurate fire difficult. In addition, and this greatly disappointed the leading assault troops, they discovered that the beach was relatively unscarred by the air bombardment. Overcast conditions had made things difficult for the Eighth Air Force Liberators, so, for safety reasons, the drop pattern had been pushed well inland. Nevertheless, some 446 aircraft were involved and over 13,000 bombs were dropped between 05.33 and 06.14hrs.

As on the other beaches the first wave, which landed just before 06.30hrs, was the Special Engineer Task Force and in certain sectors they suffered heavy casualties during landing. However, despite this, and under intense fire, they continued their demolition work, so that they achieved six complete and three partial gaps through all the obstacle bands. Casualties among the Special Engineer Task Force, including naval personnel, were 41% on D-Day, most of whom were hit during the first half hour.

Above: Canadian troops coming ashore on Juno Beach on D-Day. They were from the Stormont, Dundas and Glengarry Highlanders of the Canadian 9th Infantry Brigade and they landed at Bernières-sur-Mer. *Public Archives of Canada — PA122765*

'The infantry companies in the first wave came in by boat sections, six to a company, with an HQ section due in the next wave [07.00]. Each LCVP carried an average of 31 men and an officer. The 116th's assault craft were loaded so that the first to land would be a section leader and five riflemen armed with M-1s [carbines] and carrying 96 rounds of ammunition. Following was a wire-cutting team of four men, armed with rifles, two carried large "search-nose" cutters and two a smaller type. Behind these in the craft, loaded so that they landed in proper order were: two BAR [Browning Automatic Rifle] teams of two men each; two bazooka [anti-tank weapon] teams, totalling four men, the assistants armed with carbines; a mortar team of four men with a 60mm mortar and 15 to 20 rounds; a flame-thrower crew of two men; and, finally, five demolition men with pole and pack charges of TNT. A medic and an assistant section leader sat at the stern. Everybody wore assault jackets, with large pockets and built-in packs on the back; each man carried, in addition to personal weapons and special equipment, a gas mask, five grenades (the riflemen with the wire cutters also had four smoke grenades), a half-pound block of TNT with a primacord fuse and six and one-third rations (three K's and three D's). All clothing was impregnated against gas. The men wore life preservers (two per man in the 116th Infantry units) and equipment and weapons were fastened to life preservers so that they could be floated in.'

Few LCVPs and LCAs carrying assault troops were able to achieve a dry landing. Most grounded on sandbars 50–100m

out and in some cases the water was neck deep. They were under fire from about a quarter of a mile out, hearing the enemy fire beating on the ramps of the LCVPs as they came in and then the hail of bullets whipping through the surf just in front of the lowered ramps. Small-arms fire, mortars and artillery were all concentrated on them, but it was the converging fire from enemy machine guns which caused the most casualties. Men dived under the water or went over the sides of the landing craft, in an effort to escape the bullets:

'Stiff, weakened from seasickness and often heavily loaded, the debarking troops had little chance of moving fast in the water that was knee deep or higher, and their progress was made more difficult by uneven footing in the runnels crossing the tidal flat. Many were exhausted before they reached shore, where they faced 200 yards or more of open sand to cross before reaching the cover at the sea wall or shingle bank. Troops who stopped to organise, rest, or take shelter behind obstacles or tanks merely prolonged their difficulties and suffered heavier losses.'

It was a prime example of Rommel's oft-stated principle of the beach being the place to defeat the enemy and had this been repeated in all the other landing areas then Operation 'Overlord' might have been all over before it had properly

Above: Troops, tanks and other vehicles, having just landed, move along the beach towards a gap in the enemy wire. *IWM — B5070*

begun. In fact even on 'Bloody Omaha' there were areas where safer landings were possible. For example, several hundred metres of the low cliffs just west of the Les Moulins gully were completely obscured in heavy smoke apparently started by naval shellfire and rockets. This smoke prevented the Germans from being able to see their targets. It was the same in other 'blind spots', but they were few and far between, and undoubtedly the first wave was in the main badly hit, men being drowned as well as being hit by enemy fire. The first wave was thus held at the water's edge and subsequent waves made slow and painful progress. Indeed the 352nd Infantry Division was so convinced it had won that it advised higher headquarters that the 'Allied assault had been hurled back into the sea; only at Colleville was fighting still under way, with the Germans counter-attacking'. This reassuring view was sent up to army group. But it was not entirely accurate, being based more on wishful thinking than hard fact.

An eyewitness Staff Sergeant Harley A. Reynolds of St Petersburg, Florida, was then serving in Company B, 16th Infantry Regiment of 1st Infantry Division. He would later be awarded the Bronze Star, the French Médaille Militaire and Croix de Guerre and the Belgian Croix de Guerre, together with numerous other decorations, and was one of the first to hit the beach. As he recalled in a recording he made for the 1st US Infantry Division Museum at Cantigny:

'When the ramp went down we were in kneeling positions. Private Galenti, the radio man and I rose to exit first. At about the second or third step, I started to fan right. At this second Galenti was hit by what I believe was machine gun fire because there was more than one bullet. The radio was also hit and fragments flew from it. Galenti went down on the boat ramp. The fire seemed to come from our left front. I was maybe two feet ahead of him, saving me being hit by the same burst of fire. I don't recall getting my feet wet . . .

'I stayed to the right for a short distance. Looking for any cover, I headed for an obstacle made up of what appeared to be rails welded together. It reminded me of the Ball and Jacks we played as kids. The beach was very smooth here, showing the absence of shell holes we had been promised [to give the assault troops some cover from enemy fire]. I knelt by the obstacle to look around. From the craft to this point my constant thoughts were "What's keeping me up? I must be hit. What does it feel like when you get hit? Too many bullets flying not to be hit." While crossing the beach I felt tugs at my pants legs several times. Searching later I found too many rips and tears to identify as bullet holes. I think it is possible for bullets to pass close enough to tug at your clothing. Bullets coming so close make a hissing sound as they go by. Those you hear are not the ones that hits you . . .

'We reached the temporary shelter of the shingle and snuggled in between others already there. As the tide came in others crowded in to snuggle in with us. Our area of the beach seemed relatively safe, but only if you stayed prone behind the shingle. Many times after bursts of machine gun fire or shells landing, I called out to Sergeant Rummell and Sergeant Haughey, asking if they were OK and they said yes . . .

'Many times calls would sound out for company members. Efforts were being made to regroup without much success. One couldn't just answer: "Here", stand up and walk over to the caller. You couldn't even roll over to the man alongside. This would put you too high and you were sure to get hit. You had to crawfish backwards and side crawl like a crab with your head towards the roadbed. This didn't give you much protection and many men were hit while trying to shift along and regroup. Any movement seen above the roadbed would bring fire — rifle and machine gun. The tide was now almost lapping at our feet. Dead bodies were washing in and I'm thinking it's time to do something but what? Sticking your head up would draw fire. Occasional incoming artillery fire was

Top: HMS *Prins Leopold* en route for the beaches, carrying its force of US Rangers. *Lieutenant Tony Carter*

Top right: Aerial photograph of Pointe du Hoc showing the extent of its bomb cratered surface. *(US Army via 1st Infantry Division Museum)*

Right: Last lap of the climb up the cliffs by men from Colonel Rudder's LCA888. (US Army)

Above: Pointe du Hoc after the relief on D+2, when the Stars and Stripes had been spread out to prevent friendly fire from coming in from tanks inland of the captured gun position. Some German prisoners are being moved on after capture by the relieving force. *US Army via Real War Photos*

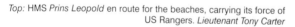

increasing. *There obviously was no way backwards, only forward. I began to raise my head up and down for real quick looks ahead. I could see a narrow pond ahead with marsh grass. Between us and the pond was a wire strung on the roadbed and beyond it a three strand wire fence with a trip wire only on the front of it. There was a sign on the fence that was in German, but two words I did understand: "Achtung Minen!"'*

The enemy fire from the beach pillboxes and other defences had now begun to slacken off somewhat and Harley decided that if they made the short dash across to the pond they could get to the base of the sheltering hill to their front — but how to get through the wire and minefield? Fortunately, they then had help from a new arrival who pushed a 4m bangalore torpedo under the wire on the roadbed. Harley recalled:

'Exposing himself to enemy fire he inserted the fuselighter, pulled the string to set it off, but it misfired. After a few seconds the man calmly crawled forward exposing himself again. He removed the bad lighter, replaced it with another and started to repeat his first moves. He turned his head in my direction, looked back, pulled the string and made only one or two movements backwards when he flinched. Death was so fast for him. His eyes seemed to have a questioning or pleading look in them. His head was maybe three feet from the explosion, but it didn't damage him. No fire from the Germans for a couple of minutes before and if only a couple of seconds later, who knows. My head was three to four feet from the torpedo and I was closest to the path it blew in the wire. Within two or three seconds I was up and thru the wire. My men were behind me better than we have ever done in practice. I went thru the trip wire high stepping just as we did on the obstacle course. I was running so fast that I hadn't made up my mind what to do about the wire fence until I faced it. I literally dove thru in a sideways dive. Hard to believe but I completely cleared those strands. Not one rip or tear in my clothes or skin. I was into the pond (on the other side of the wire) in under 10 seconds, with all my men except Schintzel and Galenti following [the former had been badly wounded on the beach and Galenti killed as he left the landing craft]. Troops on the beach seemed to be holding back but not for long. They almost beat us to the top of the hill.'

Having made it off the beach Harley began to move inland, meeting up with some paratroopers — and a fearsome German Tiger tank but fortunately it had already knocked out by the paras. He closed his graphic narrative by explaining that:

'With no other US troops ahead of our team we were the first through the wire in our area, and the biggest contributing factor to the surrender of the entrenchments west of E-1. This entrenchment controlled the beach and gave our greatest number of casualties . . . I have felt for years this story should be told while it can be substantiated. We won't live forever.'

Towards the middle of the morning the tide of battle began to change, large landing craft, despite the obstacles, forced their way to the beach and destroyers risked running aground in order to get closer and engage their targets more accurately. By last light, despite the fact that some 1,000 men had been killed

and many more had been wounded on Omaha and that they had not achieved their initial objectives, they had, nevertheless, advanced off the beach and were now holding grimly on to the villages of Vierville-sur-Mer, St Laurent and Colleville-sur-Mer, which controlled the east–west road. The GIs were determined to resist all counter-attacks.

The Rangers at Pointe du Hoc

As already mentioned, the most dangerous of all the enemy coastal batteries, as far as the troops landing on Omaha and Utah Beaches were concerned, was the one at Pointe du Hoc, where six 155mm howitzers of French origin were located, four guns in open emplacements and two casemated. Further construction work was under way. Their position was well defended from a seaborne assault by sheer rocky cliffs some 30m high, below which there was a narrow strip of beach without any cover whatsoever. The Germans reckoned the position was impregnable from the seaward side, whilst it was mined and wired on the landward side, with its flanks protected by two machine gun nests and an anti-aircraft gun on its west. A total of some 210 men garrisoned the position — 125 infantry and 85 gunners, all from 716th Infantry Division. The task of capturing the gun position was given to a Ranger group, comprising two battalions (2nd and 5th) under the command of Lieutenant-Colonel James E. Rudder. The outline plan was that three companies (D, E and F) of the 2nd Battalion (Rudder's

Below: Pointe du Hoc. *Source: US Army — Small Unit Actions*

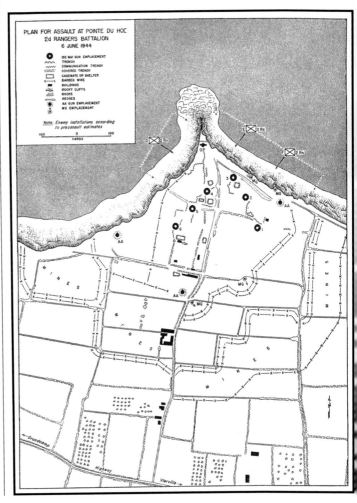

battalion) would land from the sea at H-Hour and assault the cliff position, whilst the main Ranger force (5th Battalion commanded by Lieutenant-Colonel Max F. Schneider, and Companies A and B of the 2nd Battalion) would wait off shore for a success signal, then land at the Pointe. The Ranger group would then move inland, cut the coastal road between Grandcamp and Vierville and await the arrival of 116th Infantry from Vierville before pushing on westwards.

If no word had been received by the support force by H+30, the larger Ranger force would land on the western end of Omaha Beach and proceed overland to Pointe du Hoc, avoiding all unnecessary action en route to its objective.

'After the briefing,' Tony Carter recalled,

'the ships were of course sealed and no one could communicate with the shore. Then came the delay caused by the bad weather and everyone taking part felt frustrated, having been keyed up for the operation after the long preparation. With all the Americans in the ship it was inevitable that poker schools broke out everywhere. The one in the wardroom was continuous with players leaving and others joining . . .

'Some time on the 5th June, we weighed anchor and proceeded eastwards up Channel in a great company of ships and at a very slow pace . . . It must have been some time before dawn that we had to stand to. The LCAs were lowered to deck level, the Rangers embarked and the trek to the beach started. I seem to remember that we had about eight to 10 miles to cover and I had absorbed all possible information regarding tidal set, wind strength and anything else that could affect our course to the exact spot on the beach. Boat compasses were swung and I was confident of finding the right place. But it was rough for an LCA. They are of wooden construction and armour plated. There is a small landing ramp in a square bow, behind which are steel, bullet-proof doors. The coxs'n stands in a small armoured turret on the starboard side forward and the boat has side decks covering the benches on which the troops sit. The stoker is in charge of the two V-eight petrol engines and the coxs'n can pass orders to him via an engine room telegraph. The armour plate makes the boat heavy and in a seaway the flat, square bow throws a lot of spray and sometimes solid water into the boat. LCAs had a speed of about 6–7 knots in smooth water. They had a low profile and in many ways were ideal for the job. The American equivalent were not armoured, powered by very noisy diesel engines and presented a much higher profile, but they were better seaboats.

'It must have been about half way between the ship and shore that we had to reduce speed as the pumps were unable to cope with the water coming aboard. By this time many of the soldiers were past caring what happened just as long as they got to shore, so they responded when I suggested that unless they took off their helmets and started baling we might not reach the shore. Soon after that, conditions started to improve as we began to come under the lee of the land.'

Fortunately all went well from then on and they reached the shore safely and dropped their load of Rangers, wishing them good luck — the lieutenant in charge of the troops telling Tony Carter that he really felt sorry for him having to go all the way back to the ship when he would be stepping ashore on solid land. Then, about half a mile from shore on their way back to the Prins Leopold, they found themselves in the middle of a group of soldiers in the water whom they quickly pulled aboard.

'They were from an American landing craft that had been following us in, when someone had operated the landing ramp accidentally. At full speed the boat immediately filled and sank. So we returned to the beach, where an LCI was just landing troops. To avoid the delay of beaching again, I decided to put the soldiers aboard the LCI. They made the shore in safety, but just as we were about to pull away again, I noticed that the LCI was carrying a deck cargo of petrol in jerricans and at the same moment she received a direct hit from a mortar shell. For a moment the whole boat was enveloped in flames, but we managed to pull clear without casualties.'

Tony Carter's LCA got back to the Prins Leopold safely that time, but a couple of months later the ship hit a mine halfway across the Channel and sank. Fortunately they were sailing in a convoy so the majority of the crew and passengers were rescued.

'In fact she was under tow by a tug when she finally went down. I had never realised that seeing your ship go down was like losing a close friend.'

Meanwhile, there had been some errors of direction among Colonel Rudder's column of LCAs, but these problems were overcome and they reached their objective safely but rather later than planned. The supporting naval fire had stopped before H-Hour, so the German garrison on Pointe du Hoc had had some 40 minutes to recover.

'As the LCAs neared the Point, they received scattered small arms and automatic fire, and enemy troops could be observed moving near the edge of the cliff. There was, however, no indication of artillery in action from the enemy positions. At 07.10 as the first craft were grounding under the cliffs, radio silence was broken to send Colonel Schneider the order for landing at Vierville. The message was acknowledged.

'The small assault force was not entirely alone as it came into a hostile shore. The British destroyer Talybont which had taken part in the early bombardment of Pointe du Hoc at a range of 2.7 miles, saw the flotilla heading off on the wrong course and found it difficult to understand as "Texas' [a US battleship] fall of shot on Pointe du Hoc was obvious." As the Rangers corrected course and came under fire from the cliff positions, the Talybont closed range and for 15 minutes [06.45–07.00] raked enemy firing positions with 4in and 2-pounder shells. Meanwhile, the US destroyer Satterlee, 2,500yd from Pointe du Hoc, could see enemy troops assembling on the cliffs and opened fire with main battery and machine gun fire.

'The Cliff Assault. The nine LCAs touched down on a front of about 500 yards, the right hand craft just under the tip of Pointe du Hoc, and the others spaced fairly evenly. No great distance separated some of the boat teams, but according to plan, they went into action as separate units, each facing its particular problems of escalade and opposition. In certain general respects, their problems were similar. The 30-yard strip of beach between the water and cliff had been completely cratered by bombs. The craters were to handicap the unloading of men and supplies and render the DUKWs useless after landing, for these craft were nowhere able to cross the sand and get close enough to the cliff to reach it with their extension ladders. The cliff face showed extensive marks of the naval and air bombardment; huge chunks of the top had been torn out, forming talus mounds at the base. A few grenades were thrown down or rolled over the edge as the first Rangers crossed the sand, and enemy small-arms fire came from scattered points on the cliff edge. Particularly damaging was enfilade fire, including automatic from the German position on the left flank of the beach. Once at the foot of the cliff the Rangers were better off, for the piles of debris gave partial defilade from the flanking fire and the enemy directly above would have to expose themselves in order to place observed fire or to aim their grenades.'

Once again the *Satterlee* came to the rescue and immediately began firing at the cliff tops with its 5in and 40mm guns, and undoubtedly this fire did a great deal to restrict the enemy at the decisive moment as the Rangers tackled the cliffs.

LCA861 Carrying a boat team from Company E, commanded by 1st Lieutenant Theodore E. Lapres, Jr, the craft grounded about 25yd from the bottom of the cliff. The major problem was with the men's equipment. The ropes and grapnels which were fired up the cliffs all fell short of the top because they were thoroughly soaked with seawater and thus far heavier than they should have been. The Rangers also received

casualties from the 'potato masher' grenades thrown down at them as they carried hand rockets nearer the cliffs, the first one being fired just 15yd from the cliffs.

'It went over the top and caught. Pfc Harry W. Roberts started up the hand-line, bracing his feet against the 80° slope. He made about 25 feet, the rope slipped or was cut and Roberts slithered down. The second rocket was fired and the grapnel caught. Roberts went up again, made the top (he estimated his climbing time at 40 seconds) and pulled into a small cratered niche just under the edge. As he arrived, the rope was cut. Roberts tied it to a picket. This pulled out under the weight of the next man, and the rope fell from the cliffs, marooning Roberts. However, a 20ft mound of clay knocked off the cliff enabled Roberts' team to get far enough up the side to throw him a rope. This time he lay across it and five men, including Lieutenant Lapres, came up. Roberts had not yet seen any enemy and had not been under fire. Without waiting for further arrivals, the six Rangers started for their objective, the heavily constructed OP at the north tip of the fortified area. About 10 minutes had elapsed since touchdown.'

Just then there was a heavy explosion among the rest of 861's team and one of them was half buried in cliff debris. The explosion may have been a naval shell or a German mine (many old French naval shells were hung over the cliff edges and set off by tripwires). Fortunately the explosion did not hamper them

Below: Pointe du Hoc as it is today, looking landward. *Simon Forty*

and they scrambled up to the top and then followed Roberts' party towards the same objective.

LCA862 This craft landed about 100m left of the flank LCA and despite losing four men killed and wounded crossing the beach, the team managed to get some of their ropes up the cliffs and were soon at the top and away on their mission.

LCA888 This was Colonel Rudder's craft. It was the first to hit the beach and the 21 occupants saw and engaged enemy troops on the cliff edge, as they crossed the beach craters — some were neck deep in water and difficult to climb out of because of their slippery clay bottoms None of their heavy, water-soaked ropes and grapnels was able to reach the top of the cliffs, so some of them tried free-climbing and eventually they managed to reach the top.

'From then on it was easy. As the first men up moved a few yards from the cliff edge to protect the climbers, they found plenty of cover in bomb craters and no sign of the enemy. In 15 minutes from landing all the Company E men from LCA888 were up and ready to move on . . . Five minutes later he [the communications officer] sent out the codeword indicating "men up the cliff" the "Roger" that receipted for this message . . . was Eikner's last communication of D-Day on the Ranger command net. When he sent the message: "Praise the Lord" [meaning all men up the cliff] at 07.45, no response was forthcoming.'

The Rangers on board the other five LCAs all had similar stories to tell, but in summary it is fair to say that they had successfully achieved their first two difficult operations, namely of landing and getting to the top of the cliffs, despite having problems with some of the scaling equipment, the enemy fire — which had not been as bad as expected — and the badly crated foreshore. Now they had to carry out their *raison d'être* and capture the position. The force, now of some 150 men (allowing for casualties, HQ and mortar personnel), found themselves in a:

'bewildering wasteland of ground literally torn to pieces by bombs and heavy naval shells. Expected landmarks were gone; craters and mounds of wreckage were everywhere, obscuring remnants of paths and trenches. The Rangers had studied these few acres for months, using excellent photographs and large-scale maps that showed every slight feature of terrain and fortifications. Now they found themselves in danger of losing their way as soon as they made a few steps from the ragged cliff edge into the chaos of holes and debris.'

The Rangers had a set way of doing things which at first sight appeared, to the uninitiated, to be chaotic, because each small group worked to its own agenda, moving off independently as soon as it was complete. Thus over a period of some 15–30 minutes a series of these small groups had left the cliff edge, fanning out in all directions. As it was impossible to trace their movements in an exact order or timing, then it must have been extremely difficult, if not impossible, for the Germans to spot

Right: Graphic photo taken on Red Beach (Sword Area), showing a column of tanks coming ashore about 30 minutes after H-Hour. Note that the leading tank appears to have fired off its white phosphorous 'local smoke' to escape from direct enemy fire. *IWM — B5111*

Below: A Churchill AVRE belonging to 79th Armoured Division, having just landed, is being used as a shelter by a group of infantrymen. *IWM — B5096*

their lines of attack and organise to deal with them. Yet in essence the attack did follow a definite plan and order, everyone having been given a specific mission and knowing exactly what to do and where to go.

'The outcome was an action without a clear pattern in detail, but with very clearly defined results.'

Here, for example, is an account of the way in which the men from *LCA861* dealt with the main OP:

'The first men up from LCA861 found themselves about 20 feet to seaward of the massive and undamaged concrete OP. As SSgt Denbo and Pfc Roberts crawled five feet towards a trench, small-arms fire, including machine guns, started up from the slits of the OP. The Rangers threw four grenades at the slits and three went in. The

machine gun stopped firing, but Denbo was wounded by a rifle bullet. Lieutenant Lapres, Sergeant Yardley, Pfc Bell and Tech Sergeant Gunther joined up in the trench. Yardley had a bazooka and his first round hit the edge of the firing slit; the second went through. Taking advantage of this, the group left Yardley to watch the embrasure and dashed around the OP without drawing enemy fire. On the other side of the structure they found Corporal Aguzzi watching the main entrance from the landward side. Lapres' party pushed on towards gun position No 4 and points inland.

'Aguzzi had come up from LCA862 southeast of the OP, with Lieutenant Leagans and Sergeant Cleaves. As they started away from the edge, joined by Tech 5 Thompson and Pfc Bellows, they saw a German close to the OP, throwing grenades over the cliff from the shelter of a trench. The OP was not their job, but the party decided to go after the grenadier. Bellows crawled over to No 3 gun position to cover the advance of the party. They threw grenades at the German and moved into the trench when he ducked under the entrance to the OP. Aguzzi found a shell hole from which he could watch the main entrance, while three Rangers tried to skirt the OP on the east and get at it from the rear. Cleaves was wounded by a

Below: British paratroopers board their aircraft on the night of 5/6 June for operations such as the assault on the Merville Battery. They and their American counterparts would be the first Allied troops to land in France. *IWM — CH13303*

Bottom: Part of the Merville Battery as it is today. The command post and underground HQ on the right are now a museum, whilst one of the gun casemates can be seen to the left. *Author's collection*

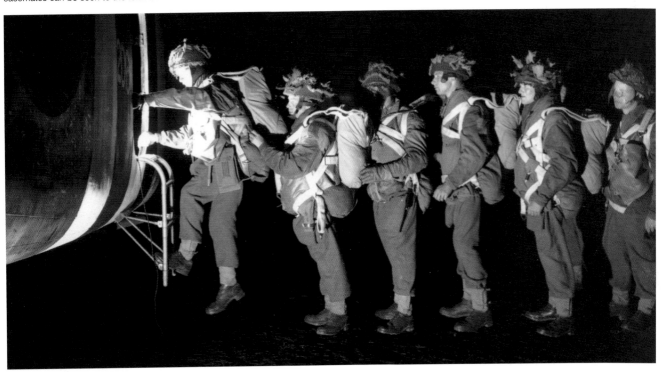

mine — the only casualty from this cause during the day. Thompson got close enough to hear a radio working inside the OP, looked for the aerial on the roof and shot it off. After throwing a grenade through the entrance, Lieutenant Leagans and Thompson decided to let the OP wait for demolitions and went off on their original mission farther inland. Aguzzi, staying to watch the entrance, was surprised by the appearance of Lieutenant Lapres' party, coming from the rear of the OP. Two small groups of Rangers had been attacking the OP from opposite sides, neither aware of the other's presence.'

When Rudder's men reached the gun positions, they found that the guns had been removed, so he divided his small command into two groups — one group to set up a defensive position while the other went off to look for the guns. Luckily they found them without difficulty, hidden in an orchard behind the position, where they had been taken for repairs following the heavy air-raids. Well camouflaged but unguarded, they were destroyed by the Rangers using thermite grenades. Later the Germans (1st Battalion of 914th Infantry Regiment) put in a series of heavy counter-attacks, which caused many casualties and forced the Americans back into a small enclave on the cliffs, just 200yd wide. Nevertheless, thanks to supporting naval gunfire, they managed to hang on and during the following night the enemy withdrew. The Rangers were relieved by tanks and infantry from 116th Infantry Regiment and the 5th Rangers. Out of the force of 225 which had landed at Pointe du Hoc, some 135 had been killed, wounded or were missing in action — a very high casualty rate, but in the circumstances considered as justified in view of the importance of the target.

The Merville Battery

Over on the other flank, where the British and Canadians would land, there were also equally important artillery batteries which could seriously threaten the Allied landings. One such battery was at Merville, where it was thought there were four 15cm guns, which would easily be able to reach the Sword, Juno and Gold beaches, especially Sword, with devastating results. The battery was located too far inland to be taken out by commandos, so it was decided to attack it using airborne troops before any landings took place. The area around the battery position had already been cleared of civilians by the Germans, who now used the nearby villages of Gonneville and Franceville Plage as troop billets. The battery had been the subject of RAF bomber raids in the weeks leading up to D-Day but aerial photographs had shown that the casemates were still virtually undamaged. It was decided that the assault on the Merville Battery position would be undertaken by men of the 9th Parachute Battalion, under Lieutenant-Colonel Terence Otway.

A fair amount of information had been obtained from aerial photographs and ground intelligence and a full scale briefing model built on which the paratroopers trained endlessly. The gun positions were formidable, being built on some 4m of concrete ballast and surrounded by 2m thick concrete walls, banked with another 4m of earth. Steel doors covered by machine guns and 20mm guns protected every entrance, while there was a 100m wide minefield and 5m of thick barbed-wire surrounding the battery position. The approaches, especially from the seaward side, had also been mined and there were random machine gun posts and anti-tank ditches. The garrison was estimated at some 200-plus troops. This then was to be the 9th Battalion's target — a formidable one.

The plan was for the battalion to be divided into two groups. The smaller group, the advance party, would land first, prepare the RV for the main body, reconnoitre the battery position and provide covering fire when the main body arrived to carry out the main assault. A bombing raid by 100 Lancasters had been fixed for 03.00hrs, so it would be essential to know what damage had been done before the main attack went in. An integral part of the main body was a party of sappers, with the necessary explosives and equipment to blow up the guns. There were five gliders packed with anti-tank guns, jeeps, scaling ladders, bangalore torpedoes and other kit, whilst three other gliders carried 50 volunteers who were a *coup de main* force that would land directly on top of the gun positions, then leap out of their gliders and attack from within, whilst the rest of the battalion stormed their way through the perimeter to join them.

The advance group would jump at 00.20hrs, the main body half an hour later. Everything was meticulously planned, but unfortunately the weather played havoc with these arrangements even before the Germans took a hand. High winds scattered the aircraft and the battalion landed all over the place. For example, the three gliders scheduled to crash-land on top of the battery never made it — one became separated from its towing aircraft and had to ditch early; the second was blown off course by the winds and landed in an orchard some 50yd outside the perimeter; the third glider was released too early and came down in a nearby village. And the main body was no more fortunate.

'We took off just after midnight,' recalled paratrooper Les Cartwright,

'and we dropped just before one. It was a beautiful flight across till we hit the coast and you've never seen anything like it in your life. It was just like going into a firework display and the old duck was going five ways at once and

Below: Merville Battery. *Source: Holt's Guide to the Normandy Landing Beaches*

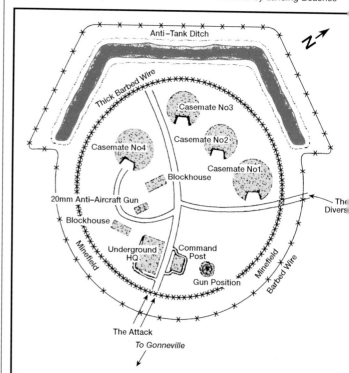

everybody was saying "let's get out of this so-and-so thing". Anyway eventually the Pilot says "Go" and puts the light on and on our way we go. And as I dropped, obviously you look round and I could see other 'chutes coming down and I hit the deck and out of my 'chute, got my Sten out, everything going, look round — couldn't see anybody. But there was one thing that got implanted in my mind — we must go to the RV. And the Colonel's orders were "You are not to have any private fire fights. You get to the RV and THAT IS IT."'

Les could just see a red Aldis lamp twinkling in the distance and decided he would make for it. Fortunately it was one of the battalion officers up a tree, shining the light in circles to bring in the stragglers.

'As soon as I saw that I knew where I was to get to. I could see the tree across the fields and I saw a bod just in front of where I knew the RV was and I yelled the password out and he yelled it back and I looked at him and it was the Colonel . . . He tapped me on the shoulder and said, "Well done lad. What company?" "C Company." "Down there." I went down there and . . . I dropped beside my lieutenant (Jackson) and had a little word with him, you know . . . It wasn't until years later that I found out that of the 550 who jumped in our battalion, only 150 got to the rendezvous.'[8]

Otway's force was still only 150 strong when H-Hour (02.50hrs) arrived and he had to make the difficult decision whether to carry on or abort. They had no 6-pounder anti-tank guns, no jeeps or trailers, no sappers, no mine-clearing equipment, no mortars and just one Vickers medium machine gun. To make things worse, the air attack had hit the battalion's advance party and they were without the field ambulance section and naval bombardment forward observation party. Despite all this, the group managed to get through the outer perimeter, blow a path through the minefield using bangalore torpedoes and then make an immediate assault on the main battery position. Almost instantly they came under heavy fire. Then things started to go right for them. First they managed to silence three of the enemy machine gun posts, their single Vickers causing heavy casualties. The German garrison had obviously called for reinforcements, but fortunately the paratroops in the glider which had landed in the orchard came upon the reinforcing platoon en route for the battery position and managed to hold it off for four hours, whilst the rest of the battalion made their assault through the two breaches in the outer perimeter and, despite strong resistance, managed to reach the centre of the gun position. Hand to hand fighting went on until nearly half the attacking force had been killed or wounded, whilst the defenders were down to only about 20 men. Just 45 minutes before the deadline when HMS *Arethusa* was scheduled to begin bombarding the Merville Battery position, the remaining Germans surrendered and Colonel Otway was able to send a success signal.

However, their job was not completely finished. The battalion, now numbering only some 80 men, reorganised, picked up any stragglers, and immediately moved on to take its second objective, the high ground near Le Plein. Despite being heavily outnumbered, they were then able to hold out in the area around Château d'Amfreville, until reinforced by men of the 1st Special Service Brigade who arrived on the 7th. Back at the Merville Battery, the Germans regained the position

temporarily, but lost it again after a fierce battle with two troops of No 3 Commando. However, this was not the end of the action. The Germans once again counterattacked and drove the British out with heavy losses. As they withdrew, the Commandos were engaged by one of the enemy artillery guns which had been brought out of its casemate and fired at them over open sights, The guns and their crews would then remain isolated in their position until 17 August, when they were withdrawn together with other German forces out of Normandy. Postwar it was discovered that the Merville battery was not of 15cm howitzers, as had been suspected, but rather Czech 105mm guns.[9] However, as these guns were capable of delivering salvos of 24 rounds a minute onto the beaches west of the River Orne, the brave and successful action by 9 Para undoubtedly played its part in enabling the Allies to achieve their vital D-Day landings.

Gold Beach — DD Tanks Come Ashore

Albert Johnson was a wireless operator/loader on a Sherman DD tank, belonging to B Squadron of the 4th/7th Dragoon Guards, who were supporting the Green Howards in 50th Northumbrian Division, who were due to land on King Green, a subdivision of Gold Beach. He recalled the landing thus:

'We had been training in our special role in DD tanks since April 1943 and were due to swim into the beach of La Rivière, four kilometres east of Arromanches, having been launched from the landing craft some 4,000 yards out. Personal equipment included a simplified version of the Davis Escape Apparatus, as a DD tank would sink like a stone if the screen collapsed. We had been on our small landing craft for over 24 hours on the morning of 6th June, owing to the postponement of D-Day. After a rough time tossing about in the heavy seas for hours before the actual crossing most of us were seasick and that didn't do much for my morale! It also accounted for my lack of concern when I inadvertently trod on my escape apparatus and bust the valve! That grey dawn was not brightened by the news that the DD tanks would not be launched on our front owing to the heavy swell. We felt our chances of being hit on the run-in were much higher when still in the LCT.

'As the sun came up an amazing sight met our eyes. The sea was full of ships as far as we could see, of all shapes and sizes. Spirits began to lift when the naval bombardment opened up and we felt that we couldn't fail as the explosions could be clearly seen on the long, low shore ahead. I remember in particular one destroyer or frigate equipped with rocket launchers firing from our rear. It seemed to be very accurate as I could see the bursts run along the beach. However, one battery of six or so kept dropping the odd rocket among the infantry landing craft in front of us.

'We went straight into the beach and as the LCT grounded, down came the door. The tank's DD screen was erect and all but the tank driver with his periscope were temporarily blind. There was a certain amount of waiting to do and it was a matter of judgement for the troop leader deciding to drop the screen. The time was around 7.30am and after interminable seconds the order came, but the screen stuck partially up. To traverse the turret the screen had to be down and I got the order to get out and clear it. As I did so a mortar shell fell on the other side of the tank. I moved rather sharpish to pull the screen down and remount!

'The tide was still out and all the beach obstacles, ramps and tetrahedra were exposed to view. All we had to do was to weave about in between them. We followed a mine-clearing flail tank of the Westminster Dragoons up and off the beach. We even crossed an anti-tank ditch before the Germans had time to blow it. In what seemed a very short time we headed inland down a lane which passed close to the Mont Fleury battery of heavy guns which could have dominated everything at sea from Arromanches eastwards had it not been destroyed by HMS Belfast.'[10]

Edgar Lawrenson was in one of the flail tanks (also known as Sherman Crabs) referred to by Albert Johnson, in B Squadron of the Westminsters and he recalled:

'During the final run-in I sat on top of our tank, giving a commentary to the three crew members inside. Captain Taylor was on the bridge checking landmarks for the lane we had to sweep through the minefields. Hostile shelling and small arms fire had started and 16 LC(R)s [Landing Craft (Rocket)] opened fire over our heads. Our tank beached safely with the other flail tank. We blew off our waterproofing and, dodging between the beach obstacles, headed for the thick wire and sandhills with the other flail tank slightly in front. We flogged through the heavy barbed-wire into the minefield, while the other tank turned right and headed for Le Hamel and its second objective. The density of mines was unbelievable and the sound of exploding mines seemed continuous. My tank was about 15–20 yards from the lateral road when we hit a mine which blew off the front bogey assembly and later we found that the front driving sprocket had been hit by an AP round. Over 40% of our chains had been blown off. The explosion had also damaged the radio so I was sent back to find Major Elphinstone, who commanded our beach party. He had been killed and the beach was now under heavy fire from strongpoints in Le Hamel.'[11]

By the end of D-Day there were seven successful breaching lanes through the obstacles, wire and minefields on the two British beaches, out of the 12 which had been attempted. Some 50 Sherman Crabs had been in action, 12 of which had been destroyed whilst many others had been damaged. They were just one form of 79th Armoured Division's 'Funnies'. Others included 120 Armoured Vehicles Royal Engineer (AVRE), 22 of which were destroyed and many put out of action temporarily, though their massive 290mm Petard spigot mortars had dealt with many seemingly impregnable enemy blockhouses, even though they had a range of only 80m. Eight fascines and 10 SBG (Small Box Girder) bridges had been dropped to make crossings over anti-tank ditches. Armoured bulldozers, Bullshorn ploughs and other strange devices had all come into their own. Without doubt General Hobart's Funnies had proved themselves invaluable, the success on the British beaches being due in no small way to them. In contrast, the Americans, who had DD tanks but no specialised armour, made much slower headway and had far more casualties.

Clearing the Beach

Right behind the assault troops came the Beach Groups, whose job it was to clear any enemy left on the beaches, secure the beach in question so as to enable the follow-up troops to pass through the beach safely and follow the assaulting troops. All members of the Beach Groups had a broad white band painted on their steel helmets to indicate that they were the only troops allowed to remain on the beaches. Peter Lovett of Swanage was a member of one such group attached to the 3rd Canadian Infantry Division, who landed on Juno Beach. He told me:

'As we approached the Normandy shore we were ordered up on deck and crouched in lines on each side of the deck roofing to await the lowering of the bow ramps. Once on deck we could see what we were going into. Landing craft were lying destroyed at various angles, bodies of Canadian soldiers were on the beach in positions that, as we were to find out, only death can produce. The landing craft slowed down, the sailors on this craft pushed the bow ramps down and it was every man for himself. As we stumbled down the ramps, sporadic machine gun fire came from the right and we went waist deep in water. Every man was wearing Field Service Marching Order, but it was amazing how fast you could travel through water when you have a good reason. It was nothing like the controlled exercise landings at Studland . . . A group to our right went off after a pillbox, a tank with a Petard mortar had just dealt with another strongpoint and I remember thinking: "never think you are safe behind a foot of concrete. It is far safer in a slit trench. Pill boxes only delay, they are always destroyed sooner or later, along with the occupants."

'We did get shelled badly, although the soft sand stood us in good stead. We also got strafed and on one occasion a bomb hit a Bofors gun close to my slit trench. It certainly emphasised the lethal side of war as our trench was showered with parts of the gun crew. The smell of death lingered for ever and never seemed to leave your clothing . . . Prisoners came through us on the beach and we just penned them inside a barbed-wire circle. There was nothing for them to do except await a place on a landing craft to take them back to England . . . A party of us were sent to check out buildings to the rear of the sand dunes. I remember a French woman waving us to come over to her that we did with extra care. On arrival however, she handed over an elderly German soldier, who was, very rightly, scared out of his wits . . . My company commander, Major Morrison, had landed near a pillbox which, with a small number of men, he attacked and cleared, killing all the occupants . . . We went on into Graye-sur-Mer and came under fire twice, winkling out three more Germans. The devastating effect of the assault troops was very clear — in this case the Winnipeg Rifles — German and Canadian dead were all over the place, including two German soldiers and their French girlfriends in a nearby slit trench. Then we returned to the beach to carry on with our primary task of securing it and clearing incoming traffic.'

Summary

By the end of D-Day, the British and Canadians had achieved a bridgehead some 30km wide by 5–10km deep, whilst the Americans had gained two smaller footholds. Some 130,000 Allied troops were now ashore in the bridgeheads, whilst a further 23,000 airborne troops were scattered over a wide area inland and were causing the harassed defenders no end of problems. In short, the Allies had initially succeeded in their bold venture, whilst Army Group B had committed its

Right: This German trench right on the beach has been captured and now shelters British troops, whilst a column of vehicles, including a Beach Armoured Recovery Vehicle (BARV), moves along the beach. *IWM — B5180*

Above: 'For you the war is over!' The first German prisoners are marched away. *IWM — B5257*

immediate reserves to little effect. The commanders of the coastal units now waited, with growing impatience, for the arrival of the panzers that would throw the enemy back into the sea. They would wait in vain, while the higher headquarters tried to decide if these were the main Allied landings or just a feint, refusing to release the armour until the situation was clarified. Of course by the time they did so, they would find that any movement towards the coast in daylight was severely hampered. It was all happening just as Rommel had foretold. Instead of hitting the enemy hard on the beaches and driving them back into the sea, they had been allowed to gain a toehold, so the battle would be much more difficult to win.

How Good Were the Defences?

From the various eyewitness reports covered, it is clear that the permanent reinforced concrete installations undoubtedly protected the German infantry, but also undoubtedly reduced their fields of fire, making them less effective, but more likely to survive, although, as explained earlier, this was not the basic German philosophy as far as building such defences was concerned, but rather that fewer men would be able to cover a greater area. Nevertheless, infantry positions close to the shoreline were generally able to inflict considerable losses upon the enemy, but were themselves extremely vulnerable to fire from the sea, be it from naval vessels or close support landing craft — such as those carrying batteries of rockets. The commander of 352nd Infantry Division said that on 6 June his division had lost one fifth of its total infantry fighting strength.

Communications between all positions were frequently broken due to the telephone wires being damaged whether or not they were buried. This was a well-known hazard in defensive positions, but still occurred constantly and led to chaos, there being insufficient modern radios to replace/back up the telephone system, whilst specialist repairmen were always at a premium. This led to runners having to be used, causing delay and casualties.

Troops held back for counter-attack purposes were never sufficient to get the job done, especially as they were usually short of heavy weapons and lacking in suitable transport — one divisional commander complaining that his troops had to march, go by bicycle or travel in old French lorries which continually broke down. There was also a shortage of heavy weapons in the forward positions, which should have been 'in the shop window', that is to say up front in protected positions — Rommel's relevant tactic being aptly described as: 'let all weapons display their effect on the water'. In some areas, the

Atlantic Wall as we imagine it today, just did not exist; for example, parts of the Bayeux sector were lacking any concrete defensive positions at all.

Artillery, both coastal and field, generally did well initially, but was then badly affected by enemy air strikes, both on gun positions and, most importantly, on forward observers (the observers could be replaced but not their equipment). However, the worst problem of all was a general shortage of ammunition, which seems to have been a major difficulty, compelling the defenders to use ammunition as sparingly as possible. All types of artillery suffered from the fighter-bomber activity, which caused many casualties, especially to flak and anti-tank artillery.

Notes

1. General Günther Blumentritt, CoS OB West in a postwar report.
2. The 15cm Nebelwerfer 41 was a 6-barrelled rocket-launcher system, mounted on the same two-wheel carriage as the 3.7cm anti-tank gun and fitted with a simple sighting system. The rockets had a range of 7,000m, contained some 2.5kg of explosive and were known as 'Moaning Minnies' by the Allies because of their distinctive droning sound when in flight.
3. Patton's impetuosity and quick temper had led to him slapping a soldier with shell-shock in a field hospital in Sicily. Whilst he was probably the best 'ass-kicker' in the whole US Army, this was clearly not the best way of trying to bring the man to his senses. The press quickly latched on to it, the resulting headlines completely overshadowing Patton's brilliant handling of his forces in Sicily.
4. As quoted in *Rommel in Normandy* by Friedrich Ruge.
5. This and subsequent short linking quotes of Lieutenant Jahnke's battle descriptions are taken from *Invasion — They're Coming!* by Paul Carell, whilst the description of the landing by 8th US Infantry Regiment, 4th Infantry Division is taken from *Utah Beach to Cherbourg* in the American Forces in Action series and the Omaha Beach quotes from *Omaha Beachhead*.
6. *Yesterday's Heroes* by Kenneth N. Jordan.
7. As quoted in *Fighting the Invasion* edited by David C. Isby.
8. As quoted in *The Visitor's Guide to the Normandy Landing Beaches* by Tonie and Valmi Holt.
9. The Skoda 105mm Model 35 was one of the most modern and well designed of the Czech Army field pieces and entered German service as the s 10.5cm K 35(t). It had a maximum range of 19,800yd and a shell weight of 18kg.
10. As quoted in *M4 Sherman* by George Forty.
11. As quoted in *D-Day 1944, Voices from Normandy* by Robin Neillands and Roderick de Norman.

Chapter 10
Dealing with the Fortresses

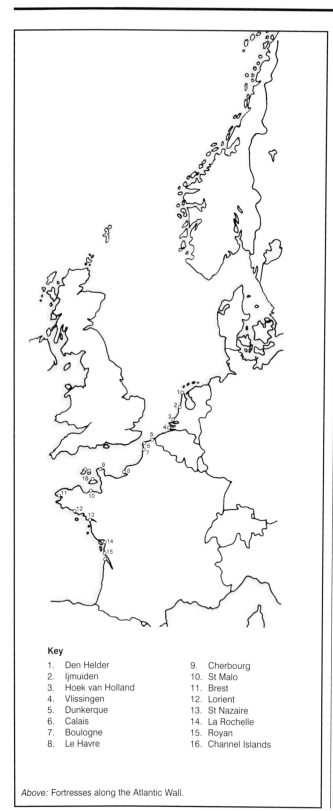

Key

1.	Den Helder	9.	Cherbourg
2.	Ijmuiden	10.	St Malo
3.	Hoek van Holland	11.	Brest
4.	Vlissingen	12.	Lorient
5.	Dunkerque	13.	St Nazaire
6.	Calais	14.	La Rochelle
7.	Boulogne	15.	Royan
8.	Le Havre	16.	Channel Islands

Above: Fortresses along the Atlantic Wall.

The Toughest Nuts to Crack

Of all the various component parts of the Atlantic Wall defences undoubtedly the designated fortresses (Festungen) were the toughest nuts to crack. Therefore it was eminently sensible for the Allies only to take them on when it was essential to the overall plan of winning the war in North-West Europe. It will be remembered that the Commander-in-Chief West had, with the Führer's full approval and backing, designated some of the fortress areas as early as 8 July 1942. These had included St Malo, Cherbourg, Le Havre, Boulogne, Calais and Dunkerque along the French Channel coast; Brest, Lorient, St Nazaire, La Rochelle and Royan along France's Atlantic coast; and Den Helder, Ijmuiden, Hoek van Holland and Vlissingen in the Netherlands. As we have seen, others, including the Channel Islands, were added later. The primary aim of the garrisons of these fortresses was to deny major ports to the Allies, and Hitler became personally involved in planning their defences, selecting and appointing their commanders and doing his utmost — albeit at long range — to ensure that they fought to the death. The appointed fortress commander had a direct line to Hitler's headquarters so that his Führer could, when necessary, keep in personal touch, whilst every one of the chosen commanders had to swear a personal oath of allegiance. This was enshrined in Führer Order 11 of March 1944, which has already been covered in Chapter 2. Suffice it here to reiterate the stipulation from Hitler that these commanders must be tough, experienced soldiers, of general rank, and not be allowed to delegate their responsibilities to anyone else.

Each of the selected fortress commanders fought his particular battle differently and naturally had to fight it at different times between D-Day and the end of hostilities. First to have to face the onslaught was the port of Cherbourg on the Cotentin peninsula, then St Malo and Brest to its south-west in Brittany. These would be followed by Lorient and St Nazaire as elements of the US First and Third Armies swung in that direction following the Operation 'Cobra' breakout, whilst, on the other flank, the Canadian First and British Second Armies began advancing up the Channel coast, from Le Havre onwards, taking on each of the Channel ports in turn. Here, they had mixed results, because the Allied advances were not always crowned with the successful capture of the requisite port. For example, they had an early setback at Dunkerque, whilst the spectacular early capture of the great port of Antwerp had to wait for Vlissingen and all the rest of Walcheren to be cleared of the enemy before the vital Scheldt estuary could be opened to shipping once again.

The Mulberry Harbours

The major task of most of the fortresses was to prevent the Allies from securing a major port, because of course the Germans did not know about the two amazing prefabricated Mulberry Harbours, which were to be towed over to the Normandy beaches soon after D-Day, the prefabricated concrete caissons then being sunk to form two harbours — they had taken almost all the UK concrete production to make. Then 59 old warships and merchantmen, known as the 'Corncob

Above: This was one of the two 'aces up the Allied sleeve', namely the pair of prefabricated Mulberry Harbours, which were towed over to the Normandy beaches, thus reducing the need to capture an intact port. This photograph was taken before the severe gales that wrecked one of the two harbours. *US Army*

Fleet' which had sailed down from Scotland to Poole harbour prior to D-Day, ready for their final journey over to Normandy, arrived and were sunk to form breakwaters. The two Mulberrys were meant to be up and running as soon as possible during the first week after the landing, but took rather longer than anticipated. Then, just as they were being got ready to operate, severe gales (the worst for 80 years) blew up early in the morning of 19 June and blew for three nights and three days without respite. Mulberry A (off Omaha Beach) was irreparably damaged, while Mulberry B (off Arromanches) was severely damaged. The two had been expected to handle some 15,000 tons of cargo daily, rising to 46,000 tons by D+90, so the damage was very worrying and put pressure on the ground forces to capture a port as quickly as possible. Eventually, however, enough was salvaged from the two artificial harbours to restore Mulberry B and to get it working again. Another revolutionary means of supply was PLUTO — the *Pipeline Under The Ocean* — which enabled fuel to be pumped from England to France.

A Selection of Battles for Fortresses

It would take another book of comparable size to this one to cover all the battles which took place in isolating and capturing these fortresses, so all I have space for are just some examples. I have therefore tried to choose four which had very different characteristics:

- The capture of Cherbourg.
- The isolation and final surrender of Dunkerque.
- The clearing of the Scheldt estuary
- The liberation of the Channel Islands

The Capture of Cherbourg

Fortress Commander Cherbourg

The Commander of 'Fortress Cherbourg' was 49-year-old Generalleutnant Karl-Wilhelm von Schlieben, holder of both the German Cross in Gold and the Knight's Cross, who was at the time commanding the 709th Infantry Division, the Cherbourg city garrison, which had been in Brittany since the spring of 1943. It would be to him that the Führer would send

a signal on 23 June, ordering him to 'defend the city to the last man and the last bullet'. Within the Cotentin peninsula there were other static divisions, elements of which had also fallen back onto Cherbourg and were now under von Schlieben's command. There was also a significant number of Kriegsmarine personnel in the port, including two Marine Artillery regiments, with seven casemated batteries, all sited to defend against a seaborne assault, but each still a self-contained small Festung needing to be taken out, and three Marine Flak Battalions (803, 804 and 805). Also located at Cherbourg was the headquarters of the German Naval Commander Normandy, Vizeadmiral Walter Hennecke.

In addition, Cherbourg had been an important German naval base, for various flotillas of E-boats (Schnellboote). For example, in 1943 there were the 5th and 6th Flotillas, but later just the 5th remained for a while and was then joined by the 9th. They and other flotillas from Boulogne and Ostend often used the Channel Islands as a temporary base whilst operating against enemy shipping. Probably their most successful operation had been on the night of 27/28 April 1944 when six E-boats of the 5th Flotilla and three of the 9th sailed from Cherbourg and in Lyme Bay unexpectedly found themselves involved in Exercise Tiger (part of the preparations for D-Day in which landings were being practised on Slapton Sands). The E-boats attacked a convoy in the bay, sinking two heavily laden LSTs and badly damaging a third. Allied losses were heavy — 441 soldiers and 197 sailors — more than would be killed on D-Day on Utah Beach.

The Attackers

General 'Lightning Joe' Collins'[1] US VII Corps was given the task of taking Cherbourg. He had advanced from Utah Beach on a three-division front (from east to west 4th, 79th and 9th Infantry Divisions), moving through Montebourg, Valognes and Bricquebec. The major effort would be in the form of a double-pronged assault by the 4th and 9th Divisions, cutting in against

Right:
This aerial photograph shows some of the damage done to the 'impregnable' defences in and around Cherbourg by the Allies in their drive to capture the port.
IWM — EA 9420

Left:
Edging along the battered streets of the outskirts of Cherbourg, this column of Sherman tanks helped to mop up the remaining German resistance. *US Army*

Below:
Cherbourg. Final surrender. Generalleutnant Karl-Wilhelm von Schlieben emerges from his underground command post under a white flag to surrender to 9th Infantry Division on 26 June 1944. *US Army*

the Cherbourg defences from east and west, with the 79th Division and the 4th Cavalry Squadron, serving as a link between the two prongs. The attack began well before first light on 19 June, without a preparatory artillery barrage to warn the enemy. However, the Germans had strengthened their positions prior to the attack and the 4th Infantry Division made little progress until after last light, when 8th Infantry Regiment carried out a well-executed double envelopment of Montebourg, supported by 12th Infantry Regiment. By midnight, both regiments were closing in on Valognes. The enemy then abandoned Valognes and fell back within the outer defensive ring around Cherbourg. They were speedily followed up by the Americans and by 21 June, the 8th and 22nd US Infantry Regiments had begun to make inroads into the German perimeter. Similarly, the 79th Division was pushing hard and meeting only light initial resistance. The attack continued into the night and forced the enemy to withdraw to the north. The 79th uncovered a major V-bomb launching site near Brix, to the north-west of Valognes — this was one of several such sites which the corps overran on the Cotentin peninsula. The 9th Infantry Division made steady progress and by 07.00 the following morning the old fortress town of Bricquebec, which it had been anticipated would be a hard place to take, had been overrun without hardly a shot being fired. By the late afternoon 9th Division, with the 4th Cavalry Squadron on its right, had reached the line Hellville–Colleville–St Martin.

Storms in the Channel

'The need for early capture of the port city was dramatized by a four-day storm that hit the Normandy beaches beginning June 19. By the 21st the ships and barges sunk or moored off-shore to form artificial harbors began to break up, and unloading of ammunition and other supplies had to be suspended. Combat operations ashore as well as the landing of additional troops would be gravely threatened if capture of the port facilities was long delayed.'

That was how General Collins summarised the situation which faced the Allies as the final assault on Cherbourg began. However, before the assault began on the 22nd, saturation bombing of the German perimeter defensive positions took place, as a prelude, designed to weaken the already shell-shocked defenders. For well over 60 minutes before H-Hour wave upon wave of American fighter-bombers plastered all the main enemy positions and this was followed by artillery and also by naval gunfire. H-Hour for the final assault was set for 14.00 on the 22nd. The evening before, a multilingual appeal had been made to urge the Cherbourg garrison to surrender by 09.00hrs, but no answer was received, so the attack went ahead as planned.

Naval Support

As the final reduction of the fortress began, it was accompanied by a synchronised naval bombardment. A task force (TF.129) had been assembled to provide the bombardment. This consisted of three US battleships (*Texas*, *Arkansas* and *Nevada*), four cruisers, two US and two British (*Tuscaloosa*, *Quincy*, *Glasgow* and *Enterprise*), with screening destroyers and two minesweeping flotillas, under the command of Rear-Admiral M. L. Deyo, USN. What the Army had requested was that the task force should close in to the coast to neutralise the very powerful shore batteries and deliver heavy fire against artillery

and protected German pockets of resistance, so as to destroy their resistance, whilst the VII Corps left the high ground south of the city and stormed the inner defences.

Despite the massive weight of bombs and shells fired at them, the garrison did not cave in, clinging tenaciously to their positions, buoyed up, perhaps, not so much by the hope of being relieved, but rather by the Führer's exhortations to defend every last bunker and to leave the enemy 'not a harbour but a field of ruins'. There was no clear breakthrough on the 22nd and progress was painfully slow. It would not be until the 25th that the brave garrison started to crack. Here is how 'Lightning Joe' described the situation in a letter to his wife:

'Yesterday was one of our great days. The evening before we had ringed around the city and I was confident that we would be able to enter Cherbourg proper sometime on Sunday . . . Right after lunch I started my usual round visiting the divisions . . . in an armored car that has been my rolling CP . . . First we went to see Tubby Barton's division. Teddy Roosevelt acted as our guide and led us to a captured German position overlooking the city from the east . . . The view of Cherbourg from this point is magnificent. Off to the left were the steep cliffs of the highlands that run right up to the back door of the city. Another of our divisions was rapidly closing in on this area from the south and we could see smoke from the fires being directed into Fort du Roule, which is the central bastion of the German defenses, on a high bluff overlooking the city. Over to the right were the inner and outer breakwaters with the old French forts guarding the entrance from the sea. Beyond the haze of smoke we could see part of our battle fleet engaged in shelling the seacoast batteries west of the town. Within this frame, the city itself lay as a bowl from which billows of smoke poured up in the places where the Germans were destroying stores of oil and ammunition. As we watched, one of our heavy batteries fired a perfect concentration onto a German position just west of the Fort des Flambards. It was a thrilling and in a sense, an awe-inspiring sight. I knew definitely that Cherbourg was ours and directed Tubby to push one of his regiments into the eastern section of the city before that night.'

General Collins then continued to describe his progress around the city visiting other positions, getting more spectacular views, then giving the other two divisional commanders orders and, at one stage, having to dodge the fire of an enemy 8.8cm gun as he made his way to the safety of a well-placed concrete OP, from which he could direct fire onto the troublesome 88 and silence it. His account of the day closed with the words:

'I directed Matt [General Manton Eddy, commander 9th Infantry Division] to push his two regiments into the city and before dark one of them had broken through to the sea, effectively cutting the last route of withdrawal of the Germans to the area they still hold in the Cap de la Hague to the north-west.'

General von Schlieben and Admiral Hennecke were both taken prisoner at Hennecke's headquarters during the afternoon of the 26th and — despite having previously exacted a 'no surrender pledge' from their men — gave themselves up to the commander of the American assaulting forces. The city arsenal held out until the following morning, whilst forces outside Cherbourg and in the north-west of the peninsula continued to resist until 1 July when they were rounded up by the US 9th Infantry Division. This action really brought to a close Operation 'Neptune', which had begun with D-Day, now that the naval position had been stabilised in the assault area and the city port of Cherbourg had been liberated.

Some 39,000 prisoners were taken in Cherbourg and work immediately began to reopen the port for Allied use.

Isolating Dunkerque

As the Allies advanced, the Canadian II Corps operated in the coastal belt on the far left flank of 21st Army Group. General Montgomery's intention was for it to clear the area west of Antwerp up to the southern shores of the Scheldt estuary. At the same time, it had to reduce the garrisons of Boulogne and Calais, while investing Dunkerque. This was the toughest nut of the three, being a major German naval base as well as a fortress. Some 20–30,000 German troops were estimated to be holding Boulogne, Calais and Dunkerque. Whilst operations for the clearing of the Scheldt were developing, Boulogne and Calais were both stormed. The assault on the former began on 17 September, the latter on 25 September. Boulogne surrendered on 22 September and Calais on 30 September, after fierce fighting in both fortresses. It was then decided that the Canadians should concentrate on clearing the Scheldt, so Dunkerque, which continued to be invested, became an army group responsibility and Montgomery put the Czechoslovakian Independent Armoured Brigade in charge of the investing forces surrounding the port. Part of its force was the British 7th Royal Tank Regiment, commanded by Lieutenant-Colonel (later Major-General) Rea Leakey, who would be awarded the Czechoslovak Military Cross for his part in the siege. In his autobiography General Leakey had this to say about his part in the battle:

'What a grand crowd those Czechs were, the more we saw of them, the more we liked them, particularly Major-General Alois Lishka. When I met him he told me, most apologetically, that my Regiment was to take over the most difficult sector because, after all, we were a regular Regiment. I later learned that in their eyes, this was a great honour! I then visited the 1st Battalion the Black Watch from whom I was to take over. They were holding some 6,000 yards of front to the south of Dunkirk and guarded the direct route to Calais. The CO, Lieutenant-Colonel John Hopwood, greeted me with joy. "Thank goodness for the few tanks in this area; we need them as things are a bit hot round here. Last night the Germans were throwing hand grenades at me here at my headquarters. Not so funny, as we are at least two miles behind the front line. Who are your infantry?" I then explained that my Regiment was to relieve them and that we were the infantry. He just roared with laughter and explained that his Battalion, up to full strength and augmented by two dismounted anti-aircraft batteries, was finding very great difficulty in holding the line.

'"How many men can you raise?" I would have to leave some men guarding our Churchill tanks, so at the most 400 officers and men would be available to man the defensive positions. And I explained that few would be armed with rifles and that we had a few Bren guns, but of course no support weapons. He told me he had well over double that figure. "If you are still holding the line in a fortnight's time, send me a signal and you will receive a crate of whisky — and I would remind you that I am a Scotsman."'

More from Rea Leakey later, but first a brief look at their opposition. The garrison was some 12,000 men, from all three services of the Wehrmacht, the Luftwaffe representatives initially being the strongest, namely the 18th Luftwaffe Field Division, whose commander, Generalleutnant Joachim von Treschow, was the original fortress commander. However, he and his division left Dunkerque on 14 August to fight in the Seine area. Nevertheless, the rest of the garrison remained determined to resist. They included Kriegsmarine Abteilung 618, plus an artillery group and a flak group. As well as occupying the port and docks, they were also located in a string

Above: The stubborn garrison in the fortress of Dunkerque was kept bottled up by the Czech Independent Armoured Brigade who had relieved the Canadians. Here a brigade patrol of engineers crosses one of the flooded areas around the town. *IWM — B15132*

Above: As Rea Leakey explains, there were also French troops attached to his regiment, helping to encircle Dunkerque. Here two of them use a captured MG42 machine gun — probably the best LMG of the war, with a very high rate of fire. *IWM — B15116*

of strongpoints some distance outside, stretching from Loon-Plage and Mardyck on the coast west of Dunkerque, to Bergues some 8km inland and thence to Bray-Dunes some 8km up the coast to the north-east. Much of the area surrounding Dunkerque had been flooded, making movement off the roads and tracks well nigh impossible. The Canadians had tried valiantly to break through the German defences, but without success. Throughout the entire siege, the Germans fought ferociously and very few surrendered, despite their impossible situation. At one stage the French Red Cross asked for a truce so as to evacuate some 8,000 civilians, and this was granted and lasted for 60 hours.

Finally, after some difficult, dangerous and extremely unpleasant (due to the conditions) offensive actions had failed to break through the stubborn defences, it was decided that at least a two-division attack, heavily supported with artillery bombardment, bombing and naval gunfire, would be needed to achieve any significant results. This rightly seemed to Montgomery to be a waste of time and effort, especially as it was far more important to clear the Scheldt, so that the much larger port of Antwerp could be opened up. So on 17 September General Henry Crerar, commander of the First Canadian Army, was ordered to call off the assaults and to hand over responsibility for continuing the investment of the fortress to a mixture of forces including, as we have already seen, the Czech armoured brigade. So now back to Rea Leakey:

'So we dumped our tanks in a small town called Gravelines, and on a dark September night took over from the Black Watch. We knew we were going to be employed as infantry for some time, so it would be necessary to have one of the squadrons out of the line in reserve. As a result, where the Black Watch had a platoon defensive post manned by 30 men, we put in no more than 10. Our sector was flat, mostly waterlogged and the only cover was one small village and a few farmhouses. Two roads led in towards the town of Dunkirk and there was also a short road leading from the small village directly to the seashore. Vehicles could not move across country. By day we saw few Germans. They had plenty of artillery, but not a lot of ammunition. By night, however, they were very active.

'I remember the night we took over; the Black Watch put on a firework display, the like of which I had not seen before. They certainly had a great variety of weapons and plenty of ammunition. As a result the Germans left us alone and the handover was completed by midnight. From then on there was silence and no doubt the enemy was anxious to know what was going on. It did not take them long to find out. Our first night was peaceful, although various positions were shelled and German patrols were active. On the second night one of our posts held by a dozen men was attacked and overrun. Two men escaped, but the rest were killed or captured. The next night the same happened to another post. And this was to be the pattern of operations for the following two nights. On the sixth night the strongest and most important of our positions astride the road leading to Calais, manned by 23 men, was attacked by a force of 500 men (so we discovered later) and this time none of our men escaped. At dawn we found the Germans had occupied the position and were holding it in strength.

'The situation was serious, because we now had little to stop the Germans pushing on to Gravelines and even to Calais, now that one of the most important posts was in their hands. By midday I had assembled a company of about 100 men armed with a variety of weapons, and 10 Churchill tanks moved forward fully crewed. We had little difficulty in recapturing the post, killed a number of the enemy and took over 50 prisoners. That certainly kept things quiet for a while, and in due course the whisky arrived, but it was a near thing.

'Before long the Germans were at us again and night after night our isolated posts were attacked. It was now becoming bitterly cold and most nights the temperature fell to below freezing point. The morale of my men in their waterlogged pits was also beginning to drop, and I realised that this state of affairs could not go on. Studying the map, I found there was a lateral road running across our front some 2,000 yards plus ahead of our positions. There were two "feeder" tracks leading up to this road from our area. This gave me an idea. If we could attack and capture this lateral road not only would we narrow our front, but it would also be invaluable for our tanks, because they could then use it to move across the front. I arranged for as many tanks as possible to be fitted with a spotlight.

'Once again I called in all the men from the forward posts and this time formed two teams; each consisted of 10 tanks and about 50 men. With this small force I launched an attack against the German position. Each team was based on one of the two feeder tracks leading up to the lateral road; the tanks were, of course, roadbound, but as the country was flat and open, they could give supporting fire to either flank for a considerable distance. We caught the Germans "napping" and within two hours we had reached the lateral road and continued to push forward. By this time we had captured quite a number of prisoners, and they were becoming a bit of an embarrassment; when we asked Brigade to come and collect them, they quite naturally asked how we had collected them. I had forgotten to tell General Lishka about the attack! He was just a little annoyed. However, later on he awarded me the Czechoslovakian Military Cross, so he must have forgiven me.

'As darkness closed in on us we fell back to the lateral road, more tanks were brought forward and we took up our future defensive positions that were to last until Germany surrendered. No longer did the men occupy damp holes in the ground; the tanks, fully manned, were spaced across the front on the lateral road and acted as pillboxes, each equipped with a spotlight. At dawn, the tanks moved back down the feeder roads and spent the day hidden around farmyards. The crews slept; at dusk they moved forward again and took up station on the lateral road. It was certainly a novel way of holding a front line and many senior officers were most sceptical. Brigadier "Wahoo" paid us a visit shortly after we had adopted these tactics and, to give him his due, he refrained from criticism. He evidently decided to wait and see!

'The Germans soon realised our game and tried every means possible to make us abandon it. Almost every night aircraft from Germany used to drop supplies to the beleaguered garrison. We used to send up recognition flares and thus received a number of these supply drops. Mostly they consisted of short-range anti tank weapons, although we did collect a proportion of their mail. Armed with these anti-tank weapons, the German patrols were out every night trying to destroy our tanks. Only once did they ever achieve any degree of success and this was early in December in a blinding snowstorm. By this time they knew the position of almost every tank, so it was not surprising that even at night in a snowstorm one patrol located a tank. From a range of a few yards, they fired a hollow-charge armour piercing shell at the tank and hit it. Fortunately the shell hit the outer edge of one of the tracks and expended its force on the track plates. It did very little damage to the tank and not one member of the crew was even scratched. The crew could of course see nothing, but opened fire in the direction where they thought the enemy patrol might be. Next morning we discovered two dead bodies.

'As a result of this novel way of holding the line, our casualty rate dropped from a high figure to nil. Also, we found that we needed fewer men actually in the line and so we could ring the changes and get people away on short leave. Before long we had trained patrol teams who would go out almost every night giving the enemy a little of their own medicine. They also made sure that no mines were laid on one of the roads which we used. One night 12 anti-tank mines were laid on one of the roads; fortunately a patrol found them.

'During the day there was very little activity and we tended to think that the Germans would not venture out of their defences in daylight. How wrong we were. One Sunday afternoon in November, my second in command, Bob Romsey, and I decided to walk down to the seashore. I now had some French soldiers under my command and they were manning a position in the sand dunes. We decided to visit them. As we arrived, all hell broke loose and I realised that the Germans were about to assault this small strongpoint. This was the first time these men had been in action and it was just as well that we had turned up, despite the fact that we were only armed with walking sticks, because they panicked and there was little chance of their escaping. Bob was slightly lame, so I told him to take command while I set off at the double across the open ground to get help. Fortunately, I was some 300 yards away before the enemy opened fire on me and once again my luck held. I was able to wake up the crews of some tanks and get them into action, but it was a close thing and taught us a lesson.'[2]

Shortly after this excitement Rea was ordered to leave 7 RTR and take command of 5 RTR who were then in action near Sittard in Holland. The Dunkerque garrison would remain invested for a further seven months, being the last French town to be liberated on 10 May 1945, by which time three-quarters of its houses had been destroyed in the siege.

Clearing the Scheldt

The capture of Antwerp on 4 September 1944, with its port facilities in good condition, did not immediately solve the Allies' supply problems, because the Germans still held the Scheldt estuary and could thus prevent shipping from using the port. SHAEF considered the opening of the port to be of vital importance and gave absolute priority to the clearing of the area. As Montgomery later wrote in his memoir *Normandy to the Baltic*:

'It had become necessary to devote the whole of our resources into getting Antwerp working at once, and

I had to shut down all other offensive operations in 21st Army Group until this object was achieved.'

Operations in the estuary area were not made any easier by the fact that much of the area consisted of reclaimed land — flat, muddy and in some places flooded. The Allies did, however, have two very useful assistants in such circumstances: one was a number of the remarkable AFVs of 79th Armoured Division, the other the Royal Navy Support Squadron, whose rocket-firing/AA/gun batteries would prove to be invaluable. Combined with the bravery and determination of the Canadian and British troops, together with excellent sea and air cover, eventual success was assured, but not before a difficult, hard-fought campaign against a tough and resolute enemy had been waged, lasting from 2 October until 8 November. Even before the fighting was over, minesweepers were already clearing the river ahead of the first convoy.

The Plan

The clearing of the estuary involved the capture of three separate but related areas:

- The coastal plain between Terneuzen and Knokke (known locally as 'Breskens Island' though it was actually part of the 'mainland') where heavy coastal batteries at Breskens and Cadzand covered the approaches to the estuary.
- The isthmus and peninsula of South Beveland, which stuck out into the Scheldt.
- Walcheren Island, where some 25 heavy batteries covered shipping in the estuary.

The area was garrisoned by tough seasoned troops, many of whom had fought on the Eastern Front. The 64th Infantry Division held the mainland south of the estuary (the division had been left isolated when Fifteenth Army had withdrawn eastwards). Walcheren was garrisoned by the 70th Infantry Division, which, as already mentioned, was known as the 'Whitebread Division' because many of its troops had stomach problems and special diets, although this did not seem to affect their fighting ability. On South Beveland there were the elements of a divisional battle group and between the estuary and Turnhout were troops from the 346th, 711th and 719th Infantry Divisions. The clearance plan was to be in three phases:

1. Clear Breskens Island, whilst sealing off the South Beveland peninsula by a thrust from Antwerp.
2. Clear South Beveland by advancing along the isthmus in conjunction with an amphibious assault across the estuary from the south.
3. Capture Walcheren by a series of concentric assaults from east, south and west (which would entail a second crossing of the estuary to take Vlissingen, together with a seaborne assault coming from one of the Channel ports).

Execution of the Plan

On 1 October Phase 1 began, with 2nd Canadian Infantry Division crossing the Antwerp–Turnhout canal and advancing westwards towards the outer suburbs of Antwerp. Resistance was scattered and by the evening of the 4th, the Canadians had cleared the Merksem–Ekkeren area and their leading troops had reached Putte, about half way to the peninsula. They continued to make steady progress, but as they approached Korteen resistance increased and they were unable to capture the village. The Germans launched a series of

Left:
The Scheldt is open! First Allied convoy to enter Antwerp did so on 28 November 1944. The great port could begin to be revitalised. This photo shows part of the empty docks — empty apart from a scuttled coaster — awaiting the convoy's arrival.
IWM — A26605

Right:
Buffaloes belonging to 5th Armoured Regiment RE, and Sherman Crabs of 1st Lothians, both of 79th Armoured Division, are loaded onto LCTs for the Westkapelle operation. Over 100 of these amphibians were used in the operation, manned by 5 ARRE and 11 RTR.
Author's collection

Left:
Smoke rises above Westkapelle as British commandos land there during the final phase of the battle to clear the Scheldt estuary, 1 November 1944. *IWM — A26271*

Right:
The 79th Armoured Division provided maximum assistance to the British troops during the Walcheren operation, as can be seen by the AFVs behind the Weasel cargo carrier. There is a Sherman Crab mine flail (the rotating drum can just been seen on the left), whilst behind it is a Churchill AVRE, which had a Petard spigot mortar, ideal for use against enemy blockhouses.
Author's collection

counter-attacks, but on 16 October the village of Woensdrecht was occupied.

Meanwhile, on the right flank of the Canadian Army, I Corps advanced on the line of the Antwerp–Turnhout Canal. The Polish Armoured Division crossed the Dutch frontier north of Merksplas on 1 October, 49th Infantry Division at this time being engaged in fighting north of St Lenaarts. By the 5th, the leading troops were only about four miles from Tilburg and held on to their positions despite continual counter-attacks. Then in late October the 4th Canadian Armoured Division and US 104th Infantry Division were switched to join I Corps and made good progress northwards, so that by late on the 23rd they had crossed the Dutch frontier near Essen and swung west towards Bergen-op-Zoom. This put pressure on Woensdrecht, successfully sealed off the South Beveland peninsula and thus opened the way for an advance along the isthmus.

Meanwhile, in the south of Breskens Island, 3rd Canadian Infantry Division was planning to assault across the Leopold Canal, due north from Maldegem. At the same time a brigade-sized amphibious landing was to take place on the north-east corner of the island. The enemy positions facing the Canadians were dug in on the reverse slope of the dyke and were clearly going to be difficult to capture, so it was decided to use the Churchill Crocodile flame-throwers of 141 Regiment RAC prior to the main attack. H-Hour was set for early on 6 October and the attacking infantry launched their assault boats as soon as the Crocodiles had finished flaming. All went well on the right, but on the other flank they suffered heavy casualties from enemy machine gun fire. Nevertheless the assault managed to gain a toehold on the far bank and to hold on to it in the face of continuous mortaring and counter-attacks. Reinforcements were ferried across on the 7th and then, about four days later, a Bailey bridge was completed and the bridgehead was at last secure.

The accompanying amphibious landing was made at about 02.00hrs on the 8th and surprise was achieved. At first light, however, the German batteries at Vlissingen and in the Biervliet area began to bombard the beach and its approaches. However, by 05.00hrs the amphibious Buffaloes which had brought the assault force across had returned to embark the follow-up echelon which began to arrive around 09.00hrs. Despite strong resistance, the troops pushed further inland, and also along the coast westwards. By last light they had achieved a beachhead some 3–5km deep.

Because of the difficulties at the Leopold Canal crossing area, it was decided to push southwards along the western bank of the Savojaards Plaat inlet, and to open an inland route via Isabella village. This was achieved by the evening of 14 October. Reinforcements in the shape of the British 52nd Lowland Infantry Division were now arriving and took over the canal bridgehead. These troops plus good air support soon speeded things up and Breskens was taken on the 22nd. Now more than half 'the island' was in Allied hands.

Phase 2 started on 24 October when the 2nd Canadian Infantry Division began its slow but steady advance along the Beveland isthmus leading to the peninsula. The going was terrible, with considerable flooding, particularly near the Beveland Canal. All unflooded roads were either cratered or mined, or both. The advance in some cases was through waist-deep water. Nevertheless, by the 25th they had reached Rilland only some 10km from the Beveland Canal.

Meanwhile, on the night of 25/26 October a brigade of the 52nd Lowland Division had sailed from Terneuzen in LCAs and Buffaloes, to make an amphibious assault near Baarland. The left-hand landing was unopposed but on the right there was

some shelling. A squadron of Sherman DD tanks had managed to cross the estuary but they were soon in trouble in the succession of dykes and mudflats. Despite the problems, the beachhead was extended beyond Oudelande in the west by 27/28 October, whilst the leading troops of 2nd Canadian Infantry Division reached the canal, only to find that all the bridges had been blown. They managed to force a crossing and to get a Class 9 bridge across the canal by midday on the 29th near Vlake. At about the same time, 4th Canadian Armoured Division captured Bergen-op-Zoom. By the 30th the Canadians had reached the eastern end of the causeway across to Walcheren Island and set about clearing any enemy pockets which remained on North Beveland. Whilst all this was taking place, progress continued on 'Breskens Island', so that by the beginning of November, Cadzand and Knokke had been liberated; then two days later, on the 3rd, Zeebrugge fell. Thus the whole of the southern bank of the Scheldt was now clear and all that remained in enemy hands was Walcheren Island.

The estimated garrison on Walcheren was some 6–7,000 men, and there were heavy coastal batteries in concrete emplacements covering the entrance to the West Scheldt. To the west and south of Walcheren were extensive underwater obstacles, whilst wire and minefields blocked all the beach exits. Vlissingen had a sophisticated perimeter fence system with a double line of anti-tank ditches. And there were the normal natural and man-made obstacles such as dykes and flooding.

However, Allied commanders realised that perhaps these features could be turned against the defenders, by breaching the sea dykes and flooding much of the island, thereby making many of the artillery positions untenable and restricting movement of anything but amphibious vehicles. Thus an assault force could then take on the enemy from the rear. Accordingly, in early October the sea defences were breached by some highly accurate bombing by RAF Bomber Command which holed the sea dykes in four places. Further bombing then gradually widened the gaps, so that by the end of October the island had been slowly flooded. The most important gap was near Westkapelle and it was 100m wide by about 3m deep at the low water mark.

Two seaborne landings were planned on Walcheren, the troops being carried and supported by the Royal Navy's Force T. One group would move from Breskens to take Vlissingen; the other, sailing from Ostend, would pass through the hole in the dyke at Westkapelle, get into the island and then link up with the first group. At the same time, a third assault would be made across the South Beveland causeway.

The operation began on 1 November, No 4 Commando landing near Vlissingen with few casualties. Luck also played its part as they hit the only section of shoreline near the town which was unmined. They were followed in by troops of 52nd Lowland in Buffaloes, but these came under heavy, direct and accurate fire from some 8.8cm guns. This caused a large number of casualties. Nevertheless, the rest got ashore and pressed on into the town, whilst reinforcements were ferried in all day long bringing in the entire infantry brigade. At the same time, the Westkapelle force approached the coast, led by 4 Commando Brigade (less No 4 Commando). They attacked the German sand dune positions on both sides of the town, clearing as far as Domburg, then joining up to assault Vlissingen. They were carried in no fewer than 102 Buffaloes, manned by 5 ARRE and 11 RTR, with a wide variety of 79th Armoured Division Funnies close behind.[3] In support were the 25 close support craft of Force T with Landing Craft Guns, Landing Craft AA and Landing Craft Rockets, whilst HMS

Warspite and two 15in gun monitors added their firepower. Overhead were rocket-firing Typhoons from 65 Group RAF.

The force had set off from Ostend at 01.00 on 1 November and seven hours later could just make out Westkapelle Tower through the rain clouds. Half an hour later the warships opened fire, but at first were hampered by poor visibility and the lack of aircraft spotters — this was rectified by using RA Air OP Auster aircraft. The Buffaloes ran ashore, being given close-range protection from Force T, despite heavy casualties from the return fire.

Ernest Carver, a 19-year-old from Nottingham, was a member of the crew of *Landing Craft Flak 36* and he later recalled:

'*The LCFs headed in in a diamond formation. 38, the flotilla leader, was now leading with 37 to starboard, us to port and at the stern was 42. As we ran in, one of the rocket craft released its deadly cargo too early and these blanketed us. We hit the deck in terror and when the smoke and spray had died down, we saw that LCF42 was in bad trouble. She was badly damaged and falling astern rapidly. The other three LCFs were OK, but by now were coming under fire from the shore batteries. The enemy was still well out of range of our light AA guns, so we kept going . . . Suddenly I felt a shockwave and looking to starboard saw that LCF37 had taken a direct hit and in a few seconds the entire boat and its crew had disappeared. Now there were only two of us left and we were close enough to see the German guns being swung up for loading and then depressed down to their minimum range as the crack German gunners fired at us over open sights . . . At the appointed distance from the beach we went into action, LCF38 turned to starboard and we turned to port, then both opened fire. Our shells bounced off the pillboxes like hail off a tin roof! Looking astern to see how LCF 38 was doing I was just in time to see her entire port side disintegrate under direct hits. I reported this to the skipper and then got a message from the flotilla leader: "Close on me". We turned about, still engaging the enemy and the captain took the craft in between the helpless LCF38 and the shore batteries. We were so close now that cannon fire was beginning to reach us. Nothing looks so harmless as tracer, curling lazily towards you and it is only the vicious crack as it passes that brings realisation of its deadliness.*

'*As we were transferring the wounded and survivors from LCF38, the Germans concentrated on us and shells pitched so close that the spray from them soaked everyone. Suddenly we were hit — I was looking at the nearest pillbox and actually saw the shell fired. I watched the big gun barrel swing down and point like a giant condemning finger. An orange flash and immediately the ship staggered as we were hit amidships on the starboard side, but there was no explosion. As quickly as possible we cast off from 38 and left her adrift with her dead, while we continued to engage the enemy.*'

At the end of the action, *LCF36* managed to limp back to Ostend, and was then ordered back to its home port of Poole. In fact, by using the hand-pumps continuously, the crew just managed to get their craft across the Channel to reach Newhaven. The skipper, Lieutenant N. E. Ellams, RNVR, was awarded the DSC and the crew an extra rum ration, whilst a lych gate at the parish church of Hamworthy, near Poole, was

built in memory of those who died in the Walcheren operation.

To return to the landing operation, the LCTs carrying the breaching teams from 79th Armoured Division came ashore with the commandos. They were met with heavy fire and soon had many casualties. However, some of the AFVs did manage to land and materially assisted the commandos in capturing Westkapelle and several of the gun batteries. By 8 November operations had been extended to reach the north end of the island, where the Domburg battery was knocked out, partly by tank shells fired very accurately through the emplacement slits. Middelburg was captured on the 8th, what was left of the garrison (some 2,000) surrendering with their commander Generalleutnant Wilhelm Daser. RN minesweepers immediately began to clear the seaway to Antwerp, but it took three weeks of continuous work by 100 minesweepers before the 120km channel was safe to use, the first convoy berthing in Antwerp on 28 November. The Germans had fought with stubborn bravery, losing many men, including some 10,000 taken prisoner. However, the Allied casualty figures were also considerable — 27,633 killed, wounded and missing.

Liberating the Channel Islands

In stark contrast to the bitter and bloody fighting involved in reducing so many of the Festungen in the battle area, the surrender of the massive German garrison on the Channel Islands came as a complete anti-climax, although I am certain that all the Channel Islanders must have been holding their breath to see what would eventually happen after some of the bellicose remarks made by the Commander in Chief of the Channel Islands (Befehlshaber der britische Kanalinseln — BdbK) the rabid Nazi Vizeadmiral Friedrich Hüffmeier. He had in fact been plotting for some time to oust his predecessor, Generalleutnant Graf Rudolf von Schmettow and succeeded at the end of February 1945. 'I have only one aim,' ranted Hüffmeier in a speech he then made to his officers in the Odeon Cinema, Jersey, 'and that is to hold out until final victory.' He also said on more than one occasion that he would make his soldiers eat grass before he allowed them to surrender.[4]

The British were naturally interested to know if the German garrison would fight or not, because although they had heard of the garrison being subject to malnutrition, it still had substantial fortifications, massive coastal defence batteries and weapons of all kinds, manned by the largest infantry division in the entire German Army. So, for some time, they assumed the worst and set about selecting and training a special force to retake the islands by assault. Under the auspices of HQ Southern Command, the relief force began training in Devon, which it was felt most resembled the Channel Islands terrain. Headquarters 115th Infantry Brigade, a TA Infantry Brigade which had been formed in September 1939, but as yet had never served outside the UK, was selected to command the force, its commander being Brigadier Alfred Snow OBE, a no nonsense 47-year-old Somerset Light Infantryman, who had served towards the end of World War 1, then postwar in India and Burma. It was soon called Task Force 135 (TF135) and the operation to retake the Channel Islands was given the code-name 'Nestegg'. TF135 initially consisted of the infantry brigade together with a number of heavy anti-aircraft and coastal artillery units which were by then not in such great demand since the threat of invasion had all but vanished. They were put at seven days' notice to move, given rigorous training in street fighting in bombed areas of Plymouth and generally prepared for the operation. However, as 1944 gave way to 1945, it became clear that it was crazy to keep a well-trained

Top:
On board HMS *Bulldog*, 9 May 1945.
Kapitänleutnant Zimmerman and
Generalmajor Siegfried Heine listen to
Brigadier Snow telling them about the terms of
the surrender. *CIOS Jersey*

Top right:
The banner says it all. Mrs Elsie Jory of
St Peter Port had painted her own 'welcome'
sign during the occupation and hidden the
Union flags, waiting to put them up on
Liberation Day. *IWM — HU25935*

Above:
Brigadier Snow with the inspection party at
Batterie Annes on Alderney, 16 May 1945.
CIOS Jersey

Right:
End of the occupation. German prisoners
wait to get onto the landing ships that had
brought the British troops of TF135 to
liberate the islands. *IWM — HU5193*

and motivated infantry brigade cooling its heels in England, when there was a continual shortage of infantry in fighting the Germans in North-West Europe. So 115 Brigade was sent over to 21st Army Group (but minus its brigadier) and its place was taken in TF135 by three artillery regiments 614, 618 and 620. The new 'infantry' brigade was given some hasty basic infantry training and made ready for action.

No 20 Civil Affairs Unit

This was a special unit within TF135, which would be of prime importance in getting the islands going again. In the run-up period, it was made responsible for collecting all manner of items which it was considered would be needed by the islanders. Food was top priority, then clothing, with some 200 tons of essential supplies ready for immediate distribution, all pre-loaded onto suitable transport. These supplies included three months' rations for the entire population (not including the German garrison) calculated to raise the diet to a healthy 2,750 calories a day, then the normal food supply chain would take over. Clothing equal to 15 months on the current UK clothing ration would be included, followed up shortly by a further 15 months' supply. The food and clothing would be sold through the shops at current UK prices, whilst, as a goodwill gesture, there was a free gift of chocolate, cigarettes and tobacco. The unit also stockpiled a large range of basic household items and to boost female morale even included a range of cosmetics.

By early May it had become clear that Germany was in total collapse and that liberation for the Channel Islands was at hand. TF135 was brought to a high state of readiness, whilst, with SHAEF approval, HQ Southern Command began trying to open surrender negotiations: 'Subject to you being satisfied as to the intentions of the German Commander, Channel Islands,' signalled SHAEF, 'you should complete mounting and launch of "Nestegg" earliest practical date.' Accordingly, TF135 was assembled at Plymouth on 7 May and married up with its fully laden ships and landing craft. At the same time GOC-in-C Southern Command signalled Hüffmeier to say that he was authorised to receive his unconditional surrender. But the Vizeadmiral was not going to submit without at least a show of defiance. He replied that he only took orders from his own government. However, in the early hours of the 7th, word was received that the Germans had signed the unconditional surrender and that all hostilities would cease at midnight on 8 May. This was followed by a signal from Hüffmeier proposing that his representatives meet the British representatives some 7km south of the Les Hanois light to sign the surrender documents. This was agreed and the time for the meeting set as 12.00hrs, Tuesday, 8 May 1945.

Each carrying a landing party of two officers and 20 other ranks, the two RN destroyers HMS *Beagle* and HMS *Bulldog* left Plymouth at 10.00. Brigadier Snow was on the *Bulldog* and reached the RV without a hitch. Kapitänleutnant Armin Zimmerman, representing Hüffmeier, came aboard. He then told Brigadier Snow that he was only authorised to discuss the armistice and could not sign anything. Snow replied in no uncertain terms that he must return and prepare for unconditional surrender. Zimmerman countered by saying that the general cease-fire did not begin until midnight and that if the destroyers did not withdraw they would run the risk of being shelled by the German coastal batteries. Rear-Admiral Starr, the Naval Force Commander, who had been ordered to avoid confrontation at all costs, decided to withdraw out of range. A signal was shortly afterwards received to say that Hüffmeier's deputy, Generalmajor Siegfried Heine, would be at the RV at

midnight and that he would be authorised to sign. This he did, signing eight copies of the surrender document at 01.14hrs on a rum cask on the quarterdeck of HMS *Bulldog*. The destroyer then moved into St Peter Port harbour and the Guernsey landing party went ashore. Meanwhile, Brigadier Snow transferred to HMS *Beagle*, then headed for Jersey, anchoring off St Helier and sending for the island commander Generalmajor Wulf to sign the surrender of Jersey. On his arrival Wulf, another fervent Nazi, was somewhat aggressive and arrogant, causing Brigadier Snow to 'express his displeasure in the most forthright language'. This completely took the wind out of Wulf's sails and he signed the surrender document without any further nonsense. The landing party then disembarked and there followed flag hoisting ceremonies on both islands, together with the reading of King George VI's royal proclamation.

TF135 Lands

'Bev' Bevins of the Royal Engineers remembered what happened when he came ashore:

'They sent me off first. They said, "Bevins, you go first. You've got 3.5 tons, so if you blow up they'll know we've arrived." I had got sandbags all around me, I could just move my hands and feet. Once ashore then our job was clearing mines that had been missed and God knows what else. When we first landed it was hugs and kisses from the ladies. The men shook our hands, patted our backs and asked if we had any cigs. We gave the children sweets — they thought it was Christmas! One thing sticks in my mind. I was standing by my lorry and the lads were clearing a Jerry store, making sure there were no booby traps, when this old lady came to me with tears in her eyes and she said: "There you are, I always said that an English soldier would have the first strawberry and you are he." And I had to stand there and eat, and I cried with her.'

Notes

1. Collins had been given this nickname early in the war at Guadalcanal, when one of his soldiers in a forward foxhole was heard to remark: 'By God, there is J. Lightning himself!' — 'Lightning' being the telephone code call for Division HQ. By the end of the campaign, word of the incident had spread on the soldiers' grapevine but 'J. Lightning' had been changed to 'Lightning Joe' and the nickname stuck thereafter.

2. *Leakey's Luck* edited by George Forty.

3. These included 10 Crab Flails, eight AVREs with Small Box Girder bridges and fascines, and four bulldozers.

4. This was an oblique reference to the severe shortage of food on the islands in the winter of 1944/45 — which became known as the 'Great Hunger Winter', which got so bad that the Red Cross had to bring in food parcels for the civilians. The German garrison had been very short of rations ever since the Normandy landings had virtually cut them off from the Continent.

Chapter 11
Conclusions

Why the Wall Failed

Having looked at aspects of the designing, building, manning and defending of the Atlantic Wall, we must now try to decide why it did not prevent the Allies from successfully invading Normandy. We need to examine this question both from the defenders' point of view as well as from that of the attackers. We need also to consider whether the German military ever thought that it would prove to be 100% effective, or rather just a means of slowing down the assault so as to give them time to defeat it in other ways.

From the German Side
Lack of a Unified Concept of Defence

First and foremost, the failure of the Germans to repulse the Allied invasion did not just depend upon the strength of the defences which formed the Atlantic Wall. It also depended upon the strategic distribution of German forces within North-West Europe. There were just under 60 divisions available in the west, but of course their strength, weaponry and fighting ability were not universally high, many of the infantry divisions being suitable only for local, static occupation use. In addition, only a few infantry and panzer divisions were up to anything like full strength, whilst many of the coastal divisions actually manning the Wall contained an alarming number of what were described as 'Eastern Volunteers' whose combat abilities and loyalties were suspect from the outset. We have already dealt with the rivalries, differences of opinion and of tactical concepts between the Heer and the Kriegsmarine, and also between various factions within both services; these were probably the most important factors which militated against a successful, unified command. The 'panzer controversy', for example, which I have highlighted, was a major expression of this internal squabbling and it was never resolved. This meant that there was never anything that could have been described as being a unified concept of defence on the Western Front.

Lack of Weapons and Equipment

As well as a shortage of forces, there was undoubtedly an acute shortage of weapons and equipment in all three services of the Wehrmacht. Almost everywhere there was a shortage of naval vessels, a shortage of fighter aircraft, a shortage of infantry weapons, a shortage of armour and artillery, and a shortage of mechanised troops, with too many horses still performing front-line duties. Despite the individual excellence of such basic items as the MG42 — probably the best light machine gun of the war — the MP40 sub-machine gun, and the Panzerfaust and Panzerschreck hand-held anti-tank weapons to name but four of the basic German weapons, they just could not compete with the overwhelming fire power of the Allies, especially the Americans. It also did not help having a mixture of captured weapons in front line service, in particular artillery, which helped to complicate ammunition supply and led to ammunition shortages even for the 'sharp end' troops defending the beaches.

Lack of Agreement on the Most Probable Site for the Invasion

Equally important was lack of agreement at high level as to the most likely location for the coming invasion. Von Rundstedt and Rommel had for a long while generally agreed that the sector north of the Seine, in particular the area between Boulogne and Le Havre, was the most likely landing area. Nevertheless, the coastline of Normandy and Brittany was a close contender and became more likely as the days of spring 1944 lengthened into early summer. However, whilst they recognised this change, the German command did very little to alter the allocation of troops, or to take any real extra precautions. Even though Adolf Hitler had seen the Cotentin peninsula and the port of Cherbourg[1] as becoming increasingly important, expressing this view at several meetings, nothing was actually done about it. These differences of opinion came to a head on 6 May, when von Rundstedt categorically turned down Rommel's requests to strengthen the Cotentin peninsula defences. Hitler's HQ supported Rommel, but in too half-hearted a manner, intimating that, whilst they agreed that the Cotentin could well be the first enemy objective, they could not agree that the western bay of the Seine had become the most probable landing area.

Other commanders at a slightly lower level also agreed that the main landing area would be Normandy — these included General Erich Marcks, commander of LXXXIV Army Corps, who would be right in the thick of it when the invasion came. Nevertheless, voices like his were crying in the wilderness as events would show.

Spies on the Atlantic Wall and other Subterfuges

As mentioned at the start of Chapter 6, the incredibly brave 'volunteer' spies and their handlers who operated in all the occupied countries, often under the very noses of the Gestapo, played an important role in ensuring that the Allies knew as much as possible about the German defences prior to D-Day. Add to this the constant flow of information obtained from Ultra, air reconnaissance and all the other methods of gaining up-to-date facts and figures and it is clear that intelligence played a vitally important role in the planning stages of 'Overlord' and thus in the Allied success. Furthermore, the mass of misinformation fed to the German intelligence services, typified by everything to do with Patton's mythical army group, waiting to strike at the Pas de Calais, also undoubtedly played its part in helping to breach the Wall.

What Leading Germans Thought

It is interesting to read what has been written about the Wall by senior Wehrmacht officers and Organisation Todt staff. Most of these views were written after the war, so are presumably given with the benefit of hindsight and the knowledge that Hitler was safely under the sod. I doubt if they would ever have been brave enough to voice such defeatist opinions whilst the Führer was still alive.

A Propagandist's Bluff

'The Atlantic Wall was a propagandist's bluff, it was not as strong as was believed abroad.' These are the words of General der Infanterie Günther Blumentritt, who was Chief of Staff OB West. He continued:

Right:
Some basic German small arms and other equipment — even these weapons were in short supply. The photo shows the earlier MG 34 which was widely used, as its replacement, the MG42, was still not available to all. *IWM — E3091*

Below:
Panthers en route from Northern France during June 1944. The Allied bombing and sabotage by the French *Maquis* helped to make it virtually impossible to move such heavy equipment by day. *J. P. Benamou Collection*

Bottom:
In 1944 there were still large numbers of horses used to tow artillery and supply wagons in front line service with the German Army. *Guernsey Museums and Galleries*

'It was very strong on the coast of Holland and in the Fifteenth Army sector on the Channel. However, the batteries of these mighty concrete works were silent when they were blanketed by pattern bombing and heavy naval artillery. The guns had only limited traverse; they were unable to fire to the rear, on the land front. The ventilation [escape for gases caused by firing] did not function. The "Wall" was a line, a chain of individual works without depth. If the enemy penetrated to a depth of one kilometre, they would be in free terrain. The installed guns were captured French, Belgian, Dutch, Polish, Russian and Yugoslavian materiel of all types and calibres with a variety of ammunition. Many had only a limited number of rounds available. Under heavy bombardment from the air and strong artillery fire from the sea, blanketed by smoke and attacked by airborne troops from the rear, the "Wall" could never have stopped an invasion. It was apparent that these concrete monsters were greatly overrated. We had to assume that these facts had been made known by the many foreign workers.'

Blumentritt goes on to explain just where the staff at OB West had considered the most probable invasion sites to be. 'The wide, jutting peninsulas of Normandy and Brittany' were one area considered, but discounted as it was thought that the route to Germany was too long from either of these locations. A landing in the Bay of Biscay in the First Army sector was possible, especially because there were 500km of coastline to be defended by just three divisions, of which two were composed mainly of recruits, but this site was just as far away. They considered diversionary assaults on the Mediterranean coast to be a distinct possibility, but only to contain the German reserves. He comments that OKW, on several occasions, considered that landings might be made in Spain and/or Portugal, but OB West considered this even more unlikely for both political and military reasons — the terrain, railways and roads were unsuitable, the Pyrenees would have to be crossed and 'the Spaniard fights well on his own soil'. After considering all these possibilities they went for the Fifteenth Army sector as being the most likely invasion location, between Calais and the mouth of the Seine.

He also had this to say about the level of support they had expected from the Air Force and Navy:

'The ratio of air strength between the Luftwaffe and the Allies on 6 June 1944 was 1:25. The Allies had not only air superiority, but complete mastery of the air, with all the obvious consequences for us. In the entire OB West area, the Navy had only 12 destroyers. I do not recall the number of E-boats. There was only a limited supply of naval mines. The Resistance movement in southern France was so strong that troop movements were delayed, communications were destroyed, and considerable casualties were sustained as the result of ambushes.'[2]

An Over-Sized Construction Project

'As a result of Hitler's distrust of the Army officer corps he narrowed their field of employment more and more. This development begins with the assignment of fortification construction [the West Wall] to Todt . . . After the West Wall, which nonetheless may have had a certain psychological importance at the beginning of the war although it was never of any strategic value, his [Hitler's] dictatorial order led to the construction of the Atlantic Wall, an over-sized construction project which caused serious damage to our Army which was fighting in the East through its expenditure of labour and materials, without presenting any obstacle worthy of the name to the enemy invasion of 1944.'

These caustic comments were written by General Franz Halder in a pamphlet he wrote entitled 'Hitler as a General' which is quoted by Franz Xaver Dorsch, Deputy Chief of the OT, in his dissertation on the Organisation Todt. Dorsch, however, as one might expect, does not agree:

'Aside from the fact that it is possible to hold a different opinion as to the psychological effectiveness of the Atlantic Wall and that at that time it was justifiable to assume that without the presence of the Atlantic Wall the invasion would have taken place considerably earlier, and precisely for this reason would have caused serious harm to the Army fighting in the East at a considerably earlier time, and aside from the additional fact that the opinion may be held that the value of a fortification can only be estimated in conjunction with an Army which is still intact and not at a time when this Army, for example, was admittedly handicapped with respect to its freedom of movement and striking power as the result of the almost complete failure of the Luftwaffe, there is the following to be said concerning Halder's statements:
'For the most part the construction of the Atlantic Wall was carried out at the same time as the construction of the submarine bases, various construction projects for the armament industry, repair work on destroyed railway installations etc. Altogether, along with many other construction achievements, the OT poured somewhat more than 15 million cubic metres of concrete and reinforced concrete — to mention only one figure — in the occupied territories. With an overall personnel strength at the most important time of around 200,000 men on the job, approximately only 18,000 OT workers were employed, the average age of whom was about 55 at the end of the war! Even if the age of the OT's organic executive personnel and that of its contracting firms, which had an average strength of 8,000 men, was substantially lower, it is nevertheless obvious that the deferment of the men eligible for military service in the above-mentioned figures could not have had a detrimental effect of any importance on the supply of manpower for the Army fighting in the East, since, as already said, this figure included workers employed in the construction of submarine bases, who could by no means be dispensed with in view of the importance ascribed to these bases at that time. The construction of the submarine bases, which was carried out at the same time as the construction of the Atlantic Wall, is mentioned because the conjunction of these two construction projects resulted in greater efficiency from the very beginning. Hitler's order in the summer of 1942 to speed up the completion of the Atlantic Wall could be acted upon so quickly because the five submarine bases were already employing a considerable number of construction workers, most of whom could be reassigned to the construction of the Atlantic Wall.'

Dorsch goes on in the same rather heavy-handed way to justify the OT use of vehicles and supplies which could have been sent to the Eastern Front, pointing out for example, that more than half of the OT vehicles were rented from the French, Belgians and Dutch with their own indigenous drivers. Nor was the quantity of steel used in the Atlantic Wall of any importance to the overall military potential, especially since Speer had issued a special order for OT to use various kinds of iron which could not be used for armament purposes without special processing. Also, as he had already pointed out, only 24,000 of the 200,000 construction workers were actually Germans.

Neither Tactically nor Strategically Proficient

Rommel's brilliant chief of staff General Hans Speidel was more scathing about the OT than he was about the Atlantic Wall itself, although we have already seen how disappointed Rommel was when he carried out his first inspection. '*The whole development of coastal defence*,' wrote Speidel in his book *We Defended Normandy*:

'*that is to say, the design and layout of the fortifications, had been entrusted to an engineer of the Todt organisation, who was neither tactically nor strategically proficient, had no knowledge of the general war situation and no experience of co-operation with the armed forces. There had been no chance of an agreed system of defences between the Army, the Navy and the Todt organisation, as between 1941 and 1943 the services had failed to agree upon basic principles.*'

He goes on later to explain how propaganda for the Atlantic Wall had begun in 1942, when the Dieppe raid had been beaten off, German propaganda had claimed a major success for the defences — in order to distract public attention from the reverses on the Eastern Front, and the high command in the West had:

'*regrettably associated itself with these optimistic claims. Goebbels had experience of "building-up" a defence line from the summer of 1938 when he put the "West Wall" of Germany on the map. Now he did the same for the Atlantic Wall. He picked on the strongest area, the heavy "offensive batteries group" at Cap Gris-Nez, and made it appear that the whole of the Atlantic Wall was of equal strength.*'

And Rommel Himself

Being an entirely practical and pragmatic soldier, Rommel did not waste his breath complaining about the failure of the Atlantic Wall to stop the Allied landings, but rather expended his energies on fighting the battle in Normandy until his disastrous encounter with Allied fighter-bombers on 17 July. This ended his command of Army Group B as he sustained severe skull injuries and had to be rushed to hospital. Sadly, his remarkable recovery from these wounds coincided with the aftermath of the witch-hunt that followed the botched attempt on Hitler's life, and led to Rommel's forced suicide on 13 October. Therefore we will never know what his frank postwar assessment of the Wall would have been. Certainly from what he did mention in various battle reports after D-Day we get the impression that he was entirely satisfied with the way the troops actually defending the Wall had performed. For example, in a situation report written on 10 June, he said:

'*As a result of the stubborn defence of the coast defence troops and the immediate counter-attacks launched by the available major reserve, the enemy attack, despite the strength of his effort, has gone considerably more slowly than he had hoped. The enemy also seems to be committing more forces than he had originally planned.*'

Elsewhere in the same report, when discussing the massive enemy use of heavy naval guns — he says that at least 640 heavy naval guns were involved — he comments:

'*The effect is so immense that no operation of any kind is possible in the area commanded by this rapid-fire artillery,*

Left: The devastation caused by Allied bombing — this is part of Calais — posed a continual threat to the German garrisons and made movement during daylight virtually impossible. *IWM — CL1298*

Above: As the General Omar N. Bradley, photographed here in London after VE Day, said: 'We had only to concentrate a force against some single point in his line. With the firepower at our disposal we could break a hole in that line and pour our follow-up forces through it.' . *Author's collection*

either by infantry or tanks. Yet, despite this heavy bombardment, the garrisons on the coast and the units who counter-attacked in the Montebourg area have held their positions with extreme stubbornness.'[3]

The Atlantic Wall Existed Only in the Pas de Calais

Finally, in these 'home-truths' on the Atlantic Wall, I have chosen German author Paul Carell, who in his book *Invasion — They're Coming!* speaks for the ordinary rankers who would have to fight the battle in Normandy. After commenting on the high average age of the soldiers, naval gun crews and others who were charged with the defence, he asks the question:

'But was this disadvantage not offset by the insuperable Atlantic Wall? By that protective shield of concrete, steel, guns and mines? Was the coastline not thick with menacing concrete fortresses equipped with powerful naval guns? And was the foreshore from Brest to Ostend not littered with ingenious death-dealing obstacles? The answer, unfortunately, was no. In the summer of 1944, the Atlantic Wall existed only in the Pas de Calais. For the rest it consisted of a string of widely spaced strongpoints, some of which were only half finished. Only a few of the heavy batteries were adequately protected or even equipped. Most of the equipment consisted of captured enemy guns, totally unsuitable against naval targets because of their calibre and their lack of fire-control equipment.'

From the Allied Side

Those at the Top

In his memoir *Crusade in Europe*, the Supreme Allied Commander, General Dwight D. Eisenhower, after explaining why the UK had been chosen as the main base for operations in Europe, goes on to say:

'From that point on we encountered the obstacle on which all discussions split and practically exploded in our faces. This was a very definite conviction, held by some of our experienced soldiers, sailors and airmen, that the fortified coast of Western Europe could not be successfully attacked. Already much was known of the tremendous effort the German was making to insure integrity of his Atlantic Wall. Moreover, a considerable amount of the German Air Force could still be disposed in those areas and important elements of his fleet were lying in the harbours of northern France, in Norway, and in the Baltic Sea. The coast-line was crowded with U-boat nests, while undersea mining was rapidly covering every possible approach . . . Many held that attack against this type of defence was madness, nothing but military suicide. Even among those who thought direct assault by land forces would eventually become necessary, the majority believed that definite signs of cracking German morale would have to appear before it would be practicable to attempt such an enterprise.'

Eisenhower explains that, fortunately, a few others took an opposite view and goes on to describe how they formulated a new concept, as he puts it:

'almost a new faith, to strategic thinking, one which envisaged the air co-operation with ground operations to the extent that a ground-air team would be developed, tending to multiply the effectiveness of both.'

Whilst he is naturally inclined to emphasise the American role in the decision to make an attack across the English Channel, it was of course a decision made between the British and American governments that this would be their principal offensive effort in Europe. The plan received President Roosevelt's blessing on 1 April 1942 and the following month a body known as the 'Combined Commanders' was set up to get to grips with the problems. Following the Casablanca conference of January 1943, it was decided to set up an Allied inter-service staff (COSSAC) to prepare a definite plan for Operation 'Overlord'.

Winston Churchill, in Volume V of his *History of the Second World War*, deals with the question of where the landing could best be made.

'There were several options, the Dutch or Belgian coast, the Pas de Calais; between the mouths of the Somme and the Seine; Normandy; Brittany . . . Normandy gave us the greatest hope. The defences were not so strong as in the Pas de Calais . . . All the coast between Havre and Cherbourg was of course defended with concrete forts and pillboxes, but as there was no harbour capable of sustaining a large Army in this 50-mile half-moon of sandy beaches it was thought that the Germans would not assemble large forces in immediate support of the seafront . . . If only there were harbours, which could nourish great armies, here was the front to strike.'

Churchill went on to explain how, as far back as May 1942, he had given the go-ahead to the building of the Mulberry Harbours, being a 'partisan of piers with their heads floating out in the sea'. Thus, whilst not discounting the strength of the Atlantic Wall, Churchill's fertile imagination had already found a major key to breaking into it.

And what of the general who would command the initial landings — General Montgomery, who had been personally responsible for the simple, clear plan which eventually became the basis for 'Overlord'? He forecast that the fighting would be extremely hard, principally because Rommel was in charge of the Atlantic Wall. Monty's intelligence experts had rightly come to the conclusion that Rommel would try to defeat them as they came ashore, pushing forward his reserves, rather than assembling them to fight in depth — the fact that Rommel would be thwarted by his own side, was of course not even considered as a possibility. However, he appreciated that Rommel would need to commit his armour. As Monty's biographer Nigel Hamilton says:

'By personalising the enemy as "Rommel", he [Montgomery] was able to clarify and simplify the scenario — alerting all to the sense of contest between opposing wills: "Since Rommel toured the Atlantic Wall the enemy has been stiffening up his coastal crust, generally strengthening his defences and re-distributing his armoured reserve. The present trend of movement of his mobile reserves is South — i.e. away from the 'Neptune' ('Overlord') area; this shows that our target is not yet known to the enemy. Rommel is likely to hold his mobile Divisions back from the coast until he is certain where our main effort is being made. He will then concentrate them quickly and strike a hard blow; his static Divisions

Left:
Even Hitler's top secret V-weapon sites were located and hit. This one was at Blendecques.
Author's collection

Below:
Bombing and accurate naval gun fire did untold damage to the supposedly impregnable Atlantic Wall, as can be seen here on this casemate containing a 5cm KWK L/42 anti-tank gun, being inspected by Allied troops. *IWM — B5252*

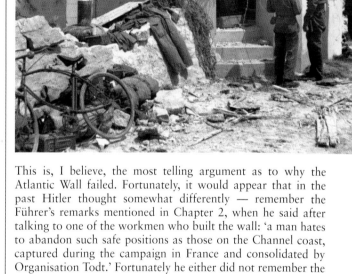

will endeavour to hold on defensively to important ground and act as pivots to the counter-attacks . . . Some of us here know Rommel well. He is a determined commander and likes to hurl his armour into the battle . . . but according to what we know of the chain of command, armoured divisions are being kept directly under Rundstedt and delay may be caused before they are released to Rommel.'

How different things might have been if Rommel had actually had control over Geyr von Schweppenburg's Panzer Group West and had been able to move it freely from the outset without the continual threat from Allied air superiority.

General Omar N. Bradley, known as the Soldiers' General, remembered one of the maxims of Frederick the Great: 'He who defends all, defends nothing. Little minds want to defend everything, sensible men concentrate on the essential.' As Bradley himself put it:

'Unable to anticipate where we might strike, the enemy had been forced to spread his strength across 860 miles of European coastline. As he continued to plant more German dead on his long line of retreat from Russia, it became increasingly difficult for him to man the Atlantic Wall. To smash our way ashore we had only to concentrate a force against some single point in his line. With the firepower at our disposal we could break a hole in that line and pour our follow-up forces through it.'

Bradley then went on to affirm that the Atlantic Wall would never have halted an intruder, but that it could, and did, slow down an attacking force whilst reserves were summoned to counter-attack. In other words, it was there to:

'blunt our assault and so split our forces so that the enemy might find time to form his reserves and strike back in counter-attack. When used to screen a mobile reserve in this fashion, the concrete fortifications of a fixed defensive line can be worth many divisions. Without these mobile reserves, however, a fixed defensive line becomes useless.'

This is, I believe, the most telling argument as to why the Atlantic Wall failed. Fortunately, it would appear that in the past Hitler thought somewhat differently — remember the Führer's remarks mentioned in Chapter 2, when he said after talking to one of the workmen who built the wall: 'a man hates to abandon such safe positions as those on the Channel coast, captured during the campaign in France and consolidated by Organisation Todt.' Fortunately he either did not remember the words of Frederick the Great with which I began this section or chose to ignore them.

'He who defends all defends nothing' — perhaps that would be the most fitting epitaph for Hitler's Atlantic Wall.

Notes
1. Cherbourg was almost completely left alone by Allied bombers in their air attacks before the invasion — an indication that they wanted to use the port facilities in due course.
2. As quoted in *Fighting the Invasion — the German Army at D-Day* edited by David C. Isby.
3. Quoted in *The Rommel Papers* edited by Basil Liddell Hart.

Chapter 12

What Remains to be Seen

Although today many of both the major and minor fortification works no longer exist, far more having been demolished since the end of the war in Europe than were ever destroyed in battle, there are still sufficient structures remaining to give anyone interested a vivid idea of what the Atlantic Wall must have looked like and how it was manned and operated. However, whilst buildings could be fairly rapidly evacuated by their erstwhile garrisons, what could not be left for posterity were the vast numbers of minefields, booby traps and other explosive devices which the Germans had sown, whilst all the defence positions had either to be rendered harmless, or in some cases their weapons and equipment (for example radar) handed over *in situ* to the Allies. Initially, therefore, there was a massive clean-up operation, much of the work being done by the German soldiers themselves — now POWs. One told me:

'Immediately after the war the soldiers of the Pionierkompanie [engineer company], and others under the age of 25 and single, had to clear the mines. The barbed-wire fences remained there . . . the mine clearing was a dangerous business and there were many casualties.'

Tourist Attractions

As the various 'owner' countries have now come to realise, there is money for their tourist industries to make out of the abiding interest of millions of people in many aspects of World War 2, including what is left of the Atlantic Wall. In addition to the general public, military historians have brought these fortifications into their studies in the same way as they have always been interested in more ancient structures such as castles, watchtowers, and defensive walls. Although it is in France and the Channel Islands where this has been most pronounced, there are excellent sites now open everywhere along the coastline of Europe which can be visited by individuals and parties, whilst organisations such as the Channel Islands Occupation societies, the Historic Fortifications Network and the Fortress Study Group, to name but a few (see Appendix I for more details) continue to research, repair and generally bring to life more and more of these fascinating sites every year. Thus after years of neglect, the Atlantic Wall has come alive again.

In this final chapter I have tried to give a general idea of what the visitor can expect to see in each country in which the Atlantic Wall was located, highlighting at least one or more 'not to be missed' sites, although in both France and the Channel Islands one is spoilt for choice. The selection of appropriate museums should be read in combination with Appendix II, which contains a more comprehensive, albeit less detailed, list.

A Word of Warning

Whilst there are plenty of recognised sites and museums for the average visitor, inevitably some people like to go 'off piste' and explore on their own, in the hope that they will discover something exciting that everyone else has missed. Not only will they invariably be disappointed, but such exploration can be downright dangerous. The Channel Islands Occupation Society always includes a word of warning in its yearly review, which I believe is well worth repeating here:

'Most of the bunkers, gun pits and defences are on private property. If you want to have a look, obtain permission from the owner. Do not enter without a strong torch or lamp. There are different designs of defences that from the outside look the same, but once inside, passages may descend without warning. Also, wellington boots may be needed as 50-plus years of dirt and dust will have blocked the drains. We would also warn you that bunkers on the coast will also have been used as unofficial toilets — so beware! Young persons should not enter without an adult, as many bunkers have awkward steps and hidden ducts that can trap the unwary. Bunkers and tunnels have been blocked up for this reason and no other; those of you who would like to find an Aladdin's Cave of war relics have been beaten to it by the scrap drive of 1947–48.'

Norway

First, two examples from Norway:

Fort Austrått As has already been mentioned, various structures along the Norwegian coast have survived well because they were built on rock. However, one of the 'jewels in the crown' must be the 28cm triple gun turret at Fort Austrått, Lundahaugen, Orland. It was originally the stern gun turret of the German battleship *Gneisenau*. Launched at Kiel in December 1936 and fully equipped two years later, the battleship had nine 28cm (11in) guns in three triple turrets (Anton, Bruno and Caesar), plus 12 x 15cm, 14 x 10.5cm dual purpose and 16 x 37mm AA guns. After seeing action during the early part of the war, the *Gneisenau* was badly damaged in February 1942, declared a partial wreck and its guns taken on shore. 'A' turret's guns were set up as individual guns at the Hoek van Holland. The undamaged 'B' turret was mounted in a mountain installation at Fjell on the island of Sotra, west of Bergen, where there now is a museum (see Appendix II). 'C' turret came to Austrått.

Before it was emplaced the necessary shafts and tunnels had to be blasted out of the mountain and comprehensive concrete work carried out. The building work was done by 300–400 Serbian POWs, who lived in terrible conditions and were roughly treated. Many died during the work, which began in 1942 and was completed the following year. Test firing of the guns took place in September 1943. Also on site were the following additional weapons: 1 x 4.7cm anti-tank gun, 3 x 40mm Bofors flak and 6 x 20mm flak guns. In the spring of 1945 the guns were jointly taken over by Norwegian and British troops and became part of the Trondelag coastal artillery brigade, later called Fort Austrått. The battery closed down in 1968, and in 1990 the Norwegian Defence Department gave 1.1 million kroner for restoration work. Once this had been completed, the battery was handed over to the municipality of Orland as a tourist attraction and was first opened to the public in May 1992.

Kristiansand Kanonmuseum, Movik Southwest of Kristiansand along Route 457 is the only remaining 38cm naval

Above: The massive triple gun turret at Fort Austrått, Norway. The 28cm guns had formerly been installed in the stern gun turret on the German battleship *Gneisenau* which was badly damaged by British bombers whilst in the floating dock at Kiel on 26/27 February 1942. Declared a partial wreck, it was used as a block ship at Gotenhafen in the spring of 1942, whilst its guns were taken on shore and used for various purposes. *Municipality of Orland*

Above: Hydraulic rammer and rear of the barrel inside the turret at Fort Austrått. The guns were first test fired in September 1943, but never saw real action. The crew comprised 10 officers and 107 men, plus a further 30 in the fire control centre at Loerbern. *Municipality of Orland*

gun of World War 2. These guns were built by Krupps as the main armament of the battleships *Tirpitz* and *Bismarck*. The complex was operational by 1943 and named Batterie Vara. Together with the gun at Hanstholm, just opposite in Denmark, its main task was to protect German supply lines and deny Allied forces access to the Baltic. The battery remained in commission until 1952 as part of Norway's coastal defences.

Denmark

All along the west coast of Jutland are considerable numbers of reinforced concrete fortifications, which are the remains of the Atlantic Wall. Some of them have been restored and have become museums. Here is a selection of the best.

Fortification 'Tirpitz' The building of this bunker at Blavand began in 1944 and it was designed to house a 38cm naval gun. However, the German surrender came before it was completed and postwar attempts to demolish it failed. The museum was opened on 1 June 1991, after a most successful project for unemployed young people who carried out a lot of the restoration work and gathered the exhibition material with the assistance of the Varde Museum, Blavandshuk Local History Record Office and Blavandshuk Regional Museum. Exhibitions describe both the function and operation of the fortification, whilst there is a film *The Atlantic Wall* (currently only in Danish and German). Conducted tours and visits outside normal opening hours can be arranged.

Museums Center, Hanstholm Immediately after the German invasion in 1940, the building of 'Fortress Hanstholm' began, naval artillery positions being established to protect supply routes to Norway and the unfinished Hanstholm Harbour, whilst flak batteries protected the approach to Ålborg air base. Four SKS/34 38cm naval guns were installed in individual casemates, each with a crew of 90 men. The battery became operational in September 1941. The Hanstholm battery was moved to its present location beginning in 1942 and completed in June 1944. The guns were never to fire in their new casemates. The civilian population was evacuated in 1942 and the area became a major defensive position, stretching from Agger to Svinkov. In the autumn of 1945 the first civilians returned, but it was not until 1959 that the fortification was declared free of mines. It can now be visited and the leaflet asks

visitors to take particular care when inside the buildings, to bring a powerful torch, be careful where they tread and, above all, mind their heads!

Fiskeri- & Søfartsmuseet, Esbjerg In the museum's open air exhibition area, a German bunker has been opened and refurnished to the original standard. An exhibition of the fortification of wartime Esbjerg is also open.

Langelands Fort Although this is an excellent and well-maintained gun position from the Cold War era, the main battery comprises four 15cm guns from the *Gneisenau*. The main exhibition highlights the fort's history and the Cold War in general.

'Stottenpunkt Hirsthals' — 10th Batterie Naval battery close to the Hirsthals lighthouse, where the bunker contains the main exhibition.

Frederikshavn 'Batterie Nord' Part of the German defensive system around this important harbour. The exhibition is housed in the fire control bunker and an emplacement complete with 10.5cm gun has been re-established.

Silkeborg Bunker Museum This was the German HQ during World War 2 and a barracks bunker has been re-opened.

There are a number of other museums listed in Appendix II and one should contact the Danish Fortification Society for further details (see Appendix I). Many of the other Danish-based fortifications, especially those built along the west coast of Jutland, are still standing and recent years have seen a growing interest in the history behind their construction. Please see the Bibliography for details of two excellent illustrated books which cover these sites in considerable detail and are published by the Blavandshuk Egnsmuseum.

Germany

There are surprisingly few signs of the Atlantic Wall left on the German coast. A few bunkers can still be found in some areas — some have even been turned into weekend seaside chalets — but in general terms, and for obvious reasons, the Wall is no more. An excellent source of Atlantic Wall material is DAWA — Deutsches Atlantik Wall Archiv, the contact address being: Harry Lippmann, Schmittgasse 151, D 51143 Köln, Germany. Herr Lippmann has himself written numerous books on the subject.

Above: Tirpitz-stillingen (Fortification Tirpitz). The bunker, designed to house a 38cm gun. was begun in 1944, but was never finished before the war ended. It is now a museum (opened in 1991), with numerous exhibits and a film showing all about the construction of the fortification. *DFS*

The Netherlands

There are various societies which want to preserve parts of the Atlantic Wall, for example Stichting Vesting Hoek van Holland, who recently dug out the remains of flak Batterie Nordmole at the Hook of Holland. Also do not forget Stützpunkt XXXVIIH at Wassenaar, described in detail in Chapter 5, which was due to open to the public in the summer of 2002.

Kustverdedigingsmuseum Housed in what was the Maasmond Fort, built to protect the entrance to Rotterdam Harbour, this is a major Dutch armour museum. Building work began on the fort in 1881 and it was completed in September 1889. It is built of concrete and brick, covered with earth. It saw action during the German invasion in May 1940. Its garrison in those days was nine officers, 26 NCOs and 246 men. Exactly

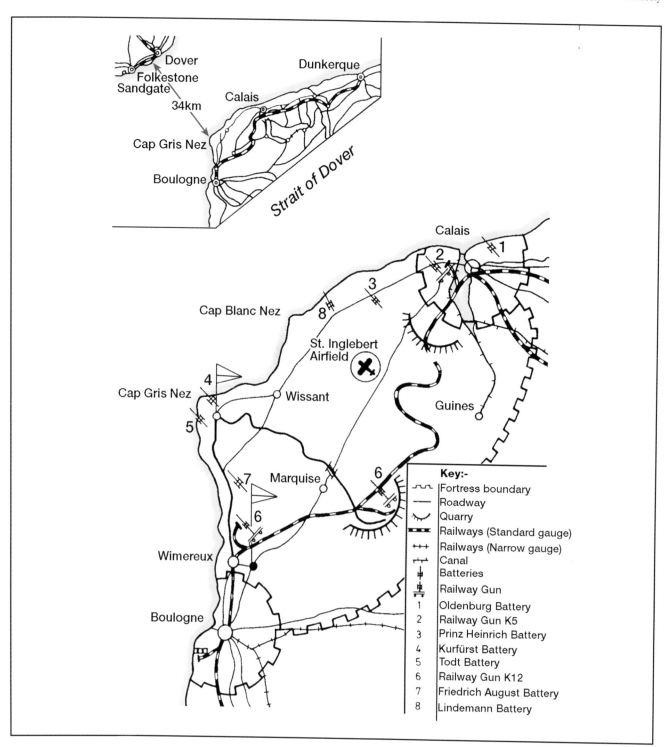

Above: English Channel coastal guns.

100 years after it was completed, on 1 September 1989, the Netherlands Kustverdedigingsmuseum was officially opened as a permanent coastal defence museum. It contains a large collection of items related to the Atlantic Wall. Postbus 9, 3150 AA Hoek van Holland (tel: 0174 382898).

Belgium

Raversijde Park Raversijde Park not only contains the Saltzwedel neu/Tirpitz naval coastal battery of 6./MAA 204 which formed part of the Atlantic Wall, but also the remains of World War 1 German coastal defences and the Prince Karel Memorial. Domein Raversijde, Duinstraat 142-B, B 8400 Oostende (tel: 059 702285). Beheerder (Curator) is Aleks Deseyne.

France
Channel Coast

Batterie Todt & Atlantic Wall Museum, Audinghen Although the turrets, armour-plating and the doors have long gone for scrap, nevertheless this famous battery remains one of the best preserved of the offensive batteries. Casemate 4 contains some of the finest wall paintings of the Atlantic Wall, and also now houses the museum, created by David Davies, with some 3,000 objects in over 10 rooms. Outside displays of vehicles, weapons and equipment, including 'K5' a 28cm railway gun (tel: 0321 329733).

War Museum, Calais 20 rooms with many relevant exhibits, including a model of the famous Batterie Lindemann, Musée de la Seconde Guerre Mondiale, Parc St-Pierre, 62100 Calais (tel: 0321 342157; e-mail: ot@calais.fr).

Normandy

Without a shadow of doubt the most comprehensive guide currently on the market is Major and Mrs Holt's *Visitor's Guide to the Normandy Landing Beaches*, the latest edition having been revised in 2000. It is a veritable mine of information and highly recommended. There are five itineraries, for example, covering the five landing beaches, plus masses of other well-illustrated information.

The following are useful addresses for information on the museums, and other sites which have collections concerned with D-Day and the Atlantic Wall:

Comité Départemental du Tourisme du Calvados,
Place du Canada, 14000 Caen (tel: 0231 279035).

Comité Départemental du Tourisme de la Manche,
Maison du Département, 50008 St Lô (tel: 0233 560703).

Comité Départemental du Tourisme de l'Orne —
88 rue St Blaise, BP 50, 61002 Alençon (tel: 0233 298160).

Comité Départemental du Tourisme de Normandie —
Le Doyenne, 14 rue Charles Courbeaux, 27000 Evreux (tel: 0232 337900).

Caen Memorial Largest of the many museums in Normandy, the Caen Memorial covers the spiral to war, the dark years of the Occupation, the D-Day Landings and the Battle of Normandy. In the International Park there is the Nobel Peace Prizewinners' Gallery. Musée Memorial, Esplanade de Eisenhower, BP 6261, 14066 Caen (tel: 0231 060644).

Musée Memorial de la Bataille de Normandie Situated in the first French town to be liberated, this large, splendid museum

tells the story of the battle of Normandy, with myriads of exhibits large and small, covering armaments, vehicles, equipment, uniforms etc, also films and dioramas. If you have time to visit only one museum in Normandy then this is the one to choose. Boulevard Fabian Ware, 14400 Bayeux (tel: 0231 929341). Conservateur (Curator) Dr Jean-Pierre Benamou OBE, MSM.

In the Sword Beach area there are:

Musée le Mur de l'Atlantique Located in the old German HQ, the 'Grand Bunker', the 16m high concrete tower has been fully restored to make it look how it was on D-Day. Avenue du 6 Juin, 14150 Ouistreham — Riva Bella (tel: 0231 972869).

Memorial Pegasus Dedicated to the men of the British 6th Airborne Division. Avenue du Major Howard, 14860 Ranville-Benouville (tel: 0231 781944).

Batterie de Merville A museum is located within the first casemate and tells the story of the assault and silencing of this famous battery (tel: 0231 914753; e-mail: museebatterie@compagnet.fr).

D-Day Landing Museum Approximately in the middle of the assault area, Arromanches was chosen by the Allies as the site of one of the two Mulberry Harbours. Now there are a number of linked exhibitions which tell the story of this remarkable achievement, including a panoramic table

Below: Le Grand Bunker Musée le Mur de l'Atlantique in Ouistreham is located in the old German HQ and 16m high fire-direction/observation tower overlooking Sword Beach, controlling the Riva Bella Battery. *Grand Bunker Museum*

located on Arromanches heights with views over what remains of the artificial harbour, a diorama about the landings in six different languages (running time 8 minutes), and a 15-minute RN archive film in seven different languages. Place du 6-Juin, 14117 Arromanches (tel: 0231 223431; web: www.normandy1944.com).

A **Juno Beach Centre** was opened in Courseulles in 2002.

In the Gold Beach area is:

Musée America-Gold Beach This dual museum covers both the historic first airmail flight from the USA to France (29 June 1927) and the D-Day landings at Gold Beach. 2 place Admiral Byrd, F14114 Ver-sur-Mer (tel: 0231 225858).

In the Omaha Beach area are:

Musée D-Day Omaha — 6 Juin 1944 Just a few yards from Omaha Beach, the museum has a collection of vehicles, weapons, uniforms and insignia found on the actual battlefield. Rue de Grandcamp, 14710 Vierville-sur-Mer (tel: 0231 217180).

La Pointe du Hoc Site of German battery position stormed by US Rangers.

In the Utah Beach area is:

Musée du Débarquement (Utah Beach) On the actual site of Utah Beach, this recently refurbished museum tells the story of the Utah landings. 50480 Ste Marie-du-Mont (tel: 0233 715335).

Musée des Troupes Aéroportées Tells story of 82nd and 101st Airborne Divisions. Place du 6 Juin, 50480 St Mère Église (tel: 0233 414135).

Musée de la Liberation The liberation of Cherbourg and the story of the port is told in this museum. In the port area of the town there is now also a road Quai General Lawton Collins so named in honour of the commander of the American troops who liberated the port on 27 June 1944. Fort du Roule, 50100 Cherbourg (tel: 0233 201412).

More museums are currently in the process of opening. These include:

H644 bunker being opened by the Musée Memorial de la Bataille de Normandie; Batterie d'Azeville — battery bunker being further refurbished.

Guided Tours of the Normandy Beaches

Although many visitors like to explore on their own there is a growing market in personal guided tours, some with expert British guides. Here is a selection:

a. **Salient Tours**. This is a British company that operates in France (NOT in the winter months) and gives a morning tour (1000-1330hrs) of the British sector and an afternoon tour (1430-1800hrs) of the American. They can be reached at: www.salienttours.com or on 0676 389689 (English spoken).

b. **Normandy Tours**. From Bayeux, picking up at hotels for tours lasting 4-5 hours (at 0830 and 1300). Book on 0231 921070.

c. **Victory Tours**. Departing daily from the tourist office in Bayeux, tours last 4 or 8 hours. Tel: 0231 519814.

There is even a 'model tour' of the beaches at: **la Forteresse Volante** in Rue de Cremel, Bayeux (0231 519235).

Atlantic Coast

Musée de la Bataille de St Malo Useful information on the battle for St Malo.

Musée de Sous-Marin Located in a former U-boat bunker at Lorient.

Above: The Rangers Memorial at Pointe du Hoc. *Simon Forty*

Above: The Naval Signals HQ at St Jacques, Guernsey, has been fully restored. *Brian Green via Fortress Guernsey*

Le Grand Blockhaus This museum has been created in an authentic command/firing control/range finding post — one of the largest bunkers built on the Atlantic Wall. Five levels, with panoramic views over the sea from the top storey which is 28m high. On the Côte Sauvage at Batz-sur-Mer, F 44740 (tel: 0240 238829).

Ecomuseum de St Nazaire Covers the history of St Nazaire, including World War 2. Avenue de Saint-Hubert, 44600 St Nazaire (tel: 0251 100303).

The Channel Islands

The best initial contacts are:
States of Guernsey Tourist Board, PO Box 23, St Peter Port, Guernsey GY1 3AN (tel: 01481 723552).
Jersey Tourism, Liberation Square, St Helier, Jersey JE1 1BB (tel: 01534 500700).

There are a number of restored sites and excellent museums in the Channel Islands, which feature all aspects of the occupation including the Atlantic Wall. The following are merely examples of the best:

Guernsey — Restored Sites
Naval Signal HQ This is a complex of three large concrete bunkers in the grounds of the La Collinette Hotel, which housed the Kriegsmarine Signal HQ. Now fully equipped and carefully refurbished.
Coast Defence Casemate A meticulously restored casemate at Fort Hommet, housing a 10.5cm K 331(f) gun.
Pleinmont Tower Direction-finding tower MP 3, unique to the Channel Islands, built in 1942 and now carefully restored.
Battery Dollmann Covering an extensive area on the headland at Pleinmont, a continuing careful restoration is in progress.

Guernsey — Other Major Sites
L'Angle Tower A massive direction-finding tower.
Flak Battery Dolmen AA battery to the west of L'Ancresse Bay.
Castle Cornet During the Occupation additional fortifications were constructed on this site which spans over 800 years of history.

Guernsey — Museums
German Occupation Museum Excellent wide-ranging museum on all aspects of the occupation, located behind Forest Church close to the airport.
La Vallette Underground Military Museum Tunnels for massive fuel storage tanks have been converted into an award-winning museum.

Jersey — Main sites
Underground Command Bunker A command post some 12m deep on two floors. Noirmont Point, St Brelade. Open every Sat and Mon morning 10.00–12.00, Apr–Oct inclusive.
Coastal Artillery Observation Tower Massive, impressive structure. Noirmont Point, St Brelade. Open most Saturday mornings 10.00–12.00, May–Sep inclusive.
10.5cm Coastal Defence Gun Casemate Contains original gun and other relics. La Corbière, St Brelade. Open every Saturday 10.00–13.00, Jul and Aug.
M19 Mortar Bunker with Tunnel System An interesting complex which once housed a rare automatic mortar. La Corbière. Open 11.00–16.30 on selected days, May–Sep.
Coastal Defence Gun and Anti-tank Casemates A twin bunker complex. La Carrière Point, St Ouen's Bay. Open 12.00–16.30 selected days, May–Sep.
Heavy MG Turret Bunker With steel cupola; one of only a few examples left intact. Val de la Mare, St Peter. Open 14.30–17.30 selected days, May–Sep.
Gun Emplacements and Underground Bunkers Meticulously restored coastal artillery battery position. Les Landes, St Ouen. Open most Sundays 10.00–15.00, Jun–Aug.
4.7cm Czech Anti-tank Gun Casemate Almost in original condition. Millbrook, opposite La Rue de Galet. Open every Thu evening 19.00–21.00, Jun–Aug, inclusive except for Battle of Flowers Day.

Most of these sites are also open on Liberation Day on 9 May.

Jersey — Museums
German Underground Hospital Largest and most spectacular 'time capsule' of the occupation. Its 'Captive Island' exhibition was the runner-up in the UK Travel Writers' Silver Unicorn Awards for the best new tourist attraction in Britain in 2001. St Lawrence (tel: 01534 863442; e-mail: info@german undergroundhospital.co.uk; web: www.germanunderground hospital.com).

Channel Islands Military Museum Housed in a restored 10.5cm casemate. St Ouen.

The Island Fortress Occupation Museum Contains many relics and a miniature cinema. St Helier.

Alderney
The Alderney Society Museum, housed in a former schoolhouse, tells the story of the island's history.

Sark
Even the tiny island of Sark has its own small **Occupation Museum**.

The Atlantic Wall in Miniature
Some years ago Spencer Pollard, the editor of *Military in Scale* wrote about the first releases from VP Studios of a range of miniatures depicting concrete bunkers from the Atlantic Wall. Although this range has remained available since the 1980s, it has now been replaced by some stunning new kits. The new 'Atlantic Wall' series will comprise a wide variety of different sizes and style of emplacement. The new kits will also differ from their predecessors in that some will be just as detailed inside as they are outside. Special items will also be available, like the guns which were used in these claustrophobic buildings. It promises to be a very interesting new series. For further details write to The Editor, *Military in Scale*, Traplet Publications Ltd, Traplet House, Severn Drive, Upton-upon-Severn, Worcs WR8 0JL.

Above:
The massive artillery control tower (Marinepeilstand) at Noirmont Point, Jersey, one of several towers still to be seen on the Islands. *CIOS Jersey*

Above right:
One of the new displays in the award-winning German Underground Hospital Museum on Jersey. *Sanctuary Inns Ltd*

Right:
Just a small part of the extensive collection of the Occupation Museum at Forest, Guernsey. *Author's collection*

Appendices

Appendix I – Useful Addresses

Alderney Society, The Museum, Alderney GY9 3TG (tel: 01481 823222).

Channel Islands Occupation Society (Guernsey), The Secretary — Major (Retd) E. Ozanne, Les Jehans Farm, Torteval, Guernsey GY8 0RE (tel: 01481 64625).

Channel Islands Occupation Society (Jersey), The Secretary — Mr W. M. Ginns MBE, 'Les Geonnais de Bas', St Ouen, Jersey JE3 2BS (tel: 01534 482089), or e-mail: mcostard@localdial.com

Casemate — Journal of the Fortress Study Group. Editor: Margaret Pinsent (tel: 01865 557631).

Danish Fortification Society, Museums Center Hanstholm, Tarnvej 23, Postbox 102, 7730 Hanstholm, Denmark.

Fortress Study Group, Bernard C. Lowry, Hon Sec FSG, 'The Severals', Bentleys Road, Market Drayton, Shropshire TF9 1LL (tel: 01630 653 433). (The group has a worldwide membership.)

Guernsey Museum and Art Gallery, Candie Gardens, St Peter Port, Guernsey GY1 1UG (tel: 01481 726518).

Historic Fortifications Network, Kent Tourism (tel: 01622 696165, e-mail: tourism@kent.gov.uk, web: www.kenttourism.co.uk).

Lieutenant-Colonel (Retd) Leif G. Ipsen, Local Historical Archivist, Kirkegade 3, DK 6840 Osbol, Denmark.

Jersey Museum Service, Jersey Museum, The Weighbridge, St Helier, Jersey JE2 3NF.

Librairie Histoire & Fortifications, 8 rue de Crussol, 75011 Paris, France (tel: 0148 057039; web: www.histoire-fortifications.com).

Société Jersiaise, 7 Pier Road, St Helier, Jersey JE2 4XW (01534 58314).

Appendix II – Museums

A selection of museums which tell part of the story of the Atlantic Wall.

Norway

MKB Fjell, Fjell/Sotra near Bergen. A museum on the site of a former bunker complex.

Austrått Fort, Orland near Trondheim. Restored gun battery and museum.

Steigen Batterie Dietl, near Steigen. Museum on site of the former battery.

Kristiansand Kanonenmuseum, Movik. Houses only remaining 38cm gun of World War 2.

There are also the Army Museum/Home Front Museum in the Archbishop's Palace in Trondheim, the Kristiansten Fort and the Hegra Fort, built to protect the main approach from Sweden. All have some exhibits to do with aspects of World War 2.

Denmark

Fortification Tirpitz, Blavand. Bunker designed for 38cm gun. Tirpitz-Stilligen, Tane Hedevej, DK-6857 Blåvand (tel: 45 7522 0877).

Museums Center, Hanstholm. Major museum in 'Fortress Hanstholm'. Also 38cm gun emplacement, Batterie Hanstholm. Tårnvej og Molevej, 773 Hanstholm (tel: 9796 1736).

Varde Artillery Museum, Varde. Danish artillery mainly.

Tøjhusmuseet, Copenhagen. Major Danish military museum.

Fiskeri- & Søfartsmuseet, Esbjerg. Open air displays of German barracks bunker.

Museum Langelands, Fort Bagenkop. 15cm guns from Gneisenau.

Stottenpunkt Hirsthals, Hirsthals. Lighthouse bunker and 10.5cm gun battery position.

Batterie Nord, Frederikshavn. Gun battery position.

Bunker Museum, Silkeborg. German HQ bunker.

Freedom Museum, Skanderborg. German HQ bunker.

Radarstellung Robbe, Romo. Radar station.

Historiecenter, Beldringe. Command bunker for aerodrome.

There are also small, free admission, unattended sites at Bulbjerg (fire control and barracks bunkers); Thyboron (10.5cm coastal battery position and radar site); Rom (hospital bunker); Dueodde (incomplete 38cm casemate); Oddesund (AA battery).

The Netherlands

Kustverdedigingsmuseum, Fort aan den Hoek van Holland. Located in an old Dutch armour museum, with many Atlantic Wall related items.

Stichting 1939–1945, Sinoutskerke. A private museum with a large collection of military equipment and Atlantic Wall related items.

Belgium

Atlantic Wall Museum,* Domein Raversijde, Duinstraat 142-B, 8400 Oostende. An open air museum at the location of Batterie Tirpitz.

France

Tourcoing WWII Museum,* 4 bis avenue de la Marne, Tourcoing 59200. Museum in the former HQ Bunker of Fifteenth Army.

Channel Coast

Musée de la guerre,* Calais. A museum in a mid-town bunker (in the St Pierre Park opposite town hall).

Musée du Mur de l'Atlantique,* Audinghen 62179. Batterie Todt museum.

Le Blockhaus d'Eperlecques,* Eperlecques 62910. Large bunker built to launch V-2 rockets.

La Coupole, Wizernes. Large dome-shaped bunker built to launch V-2 rockets.

Musée de la Batterie de Merville, Merville. Museum on the site of the Merville Battery.

* There is also a '39/45 Route association' which gives special prices at the four French and one Belgian museum starred above, plus museums at Ambleuteuse CD 940 62164 (World

Above: One of the four gun positions (Type M272 bunkers) belonging to the Longues-sur-Mer battery still has its 15cm C/36 torpedo boat cannon in position. There was also a 122mm K/390/1(r) gun for illumination. *Jonathan Forty*

War 2 soldiers), *Mimoyecques* (Base V-3 which sheltered 5 x 130m long cannons to shell London — never used) at 62250 Landrethun le Nord, and *Fortress Breendonk* (transit concentration camp) 62830 Willebroek, Belgium.

Normandy

Pegasus Bridge, Benouville. Museum at this important bridge captured by 6th Airborne Division.

Musée de No 4 Commando, Place Alfred Thomas, Ouistreham. Tells the epic story of the commandos — first to land on Sword Beach.

Le Grand Bunker Musée le Mur de L'Atlantique, Ouistreham. Former artillery range-finding post.

Musée Radar, Douvres la Deliverande. First museum to tell the story of German radar with two preserved bunkers.

Musée du Débarquement, Arromanches. Mulberry artificial harbour.

Arromanches 360, Arromanches. 18-minute film 'The Price of Freedom'.

Juno Beach Centre, Courseulles. New.

Batterie de Longues, Longues-sur-Mer. Only battery to have kept its guns.

Musée des Epaves Sous-marines du Débarquement, Port-en-Bessin. Tanks etc dredged up from the sea.

Musée Memorial de la Bataille de Normandie, Bayeux. First-rate museum with AFVs, weapons, uniforms, etc, telling the story of D-Day and the battle of Normandy that followed.

Below: The size of one of the massive gun pits which housed the enormous 30.5cm guns of the Mirus Battery on Guernsey can be seen by comparing it with the two men standing alongside. *Brian Matthews, Tomahawk Films*

Cimetière américain, Colleville-sur-Mer. Omaha Beach cemetery.

Musée Omaha, St Laurent-sur-Mer. Omaha Beach museum.

La Pointe du Hoc. Gun position taken by US Rangers.

Cimetière militaire allemand, La Cambe. German cemetery.

Musée des Troupes Aéroportées, St Mère Église. Tells the story of US 82nd and 101st Airborne Divisions.

Musée du Débarquement (Utah Beach), St Marie-du-Mont. Utah Beach museum.

Borne de la Voie de la Liberté, Utah Beach. Milestones of liberty from Utah Beach onwards.

Musée de la Liberté, Quineville. Life during the occupation.

Musée de Liberation, Cherbourg. Liberation of Cherbourg.

Le Memorial, Caen. Spectacular museum giving a journey through the 20th century with the theme of peace.

Musée de la Seconde Guerre Mondiale, Avranches. Site of breakout.

Musée Leclerc, Alençon. Located in General Leclerc's command post.

Memorial de Montmorel, Montmorel. Battle of Falaise pocket.

Musée 'Juin 44', L'Aigle. Historical scenes.

Other appropriate Normandy-based museums are at Ver-sur-Mer (*Musée America-Gold Beach*); Bayeux (*Musée Memorial du General de Gaulle*); Grandcamp-Maisy (*Musée des Rangers*); Crisbecq (*Marine Batteries of Crisbecq*); Tilly-sur-Seulles (*Musée de la Bataille de Tilly*); St Martin-des-Besaces (*Musée de la Percée du Bocage*); Nehou (*Patton's HQ*); Falaise (*Musée Août 44*). In addition to those listed above there is also another American cemetery, 16 British cemeteries, four more German cemeteries, two Canadian, one Polish and one French.

Atlantic Coast

Musée de la Bataille de St Malo, St Malo. Tells the story of the battle for St Malo.

Musée de Sous-Marin, Lorient. U-boat bunker.

Le Grand Blockhaus, Batz-sur-Mer. Massive bunker/CP.

Ecomuseum, St Nazaire. Tells the story of the town.

Channel Islands

Castle Cornet, St Peter Port, Guernsey. Includes museum and art gallery.

German Occupation Museum, The Forest, Guernsey. Excellent museum, with masses of exhibits.

La Vallette Underground Military Museum, Guernsey.

German Occupation Hospital, Jersey. Largest 'time capsule' on the islands.

Channel Islands Military Museum, St Ouen, Jersey.

La Hougue Bie, St Saviour, Jersey. This was a museum, but is now a memorial to the forced and slave workers of the OT.

The Island Fortress Museum, St Helier, Jersey.

The Alderney Society Museum, Alderney.

Occupation Museum, Sark.

Bibliography

Andersen, Jens, *The Atlantic Wall — from Agger to Bulbjerg*, Blavandshuk Egnsmuseum, 1999.

Atkin, Ronald, *Dieppe 1942, the Jubilee Disaster*, Macmillan, 1980.

Blumentritt, Günther, *Von Rundstedt, the Soldier and the Man*, Odhams Press, 1952.

Bradley, Omar N., *A Soldier's Story*, Henry Holt, 1951.

Breuer, William B., *Hitler's Fortress Cherbourg*, Stein & Day, 1984.

Carell, Paul, *Invasion — They're Coming!*, George G. Harrap, 1962.

Christensen, Peter Thorning, 'Coast Fortifications in Denmark' in *Europa Nostra* Bulletin 51, 1999.

Churchill, Winston S., *History of the Second World War*: Volume II — *Their Finest Hour*; Volume IV — *The Hinge of Fate*; Volume V — *Closing the Ring*. Cassell, 1949.

Collins, General J. Lawton, *Lightning Joe, an Autobiography*, Louisiana State University Press, 1979.

Croll, Mike, *The History of Landmines*, Leo Cooper, 1998.

Davis, Brian Leigh, *Badges & Insignia of the Third Reich 1933–45*, Blandford Press, 1983.

Ebert, Vibeke B., *The Atlantic Wall — from Nymindegab to Skallingen*, Blavandshuk Egnsmuseum, 1992.

Eisenhower, Dwight D., *Crusade in Europe*, William Heinemann, 1948.

Foot, M.R.D., *Resistance — European Resistance to Nazism 1940–45*, Eyre Methuen, 1976.

Forty, George, *Channel Islands at War — a German Perspective*, Ian Allan Publishing, 1999.

The Armies of Rommel, Arms & Armour Press, 1997.

The Armies of Patton, Arms & Armour Press, 1996.

ed, *Leakey's Luck*, Sutton Publishing, 1999.

Fraser, David, *Knight's Cross*, Harper Collins, 1993.

Ginns, Michael, *The Organisation Todt and the Fortress Engineers in the Channel Islands*, Clos (Jersey), 1994

Grieken, Gilbert van, *Destination 'Gustav' — a Wartime Journey*, The Guernsey Press, 1992.

Holt, Major and Mrs, *Visitor's Guide to the Normandy Landing Beaches*, Leo Cooper, 2000.

HMSO, *Combined Operations 1940–42*, HMSO, 1943.

Irving, David, *The Trail of the Fox*, Weidenfeld & Nicolson, 1977.

Isby, David C, ed., *Fighting the Invasion — The German Army at D-Day*, Greenhill Books, 2000.

Jordan, Kenneth N., Sr, *Yesterday's Heroes*, Schiffer Military History, 1996.

Kupka, Vladimir, *Atlanticky Val*, Skoda Fortprint, 1997.

Lucas, James, *The Last Year of the German Army*, Arms & Armour Press, 1994.

Lucas Phillips, C. E., *The Greatest Raid of All*, William Heinemann, 1958.

Maass, Walter B., *The Netherlands at War 1940–45*, Abelard Schuman, 1970.

Mitcham, Samuel W., *Hitler's Legions*, Stein & Day, 1985.

Mitcham, Samuel W., *Rommel's Last Battle*, Stein & Day, 1983.

Nansen, Odd, *Day after Day*, Putnam, 1949.

Neillands, Robin, and Norman, Roderick de, *D-Day 1944, Voices from Normandy*, Weidenfeld & Nicolson, 1993.

Pantcheff, T.X.F., *Alderney, Fortress Island*, Phillmore, 1981.

Parker, John, *The Paras*, Metro, 2000.

Perbellini Gianni, ed, 'The Military Defence at Waterways' in *Europa Nostra* Bulletin 51, 1999.

Ross, Al, *The Destroyer Campbeltown*, Conway Maritime Press, 1990.

Ruge, Friedrich, *Rommel in Normandy*, Presidio Press, 1979.

Schenk, Peter, *Invasion of England 1940*, Conway Maritime Press, 1990.

Seidler Franz W., *Die Organisation Todt — Bauen fur Staat und Wehrmacht 1938–1945*, Bernard & Graefe Verlag, 1998.

Speer, Albert, *Inside the Third Reich*, Weidenfeld & Nicolson, 1970.

Speidel, Hans, *We Defended Normandy*, Herbert Jenkins, 1951.

Thomas, Nigel and Jurado, Carlos Caballero, *Wehrmacht Auxiliary Forces*, Osprey Publishing, 1992.

Trevor-Roper, Hugh R. (ed), *Hitler's Secret Conversations 1941–1944*, Farrar, Strauss & Young, 1953.

Hitler's War Directives, Sidgwick & Jackson, 1964.

Wilt, Alan F., *The Atlantic Wall, Hitler's Defenses in the West, 1941–1944*, Iowa State University Press, 1975.

Ziegler, Philip, *Mountbatten — The Official Biography*, Guild Publishing, 1985.

American Forces in Action Series: *Omaha Beach, Utah Beach to Cherbourg*, both published by the Department of the Army Historical Division, in 1947 and 1945 respectively.

Small Unit Actions also published by the Army Historical Division, in 1946.

World War II German Military Studies, Volume 12 Part V, *The Western Theater*, published by Garland Publishing Inc, 1979 for the National Archives of the United States.

US Army Training Manual TM-E 30-451.

MS P-037 Organisation Todt — by Franz Xaver Dorsch (Deputy Chief OT), published by the Historical Division, European Command Foreign Military Studies Branch, dated 1950.

Documents held by the PRO, Kew, Surrey, all of which are reports by MI19 (RPS) on debriefings of ex-slave workers and other labourers who worked for the Organisation Todt.

Index